Power in Peacekeeping

United Nations peacekeeping has proven remarkably effective at reducing the death and destruction of civil wars. But how peacekeepers achieve their ends remains under-explored. This book presents a typological theory of how peacekeepers exercise power. If power is the ability of A to get B to behave differently, peacekeepers convince the peacekept to stop fighting in three basic ways: they *persuade* verbally; *induce* financially; and *coerce* through deterrence, surveillance and arrest, but not the offensive use of force. Based on more than two decades of study; interviews with peacekeepers; unpublished records on Namibia; and ethnographic observation of peacekeepers in Lebanon, DR Congo, and the Central African Republic, this book explains how peacekeepers achieve their goals and differentiates peacekeeping from its less effective cousin, counterinsurgency. It recommends a new international division of labor, whereby actual military forces hone their effective use of compellence, while UN peacekeepers build on their strengths of persuasion, inducement, and coercion short of offensive force.

LISE MORJÉ HOWARD is an associate professor in the Department of Government at Georgetown University. Her work on peacekeeping, civil war termination, and US foreign policy has appeared in such journals as *International Organization*, *International Security*, *International Studies Quarterly*, and *Foreign Affairs*. Her book, *UN Peacekeeping in Civil Wars* (Cambridge University Press, 2008), won the Best Book Award from the Friends of the Academic Council on the UN System.

T0371080

Power in Peacekeeping

Georgetown University, Washington DC

CAMBRIDGE
UNIVERSITY PRESS

University Printing House, Cambridge CB2 8BS, United Kingdom

One Liberty Plaza, 20th Floor, New York, NY 10006, USA

477 Williamstown Road, Port Melbourne, VIC 3207, Australia

314-321, 3rd Floor, Plot 3, Splendor Forum, Jasola District Centre, New Delhi - 110025, India

79 Anson Road, #06-04/06, Singapore 079906

Cambridge University Press is part of the University of Cambridge.

It furthers the University's mission by disseminating knowledge in the pursuit of education, learning and research at the highest international levels of excellence.

www.cambridge.org
Information on this title: www.cambridge.org/9781108457187
DOI: 10.1017/9781108557689

First published 2019

A catalogue record for this publication is available from the British Library

Library of Congress Cataloging in Publication data
Names: Howard, Lise Morje, author.
Title: Power in peacekeeping / Lise Howard.
Description: Cambridge, United Kingdom ; New York, NY : Cambridge University Press, 2019. | Includes bibliographical references and index.
Identifiers: LCCN 2018052006| ISBN 9781108471121 (hardback) |
    ISBN 9781108457187 (pbk.)
Subjects: LCSH: United Nations–Peacekeeping forces. | United Nations–Peacekeeping forces–Case studies.
Classification: LCC JZ6374 .H69 2019 | DDC 341.5/84–dc23 LC record available at https://lccn.loc.gov/2018052006

ISBN 978-1-108-47112-1 Hardback
ISBN 978-1-108-45718-7 Paperback

Contents

Figures

Tables

Photos

Preface and Acknowledgments

On patrol with the Congo-Brazzaville battalion in the Central African Republic, I asked the captain how he protects civilians. He replied, "well, there is no state here. No hospital or ambulance services. We prevent people from dying by delivering first aid, and bringing them to the hospital if they get injured in fighting. That is how we keep civilians alive." I then inquired, "what do you do when you confront rebels?" He answered simply, "we talk to them."

Civil warfare is on the rise not only in the Central Africa Republic, but across the globe, and the only effective "third party" technique that humans have devised to put an end to these bloody, destructive conflicts is peacekeeping. Today, there are more peacekeepers deployed in conflict zones than any other type of troop. Peacekeepers cost 10 times less than sending American or NATO forces. At the same time, the record of UN peacekeeping is truly remarkable. Peacekeepers have saved millions of lives. Unlike most other types of foreign intervention, two-thirds of all complex, completed UN peacekeeping operations succeeded (and not because they were sent to the "easy" conflicts).

United Nations peacekeeping is effective and relatively inexpensive, yet peacekeepers are facing an array of challenges. Blue helmets, of late, are dying in large numbers. Media hardly ever report the positive stories about peacekeeping, favoring instead sensationalized accounts of sexual abuse. Most of the qualitative scholarship on peacekeeping zeroes in on dysfunction. And the current American administration has made it a point of pride to cut UN peacekeeping budgets.

Most of these challenges fall well beyond anything one lone professor could expect to analyze or confront, but there is one area in which I can make a contribution. The scholarly literature on peacekeeping has been better at documenting empirical trends than at theorizing *how* peacekeepers keep the peace. Probably because peacekeepers wear uniforms and are trained as soldiers, many observers think these troops wield military force as part of their regular practice. Peacekeepers, however, by their very makeup, do not have the capacity, resolve, nor do they often employ, compellent force to accomplish their goals. Instead, they wield a variety of other types of power that, I contend, fall into three basic categories: verbal persuasion, financial and institutional inducement, and coercion short of offensive military force. This book provides a theoretical anchoring of the ways in which peacekeepers exercise power. By better understanding how peacekeepers cause peace, and how peacekeeping differs from other, less successful forms of military intervention, it might be possible to build on peacekeeping's strengths.

Conducting the research for this book was not simple. I wanted to interview peacekeepers, and witness them while on active duty, in several conflict zones: southern Lebanon, which is home to the oldest, interstate peacekeeping operation; Democratic Republic of the Congo, which houses the largest and arguably most complex of the current multidimensional missions; and finally, the Central African Republic, with the youngest and most innovative of the current, complex missions. I reasoned that these cases – which are at once unique but also representative of others – would help me to demonstrate different causal pathways to effectiveness (or its absence) in peacekeeping.

As I was trying to figure out how to conduct this research, a documentary filmmaking friend of mine, Pierre-Olivier François, was planning to compose a film about peacekeeping. He had been commissioned by Arté, a French-German public television company – working also with the production company Alegria – to create a one-hour film about peacekeeping for the 70th anniversary of the United Nations, in the fall of 2015.

Pierre-Olivier and his colleagues agreed to incorporate me into their filmmaking team. In exchange, I helped them with background information, interview questions, structuring the case studies, thinking through the overall narrative, and translating the final product from French into English. Journalists may gain permission to be "embedded" with peacekeeping battalions, observing them in their work, in a way that scholars generally cannot. Because of this distinctive form of access, I was able to witness peacekeepers in their daily practices and routines while enjoying transportation and protection by UN troops in unstable security contexts (and without having to seek employment directly with the UN, which could have compromised my objectivity).

Thus, I both watched peacekeepers at work, as a form of ethnographic research, and also conducted more traditional, semi-structured interviews with approximately 100 key figures in peace-keeping in Lebanon, Democratic Republic of the Congo (DR Congo) and the Central African Republic, as well as in Washington, New York, Jerusalem, Brussels, and Paris. I had previously conducted field research in Namibia for another scholarly project; I draw on some of those materials for this manuscript as well. I asked questions about the utility of force, and how peacekeepers keep the peace. What I constantly heard was something along the lines of the following: "we have the mandate to use force, and that is fine, but we don't use it. We protect civilians in other ways."

Peacekeepers exercise power in three basic ways. They persuade, induce, and coerce. I match each ideal type with one key case that demonstrates the ways in which the type of power has worked: persuasion in Namibia, inducement in Lebanon, coercion in the Central African Republic. Central Africa offers both a positive case of coercion, for a time, and then a negative example of all three types. I dropped my study of the Democratic Republic of the Congo (I plan to publish this research separately). Weeding through cause and effect in Congo is difficult because failure is overdetermined. In other words, it has multiple sources, many of which have little to do with the peace-keeping mission. In my original research design, the Force Intervention Brigade (FIB) in DR Congo provided an example of the UN's effective use of force. But that one instance of the UN's use of physical compel-lence remains the only well-documented example of such action. I can sum it up in a few sentences rather than in a drawn-out case study: in March of 2013, a unique, three-nation brigade of troops wearing blue helmets, in coordination with the *Forces armées de la république démocratique du Congo*, defeated a Rwandan-sponsored, small, hier-archically organized armed group – the M-23 – after it had taken control of the eastern town of Goma. The FIB helped to remove the M-23, but since that time it has not had success in facing the growing number of armed groups in DR Congo – some 140 by most recent counts. The FIB had one success many years ago, but the results since then suggest that this example is not generalizable.

According to Dahl's classic definition of power – when A has the ability to get B to do something s/he would not otherwise do – in order to assess whether an act of power achieved its intended behavior change, the researcher must understand very well the positive cases, when B did what A wanted. In the negative cases, it is hard to trace causal pathways because, for example in peacekeeping, the negative state is the status quo. Moreover, if fighting continues, or the number of armed groups increases as in the case of DR Congo, then peacekeeping, along with many other things, is not working well. In order to see power at work in peacekeeping, the researcher must choose cases where B has changed behavior (ceased the perpetration of violence), and then s/he must link the behavior change to what A tried to do. Some scholars might condemn this strategy for selecting on the dependent variable, but for the purposes of this study, it makes sense. All of the cases are instances when the UN's mechanisms of power generally worked (contrasted with in-case variation, when things fell apart in the Central African Republic). In other words, this book is about theory-building and small-n testing. The next step is to figure out how to assess my propositions more broadly. I welcome suggestions on this front.

But before then, there are many people to thank for getting me this far. I have studied peacekeeping since the early 1990s, when I worked at the UN in New York, before beginning my PhD at the University of California, Berkeley. At Berkeley, I had the distinct pleasure of taking a course co-taught by my mentor, the late Ernst B. Haas, and Sir Brian Urquhart, the former UN Under-Secretary-General who helped to create the UN's Department of Peacekeeping Operations. I am forever grateful to have had the opportunity to study with two giants – one in academia and the other in the UN system. Since that course, I have observed changes in peacekeeping both from a distance – while teaching undergraduate, masters, and doctoral courses in peacekeeping and related topics at Georgetown University – and more closely, by conducting interview-oriented fieldwork every few years for a variety of scholarly projects. I owe a huge debt of gratitude to my students for their probing questions and to those in the UN system for answering my questions.

During my fieldwork for this book, I would like to thank many friends and colleagues who answered my unceasing queries, and helped me to navigate my way through many obstacles. At UN headquarters, and in other locations, thank you so much, Dorian Lacomb and Hervé Ladsous. In Lebanon, huge thanks to Gheith Al-Amine, Loubna El Amine, Nada Awar Jarar, Kevin McDonald, Daniel Neep, Leila

Nicholas, Andrea Teneti, and Karim Makdisi, Ruth Putze, and Imran Riza. In DR Congo, thank you Maqsood Ahmed, Félix Prospère Basse, Alice Crowley, Carlos Alberto dos Santos Cruz, Sebastian Fasanello, Adèle Lukoki Ikola, Erik Kennes, Grace Kpohazounde, Martin Koebler, Hervé Lecoq, Jonathan Lorrilland, Jennifer Poidatz, Hany Salah, Marylène Seguy, and Bernard Van Dieren. In the Central African Republic (and in preparation for going there and in keeping track of changes in general), thank you, Nannette Ahmed, David Anderson, David Brownstein, Chandrima Das, Samuel Gahgi, Babacar Gaye, Brennan Gilmore, Kenneth Gluck, Aditi Gorur, Rebecca Hunter, Maria Jessop, Mike Jobbins, Grace Kpohazounde (again), Louisa Lombard, Parfait Onanga-Anyanga, Najat Rochdi, Rachel Sullivan, Juan-Gabriel Valdés, Rebecca Wallace, Kemi Lombardo Yai, and Marie-Joelle Zahar. Bienvenu Bitta was the most amazing "fixer," and Jean Pascal Darlan the most skilled driver one could imagine; thank you so much for your help.[1]

In recognizing the tremendous privilege accrued by circumstance of birth, which enables the ability to live and work in places at peace, I am very grateful to have benefited from audience feedback from various public presentations of earlier versions of this work. I presented parts of this book at the annual conferences of the Academic Council on the UN System (ACUNS), the American Political Science Association (APSA), the International Studies Association (ISA), and the International Security Studies Section of ISA and APSA, as well as during invited talks at Connecticut College, Georgetown University, a Folke Bernadotte Academy workshop in California, the US Military Academy at West Point, the UN University in Helsinki, Vesalius College in Brussels, and Yale University.

In the summer of 2017, I held a book incubator workshop at Georgetown with Michael Barnett of George Washington University, Andrew Bennett of Georgetown University, Susanna Campbell of American University, Paul F. Diehl of the University of Texas-Dallas, and Dr. Renata Dwan, Chief of Policy and Best Practices Service, Department of Peacekeeping Operations, United Nations. Each participant brought to the table different strengths in theory, methods, and real-world experience. This manuscript is infinitely better for their

---

[1] Bienvenu Bitta was forced to seek refuge in neighboring Cameroon in 2016 due to the fighting. He has not yet been able to return home.

input, and I cannot thank them enough for reading (re-reading), and commenting. I would also like to thank the anonymous manuscript reviewers for Cambridge University Press, Tobias Ginsberg, Elizabeth Kelly, Vinithan Sethumadhavan, and my editor, John Haslam.

For helpful conversations and comments, thank you so much, Mayesha Alam, Pat Antonietti, Séverine Autesserre, Nick Birnback, Robert Art, Kyle Bearsdley, Arthur Boutellis, Patrick Cammaert, Tatiana Carayannis, Katharina Coleman, Diane Corner, Chet Crocker, Sarah Zukerman Daly, Robert Darst, Anjali Dayal, Eric Degila, Karl DeRouen, Cedric de Coning, Sophia Dawkins, Michael Doyle, Bill Durch, Page Fortna, Linnea Gelot, Alison Giffen, Rachel Gisselquist, Desha Girod, Aditi Gorur, Richard Gowan, Ken Greene, Michèle Griffin, David Haeri, Jordie Hannum, Tori Holt, Dick Howard, Donald Horowitz, Lisa Hultman, Lauren Javins, Bruce Jones, Sabrina Karim, John Karlsrud, Peter Katzenstein, Joachim Koops, David Lake, Roy Licklidder, Robert Loftis, Princeton Lyman, Kathleen McNamara, Barak Mendelsohn, Joshua Mitchell, Daniel Nexon, William Nomikos, Alexandra Novosseolff, Mateja Peters, Richard Ponzio, Matthew Preston, Babu Rahman, William Rose, Carole Sargent, Jamie Shea, Karim Al Awar Smither, Liz Stanley, Alex Stark, Rachel Sullivan, Isak Svensson, Theirry Tardy, Ramesh Thakur, Erik Voeten, Sarah Von Billerbeck, James Vreeland, Barb Walter, Abiodun Williams, Paul Williams, and Devlin Winkelstein (with sincere apologies to anyone I have missed).

Special thanks to my research assistants Filip Savatic, Zachary Karabatak, Alesandro Ceretti, Noah Clarke, Rachel Levine, and Brian Xu. Filip and Zac read every word, and I am forever grateful for their help in the final stretch. I presented an earlier version of the argument as a TEDx talk at Georgetown University in the fall of 2017. Susan Allen, Gigi Grimes, Jesse Jacobs, Drew Joseph, and Lauren Stricker, thank you so much for helping me to prepare. Thank you also the film crew at Arté-Alegria for enabling this research (and teaching me about documentary filming!): director Pierre-Olivier François; cameramen Mathieu Pansard, Luca Chiari, and Eric Bergeron; editor Stéphanie Dréan; and producers Christine Camdessus and Serge Gordey. Thank you, Writers Room D.C. owner Lauren Francis-Sharma for providing a quiet, contemplative space for writing. I am also deeply grateful to have received financial support from Georgetown University and the United States Institute of Peace.

No project like this is possible without steadfast support from close family and friends. My sister and her husband and daughter, my parents, and my husband's parents helped me in more ways than they know. Thank you also, my huge extended family. My teenage children, Zoe and Julien, inspire me every day. My husband, Marc Morjé Howard, remains the light of my life. Nothing would be possible without him. I dedicate this book to my mother, Patricia Vidil. When it's all said and done, she is the person who motivates me to keep searching for ways to find peace, always seeking intellectual and personal integrity while doing it. I will never be able to thank her enough.

Acronyms

A4P	Action for Peacekeeping
CAR	Central African Republic
CIMIC	Civil-Military Cooperation
CIVPOL	Civilian Police
DDR	Demobilization, Disarmament, and Reintegration
DDRR	Disarmament, Demobilization, Reintegration and Repatriation
DPKO	Department of Peacekeeping Operations
DR Congo	Democratic Republic of the Congo
DSRSG	Deputy Special Representative of the Secretary General
DTA	Democratic Turnhalle Alliance
ECOMOG	Economic Community of West African States Monitoring Group
FACA	Forces Armées Centrafricaines
FIB	Force Intervention Brigade
FPRC	Front Populaire pour la Renaissance de la Centrafrique
HDI	Human Development Index
HIPPO	High-Level Independent Panel on Peace Operations
IDF	Israeli Defense Forces
ICRC	International Red Cross and Red Crescent Movement
INTERFET	International Force East Timor
LAF	Lebanese Armed Forces
MICOPAX	Peace Consolidation Mission in the Central African Republic
MINUGUA	United Nations Verification Mission in Guatemala
MINUSCA	United Nations Multidimensional Integrated Stabilization Mission in the Central African Republic
MINUSTAH	United Nations Stabilization Mission in Haiti
MISCA	International Support Mission to the Central African Republic

NAMSO	Namibian Student Organization
NATO	North Atlantic Treaty Organization
ONUB	United Nations Operation in Burundi
ONUC	United Nations Operation in Cambodia
ONUMOZ	United Nations Operation in Mozambique
ONUSAL	United Nations Operations in El Salvador
OSRSG	Office of the Special Representative of the Secretary General
PLAN	People's Liberation Army of Namibia
PLO	Palestinian Liberation Army
QIP	Quick Impact Project
SADF	South African Defense Forces
SEA	Sexual Exploitation and Abuse
SLA	South Lebanese Army
SRSG	Special Representative of the Secretary General
SWABC	South West African Broadcasting Corporation
SWAPO	South West African People's Organization
SWATF	South West African Territorial Force
UCDP	Uppsala Conflict Data Programme
UN	United Nations
UNAMIR	United Nations Assistance Mission for Rwanda
UNAMSIL	United Nations Mission in Sierra Leone
UNAVEM II	United Nations Angola Verification Mission II
UNDP	United Nations Development Programme
UNEF	United Nations Emergency Force
UNHCR	United Nations High Commission for Refugees
UNICEF	United Nations Children's Fund
UNIFIL	United Nations Interim Force in Lebanon
UNMIL	United Nations Mission in Liberia
UNMISS	United Nations Mission in South Sudan
UNMIT	United Nations Mission in Timor-Leste
UNOCI	United Nations Operation in Côte d'Ivoire
UNOSOM II	United Nations Operation in Somalia II
UNPOL	United Nations Police
UNPROFOR	United Nations Protection Force
UNSC	United Nations Security Council
UNTAC	United Nations Transitional Authority in Cambodia
UNTAES	United Nations Transitional Administration for Eastern Slavonia, Baranja and Western Sirmium

UNTAET	United Nations Transitional Administration in East Timor
UNTAG	United Nations Transition Assistance Group (Namibia)
UNTSO	United Nations Truce Supervision Organization
WFP	World Food Program

1 | *Power and United Nations Peacekeeping*

From the advent of the modern state system in 1648 until recent decades, states fought wars and sued for peace with few intermediaries. Today, however, most wars are fought not between but *within* states, and the United Nations (UN) fields the world's largest uniformed force in conflict zones (United Nations 2018f).[1] Approximately 100,000 uniformed UN troops keep the peace in 14 different hot spots around the world. In other words, rather than states serving as the units in the international system that monopolize the legitimate use of force – as was the case for hundreds of years – the UN is moving into that role.

Unlike national militaries, however, UN peacekeepers do not draw on compellent military force as their main means of power. Although peacekeepers wear uniforms and they are trained by their national governments to be soldiers, once they don the blue helmet, they swear to function by a set of rules that almost always precludes the use of military compellence. Peacekeepers are "soldiers for peace" (United Nations 1988). As a result, the concept of peacekeeping is profoundly confusing for observers, practitioners, and the "peacekept" alike.

This book presents an attempt to cut through the confusion. I devise a typology – a classification scheme – of how peacekeepers wield power. According to Robert Dahl's classic definition of power, "A has power over B to the extent that he can get B to do something that B would not otherwise do" (1957). I ask, how do peacekeepers convince the peacekept – warring parties, governments, and civilians – to behave as they otherwise would not?

I argue that peacekeepers exercise power in three basic forms: coercion, inducement, and persuasion; I devote a chapter to each concept. *Coercion* is about limiting choice. In this study, it is wielded by uniformed troops. Importantly, however, compellence – the use of

---

[1] The United States has more troops stationed abroad, but as of mid-2018, the majority of them are not on battlefields.

offensive, kinetic force to coerce an actor into action – is only one dimension. Military and peacekeeping forces may also deter, defend, surveil, and arrest (Art 1980; Foucault 1977; Schelling 1966). National militaries and regional organizations may (and must) compel, but not the UN. *Inducement* refers to the carrots of aid and employment in a variety of different forms, the restriction of markets, as well as the construction of institutions to regulate behavior. Coercion and inducement are both material in nature, rendering it easier for a researcher to detect and trace lines of causality. *Persuasion* is the slipperiest of the types because it lies purely in the realm of ideas. From Sun Tzu's ancient bid to learn the "minds" of opponents (1971) to Joseph Nye's concept of soft power and the "attraction to shared values" (2004, 7), using ideas to change behavior is a crucial, if still under-studied, form of power. When exercised consistently and without hypocrisy, persuasion tends to prove the deepest and longest-lasting means of changing behavior, whether in peacekeeping or in other domains (Carr 1946).

Peacekeepers exert intentional power in these three basic forms, and, for the most part, they are successful. There are many ways to measure success and failure in peacekeeping, as I explain later. Although by most assessments peacekeeping is effective, peacekeepers do not consistently achieve the results they seek. Peacekeepers sometimes exercise unintentional forms of power, which result in a variety of often self-defeating and unintended consequences, although not all unintended consequences are negative.

In this chapter, I introduce the origins of the concept of UN peace-keeping. I then assess the current state of peacekeeping, showing that, for all the problems reported in the media as well as in many qualitative scholarly studies, peacekeepers generally have positive effects. I then turn to the current literature about how peacekeeping works, delineating the two primary alternative arguments regarding basic causal pathways in peacekeeping. I also survey the scholarly literature about power in general and specify how it intersects with power in peacekeeping in particular. I conclude by explaining my methodological approach and the logic of the chapters.

This study is theoretical and scholarly in nature, but it has important policy implications. The main purpose is to clarify how the UN exercises power in order to achieve peace. I fulfill this goal by diving deeply into three cases of UN peacekeeping, each of which exemplifies the use of a different form of power: *persuasion* through mediation, and information and outreach campaigns in Namibia; financial *inducement* in southern Lebanon, where the UN is the largest employer; and *coercion* in the Central African Republic, where UN peacekeepers innovated in the application of the power of arrest, alongside the compellent use of force exercised by French (and American) special forces. These examples together paint a picture of the essential ways in which peacekeepers differ from military forces. For policy purposes, I show that peacekeeping has been, and may continue to be, a surprisingly effective form of intervention, especially when peacekeepers adhere to their original conceptualization, which calls for the careful application of all forms of power short of military compellence.

The Origins of Peacekeeping

From its inception in 1948, the inventors of peacekeeping sought to form a multinational, pacifying mechanism to step back from war fighting. The idea of peacekeeping arose after the devastation of World War II and was profoundly influenced by the decolonization movement, Gandhi's principles of nonviolent resistance, and the civil rights movement in the United States. Dr. Ralph Bunche, an active player in the American civil rights and universal human rights movements, and the head of the UN's decolonization office, came up with the basic concept of peacekeeping while mediating the first successful armistice deal between Israel and its neighbors (Urquhart 1998). In the course of pursuing new forms of power for establishing peace, Bunche explained,

The United Nations exists not merely to preserve the peace but also to make change – even radical change – possible without violent upheaval. The United Nations has no vested interest in the status quo. It seeks a more secure world, a better world, a world of progress for all peoples … The United Nations is our one great hope for a peaceful and free world. (Bunche 1950)

During the 1948 armistice negotiations, Bunche introduced the idea of using impartial soldiers from multiple third parties to keep the peace after violent conflict as a means of bringing about a nonviolent, mediated resolution.[2] Several years later, following the efforts of former UN Secretary-General Dag Hammarskjold, Canadian Prime Minister Lester Pearson, and Bunche, this phenomenon assumed the label of "peacekeeping." Hammarskjold proclaimed, "Peacekeepers are the front line of a moral force which extends 'round the world'" (BBC 1995).[3] The creators envisioned peacekeeping along a police-like "constabulary model," which "deemphasizes the application of violence in order to attain viable political compromises" (Moskos 1976, 2–3). Under such a model, the peacekeeper would "favor persuasion over punishment, compromise over capitulation, and perseverance over conquest" (Moskos 1976, 132). The originators of peacekeeping forwarded these novel ideas and, in a classical constructivist causal sequence (Finnemore and Sikkink 1998; Keck and Sikkink 1998), convinced the other powerful member states of the United Nations to institutionalize the unusual proposition of using soldiers for peace.

Three doctrinal rules anchored this new instrument of peacekeeping: (1) impartiality, (2) consent of the warring parties, and (3) the use of force only in self-defense. Impartiality was meant to shield peacekeepers from the vagaries of great power political and ideological conflicts and to enable them to avoid the expression of favoring any particular side in a dispute (Boulden 2015; Paddon Rhoads 2016). By not taking sides, peacekeepers would deploy with the consent of the belligerents after the parties had reached an agreement that specifically requested UN assistance. The UN's forces were to be comprised of troops from any *but* the great powers, and preferably not from former colonial states, in order to uphold the principles of impartiality and consent (Cunliffe 2013). Finally, although peacekeepers would carry light weapons for self-defense, they were meant to keep the peace without resorting to violence.

These principles of impartiality, consent, and the limited use of force are precisely what distinguish peacekeeping from other forms of military intervention. They remained in place during the Cold War, even as the United States and the USSR ceased to be able to agree on most issues confronting the United Nations. Hostile bipolarity meant that, despite the ignition of numerous conflicts worldwide, the United

---

[2] For negotiating the first armistice deal in the Middle East, Bunche won the Nobel Peace Prize in 1950.

[3] Hammarskjold was referring to the 1956 mission in Suez.

Nations did not field a single new mission between 1978 and 1988 (Fortna and Howard 2008). However, the rise of Mikhail Gorbachev in the Soviet Union and end of the Cold War changed everything.

With the end of international ideological deadlock in 1992, the great powers gathered in the UN Security Council at the level of heads of state for the first time in history and decided to halt horrific conflicts around the globe by mediating the end of civil wars and deploying UN peacekeepers to help implement the agreements. The Council requested input from the UN Secretariat. Then-Secretary-General Boutros Boutros-Ghali advanced the United Nations' efforts to establish peace by drafting *An Agenda for Peace,* which lays out the concepts and aspirations of post-Cold War peacekeeping and related activities (peace enforcement, peacebuilding, preventive diplomacy, etc.). In the introduction, Boutros-Ghali outlined the UN's plan for a "United Nations capable of maintaining international peace and security, of securing justice and human rights, and of promoting, in the words of the Charter, 'social progress and better standards of life in larger freedom'" (Boutros-Ghali 1992, para 3). Peacekeeping was reborn.

Although wars differ and change over time, we can classify them into two broad types – inter- and intrastate war.[4] Scholars have classified peacekeeping operations in a variety of ways, but we might collapse these categories into two basic types of operations that match the two essential types of war. For the interstate wars, "traditional" peacekeeping missions monitor troop demobilization and ceasefires along borders. Since the wars are between states, there is less need for externally supported state building upon the war's conclusion. Civil wars, however, are much more complex and difficult to conclude because the basic question is not how to separate but *merge* warring parties. Intra-state peacekeeping mandates mirror this complexity. Peacekeepers are charged not only with observing ceasefires and troop demobilization but also with human rights monitoring, protecting and delivering humanitarian aid, retraining troops, reforming military and police forces, protecting civilians, reforming legal systems, assisting in economic reconstruction, and sometimes administering the entire state until a new government can take over. In other words, after civil wars,

---

[4] These types contain within them several subtypes (e.g., wars of political inclusion, secession, or conquest) and may bleed into one another (e.g., externally waged counterinsurgency).

peacekeepers are often mandated by the UN Security Council not only to monitor ceasefires but also to help reform the essential institutions of the state so that all parties may be included in the political process. The idea is not to allow one side to win but to restore order by enabling politics to usurp violence.

Peacekeeping differs significantly from other forms of military intervention, but it is sometimes confused with internationally sponsored counterinsurgency (Friis 2010). While both concern the use of external military forces to protect a given population, counterinsurgency operations seek to establish order by defeating the insurgents. This crucial goal directly contradicts the basic purpose of peacekeeping in civil wars, which aims to bring about peace and reconciliation between warring parties. Counterinsurgency negates the peacekeeping principles of impartiality, consent, and the limited use of force.[5]

Although national governments are often the central actors in countering their own insurgent rebellions, for internationally sponsored counterinsurgency, such as the missions in Afghanistan and Iraq, external forces – American and allied forces in these cases – intervene to help the government. Counterinsurgency efforts have proven effective when they employ *compellence* as their essential form of power (Hazelton 2017). But recently, they also have tried to do much more. The Former Commanding General in Afghanistan, and former US Ambassador to Afghanistan, Karl Eikenberry, describes a village where Marines were "building a school, establishing a health clinic, creating a local government center, training and reforming the police force, helping the people with grievance resolution, actively supporting gender rights ... improving agricultural productivity and more" (Eikenberry 2013, 61). These are all classic multidimensional peacekeeping tasks. However, as Eikenberry lamented, "The typical 21-year-old marine is hard-pressed to win the heart and mind of his mother-in-law; can he really be expected to do the same with an ethnocentric Pashtun tribal leader?" (2013, 64). Unlike counterinsurgency, peacekeeping works

---

[5] Counterinsurgency is also much more expensive than peacekeeping. The annual peacekeeping budget for 14 peacekeeping missions in 2018–2019 stands at nearly $6.7 billion for about 100,000 troops (United Nations 2018c). In contrast, for the Afghanistan mission alone, "At the height of the surge, Washington had about 100,000 troops in theater, costing about $100 billion annually" (Eikenberry 2013, 64). Peacekeeping is more than 10 times less expensive than counterinsurgency (see also General Accounting Office 2018).

according to a hearts and minds logic precisely because of its founding principles of consent, impartiality, and the limited use of force. The individual peacekeeper does not have to woo anyone on his/her own, because the entire mission – multinational troops wearing blue hats, driving in white vehicles – is designed to signal consensual relations. Counterinsurgency, on the other hand, works according to a military-based, compellent logic. In recent years, there have been moves to merge the tools of counterinsurgency and peacekeeping, without much success for either form of intervention. I explore this phenomenon further in the concluding chapter.

Assessing Peacekeeping Outcomes

Studies of international interventions and peace operations have employed a wide variety of methods for measuring success and failure – the endeavor of measurement is notoriously difficult (Caplan 2019). In 2010, Paul Diehl and Daniel Druckman published a 234-page book entitled *Evaluating Peace Operations*, elaborating the myriad ways in which scholars can, and might better, assess success and failure. The overall picture of peacekeeping is difficult to evaluate in part because we must decide at what point in the history of the operation we make the assessment. Do we wait until the mission has concluded, or do we attempt to gauge progress while the operations are in motion? I explore both ways of measuring here.

If we wait until the operations close, the UN's record is remarkably successful. Since the end of the Cold War, the UN has concluded 18 mandates in internal conflicts. Of those, two-thirds were successful at mandate implementation. UN peacekeepers fulfilled most components of their mandates in, and then departed from, Namibia, Cambodia, Mozambique, El Salvador, Guatemala, Eastern Slavonia (in Croatia), Timor Leste, Burundi, Sierra Leone, Côte d'Ivoire, and Liberia (see Table 1.1). Although these countries are not all model democracies today (Fortna and Huang 2012), none has returned to the full-scale war experienced before peacekeepers deployed.[6]

---

[6] The standard definition of civil war comes from the Correlates of War dataset, where civil war entails sustained combat, involving organized armed forces, resulting in a minimum of 1,000 battle-related fatalities within a 12-month period (Small and Singer 1982, 205–206).

Table 1.1 *Completed Multidimensional UN Peacekeeping Operations*

Number	Country and Multidimensional[a] Mission	Year PKO Began	Year PKO Ended
SUCCESSFUL			
1	Namibia UNTAG	1989	1990
2	Cambodia (mixed success) UNTAC	1992	1993
3	Mozambique ONUMOZ	1992	1994
4	El Salvador ONUSAL	1991	1995
5	Guatemala MINUGUA	1997	1997
6	E. Slavonia/Croatia UNTAES	1996	1998
7	Timor Leste UNTAET	1999	2002
8	Sierra Leone UNAMSIL	1999	2005
9	Burundi (mixed success) ONUB	2004	2006
10	Timor Leste UNMIT	2006	2012
11	Côte d'Ivoire UNOCI	2004	2017
12	Liberia UNMIL	2003	2018
UNSUCCESSFUL			
1	Congo ONUC	1960	1964
2	Somalia UNOSOM II	1993	1995
3	Angola UNAVEM II	1991	1995
4	Rwanda UNAMIR	1993	1996
5	Bosnia (Srebrenica) UNPROFOR	1992	1995
6	Haiti MINUSTAH	2004	2017

[a] In order to count here as "multidimensional," the mission had to have at minimum military, police, civilian, human rights, and elections divisions. Many other missions have started and ended, but they were not as multidimensional (or difficult).

Alongside the remarkable and under-studied cases of success, we have the vivid and devastating examples of failed UN multi-dimensional operations in the Congo in the 1960s, and after the Cold War in Somalia, Rwanda, Angola, Bosnia-Herzegovina, and Haiti. These are all countries where the UN mission downsized or departed before fulfilling its peacekeeping mandate. In both Rwanda and Srebrenica, the UN adhered to the three peacekeeping principles, which meant that genocide could occur while UN peacekeepers merely observed. No capable militaries – a single state, a coalition of the willing, or a regional force – acted in time to halt the slaughter. Because

UN blue helmets were present, however, they took the blame (Dallaire with Beardsley 2005). In all of the most recent, successful missions, UN peacekeepers were often aided by actual ad hoc military forces. In other words, we had violent and nonviolent external interveners working together, each exercising their most effective tools of power. I will return to this insight in Chapter 4, on coercion, and in Chapter 5, the book's conclusion.

There is no single, universally accepted way to measure peacekeeping effectiveness. Many scholars contend that mandate implementation is a fair standard by which to evaluate UN missions (Bellamy and Williams 2005; Howard 2008; Ratner 1995). Given the individual components or benchmarks in a mandate, researchers may assess how many of the tasks the UN fulfilled by the time of its departure (Diehl and Druckman 2018). I have used this measure in previous work, I use it here in Table 1.1, and I appreciate it. In recent years, however, mandates have become more homogenous, longer, and less implementable (Guterres 2018; Howard and Dayal 2018). Members of the UN Secretariat like to refer to the newer directives as "Christmas Tree" mandates, whereby many players in the UN system receive the "present" (task) they would like. Most notably the current, "big five" missions in the Democratic Republic of Congo (DR Congo), Darfur, South Sudan, Malí, and the Central African Republic – each with more than 14,000 personnel deployed – have very long and involved mandates.[7] The end point of these missions, as well as the longstanding traditional operations, is very unclear. Table 1.2 lists the ongoing traditional and multidimensional missions and the year they began.

Scholars using quantitative methods have devised a wide variety of measures to evaluate both concluded and ongoing peacekeeping missions. Although earlier work suggests that peacekeepers inhibit conflict resolution (Greig and Diehl 2005), most studies find that, all else equal, the effects of peacekeepers are largely positive. UN peacekeepers tend

---

[7] The "big five" are considered to be the most difficult of the current UN missions. They are housed in DR Congo (with 22,000 personnel), the Central African Republic (14,000), Mali (14,500), and South Sudan (17,000). The UNAMID Mission in Dafur also has more than 14,000 personnel; it is co-run by the African Union and the United Nations.

Table 1.2 *Current UN Peacekeeping Operations: Traditional and Multidimensional*

Number	Multidimensional Peacekeeping Acronym	Country or Region of Operation	Year Operation Began
TRADITIONAL			
1	UNTSO	Middle East (Lebanon, Israel, Egypt, Syria)	1948
2	UNMOGIP	Kashmir, India/Pakistan	1949
3	UNFICYP	Cyprus, Greece/Turkey	1964
4	UNDOF	Golan Heights, Syria/Israel	1974
5	MINURSO	Morocco/Western Sahara	1991
6	UNISFA	Abyei, South Sudan/Sudan	2011
MULTIDIMENSIONAL AND OTHER[a]			
1	UNIFIL	Lebanon	1978/2006
2	UNMIK	Kosovo	1999
3	MONUC/MONUSCO	DR Congo	1999/2010
4	UNAMID	Darfur	2007
5	UNMISS	South Sudan	2011
6	MINUSMA	Malí	2013
7	MINUSCA	Central African Republic	2014
8	MINUJUSTH	Haiti	2017

[a] UNIFIL began as a traditional, cease-fire observational mission between Israel and Lebanon (confusingly, during the Lebanese civil war). But the mandate became multidimensional after the 2006 Israeli invasion (also, confusingly, during an interstate crisis). In DR Congo, in 2010, MONUC transitioned into MONUSCO, but the mandate did not change significantly.

to be sent to the more difficult cases – countries that show the fewest prospects for peace prior to the peacekeeping mission (Doyle and Sambanis 2006; Fortna 2008; Gilligan and Stedman 2003; Kathman and Wood 2016; Melander 2009). And yet, the presence of peacekeepers still correlates with numerous positive developments such as a decrease in civilian casualties (Hultman, Kathman, and Shannon 2013), a decrease in military deaths (Hultman, Kathman, and Shannon 2014), a reduction in the geographic scope of conflict (Beardsley and Gleditsch 2015), and a reduction in local or subnational conflict (Ruggeri, Dorussen, and Gizelis 2017).

Peacekeepers protect civilians when rebels attack (Fjelde, Hultman, and Nilsson 2019). Although we know that civil wars spread across borders (Braithwaite 2010; Buhaug and Gleditsch 2008; Salehyan 2009; Salehyan and Gleditsch 2006), peacekeepers reduce the potential for contagion of war spreading across boarders (Beardsley 2011; Collier, Chauvet, and Hegre 2008); they also reduce the occurrence of civil wars (Cunningham 2016). Once a war has begun, the presence of peacekeepers shortens the duration of violence (Beardsley 2014; Gilligan and Sergenti 2008). Other studies have also found that, for the completed missions, peacekeepers reduce the risk of violence recurring (Diehl, Reifschneider, and Hensel 1996; Doyle and Sambanis 2000; Fortna 2008; Gilligan and Sergenti 2008; Walter 2002).

The vast majority of quantitative studies of peacekeeping come to a similar conclusion: UN peacekeeping is effective. Using different datasets and statistical models, leveraging different time periods, and measuring peacekeeping in different ways, the most rigorous empirical studies have all found that peacekeeping has a large, positive, and statistically significant effect on containing the spread of civil war, increasing the success of negotiated settlements to civil wars, and increasing the duration of peace once a civil war has ended (Walter, Howard, and Fortna 2019). In short, peacekeepers save lives, and they keep the peace.

In contrast, if we explore individual cases – especially the large, ongoing missions that tend to capture headlines – the view is less rosy. The qualitative literature is both less positivist in the research methods employed and less positive in the main findings. Most qualitative studies examine peacekeeping and peacebuilding missions while they are in motion and focus on the problems inherent in peacekeeping rather than the overall results. The pervasive focus on failure and dysfunction leads to conclusions that mirror the objects of study.

The richest, theoretically oriented qualitative studies of peacekeeping (and the related topics of peacebuilding and statebuilding) tend to select failed or failing episodes and missions, and dysfunctional or unfair practices, as their central objects of analysis (Autesserre 2010 and 2014; Barnett and Finnemore 2004; von Billerbeck 2017; Campbell 2018; Caplan 2005; Cunliffe 2013; Lake 2016; Marten 2006; Paddon Rhoads 2016; Paris 2004; Pugh 2005; Williams 2018). I do not dispute these findings or arguments. Peacekeeping and related endeavors involve a stunning array of costly, questionable, and self-defeating practices, processes, and outcomes.[8] However, because so many studies focus mainly on negative cases and practices, they cannot account for the essential findings from dozens of quantitative studies that show that, in the grand scheme of things, peacekeeping seems to save lives and have broad, positive effects on civil wars.

In sum, many scholars have studied peacekeeping outcomes. Those employing quantitative methods generally find that, all else equal, peacekeeping has constructive results – fewer deaths, less contagion both within and across borders, shorter civil wars, and less recurrence. The qualitative literature tends to be less positive. I accept the findings in both literatures, recognizing that peacekeeping has numerous beneficial effects even though the endeavor is rife with problems and contradictions. The central contribution I seek to make here lies in *how* peacekeepers produce these varying outcomes. How have other scholars explained the *causes* of these varying results?

How Peacekeeping Works

The literature on the effects of peacekeeping is bifurcated largely along methodological lines. Similarly, analysis of the causal pathways to those outcomes generally falls into two scholarly traditions: rationalism and constructivism.[9] Rationalists (usually analyzing a large number of observations) argue that the "security guarantee" is the main causal mechanism that allows peacekeepers to secure the peace. Constructivists (often using single case or other qualitative methods) are generally less interested in explicating causal mechanisms, or framing in

---

[8] Howard (2008) and Newby (2018), both qualitative studies, analyze function as much as dysfunction.

[9] Note, however, that there are some exceptions. Lake (2016) and Marten (2006) both draw on rational assumptions in their qualitative comparisons.

terms of hypotheses, but often point to the absence of "local ownership" as an important source of dysfunction. Where some scholars in both traditions converge is on an inaccurate assumption that the use of force by the UN enables successful peacekeeping. I address each literature in turn before presenting a more general discussion of power and my own typology of the three basic mechanisms by which peacekeepers exercise power.

The principal hypothesis in the rationalist literature on peacekeeping contends that the core mechanism of power in UN peacekeeping is the security guarantee, which prevents security dilemma spirals and overcomes credible commitment problems because peacekeepers serve as a military deterrent (Beardsley and Gleditsch 2015, 84; Cunningham 2011; Hultman, Kathman, and Shannon 2013; Hultman, Kathman, and Shannon 2014, 737; Joshi 2013, 366; Ruggeri, Gizelis, and Dorussen 2012). Lisa Hultman, Jacob Kathman, and Megan Shannon elaborate:

When UN forces are deployed to a civil conflict, they function to resolve the security dilemma that exists between the belligerents. By providing security guarantees, UN missions assist the combatants in overcoming commitment problems that would otherwise make peaceful forms of resolution difficult to pursue ... Military troops are the most likely to prevent battlefield violence because they offer the strongest means by which the UN can guarantee security. (2014, 737–738)

The security guarantee hypothesis stems from James Fearon's seminal article, "Rationalist Explanations for War," in which he argues that commitment problems, emerging from the structural condition of anarchy in the international system, can lead to war (1995). Security guarantees can overcome commitment problems in wars between states. Extending this hypothesis from interstate wars to the realm of civil wars, Barbara Walter argues in a similarly influential piece that "when groups obtain third party guarantees for the treacherous demobilization period that follows the signing of an agreement ... they will implement their settlement" (Walter 2002, 3). Thus, in civil wars characterized by anarchy and the domestic security dilemma (Posen 1993), third parties provide guarantees of compellent military force that allows belligerents to disarm.

Several important assumptions underlie this type of argument: there are two main actors; they are rational; and the side with greatest capabilities will possess a decisive military advantage (Doyle and Sambanis 2006, 4; Fortna 2008, 81; Jakobsen 2000, 44).

Although often a security guarantee – provided by an actual military force – is important during difficult transitions, most UN multidimensional peacekeeping missions do not have either the capacity or the resolve to provide military-based guarantees. UN peacekeeping missions are composed of troops from, currently, 124 different countries (United Nations 2018c). Each mission contains troops from dozens of different states. The troops do not speak each other's languages, train together before deployment, or possess equipment that would allow them to perform standard military maneuvers. Command and control structures do not function like national militaries: a battalion commander from country X is not legally obligated to carry out the orders of a superior from country Y. The multinational makeup of peacekeepers promotes their acceptance and legitimacy, but not effectiveness as a fighting force. Unlike standard militaries, UN peacekeepers are not designed to, nor are they capable of, supplying military or compellence-based security guarantees.

Moreover, many of the assumptions undergirding the security guarantee hypothesis often do not match today's battlefields. Few civil wars have only two sides, and allegiances often shift (Kalyvas and Balcells 2010). Assuming the rationality of actors ignores many types of perplexing actions and outcomes, and well-established theoretical causes.[10] Finally, as US counterinsurgency doctrine so eloquently describes, in the section on the paradoxes of counterinsurgency operations, "stronger means" do not necessarily translate into better results: "sometimes, the more force is used, the less effective it is" (United States Army et al, 2006, 48–49; see also Chivers 2018, 340; and Byman and Waxman 2002). Even the United Nations' own internal studies demonstrate that most of the time, peacekeepers do not use their weapons when confronting violent rebels (United Nations 2014a). Security guarantees in the form of compellent UN force are not how peacekeepers tend to exercise power or achieve their goals.[11]

[10] Note that even Stathis Kalyvas (2006, chapter 6), a scholar writing in the rationalist tradition, acknowledges that much of the violence in civil wars, puzzlingly, is not strategic (see also Balcells 2017).
[11] Fortna (2008, 102) lists more than two dozen activities that help to keep the peace. I agree that these are important means by which peacekeepers keep peace, but since peacekeepers are constantly improvising and learning, the variety of tools and mechanisms is potentially infinite. Instead, what I attempt here is to theorize and categorize the three essential forms of power into which these and other tools/mechanisms may fall.

In contrast to the rationalist literature, constructivist scholars adopt a reflexive and/or critical lens to study peacekeeping (Autesserre 2010 and 2014; Bhatia 2005; Pugh 2004 and 2005; Whalan 2013). A common theme in this alternative literature stresses the importance of "local ownership" (see especially Autesserre 2010; von Billerbeck 2017; Dinnen and Peake 2013; Pouligny 2006; Sending 2010).[12] The most celebrated works in this tradition are authored by Séverine Autesserre. Her books employ ethnographic methods and seek to shed light on the deep irrationality and self-defeating practices that appear in current international peacebuilding culture – problems that span most international organizations in conflict zones, from humanitarian NGOs to development agencies to peacekeepers. Her first book focuses on international efforts in DR Congo, and a shared peacebuilding culture that ignores or prevents grassroots conflict resolution, resulting in failed peace operations.

In her second book, Autesserre widens her empirical scope to look across cases of peacebuilding and the practices, habits, and narratives in what she terms "peaceland." Autesserre argues that western "security routines, obsession with quantifiable outputs, and rituals of visibility, reporting, and impartiality... widen the chasm between interveners and their local counterparts, often emphasizing the superiority of the former. These dominant modes of operation prevent local authorship and decrease local ownership," which in turn decrease international effectiveness (Autesserre 2014, 250).

My argument here differs in three important ways from Autesserre's. I agree that she is bitingly accurate in her depiction of the self-defeating aspects of peacebuilding culture (2010) and the everyday practices, habits, and narratives of international peacebuilders who inhabit "peaceland" (2014). However, most of Autesserre's insights and evidence derive from observing civilian NGO practices. What these excellent books miss is a focused exploration of the *military* dimensions of multinational intervention. The most numerous international representatives in the peacebuilding landscape are uniformed UN troops and police, yet what they do, how they do it, and why their results often seem to be positive remain largely unexamined.

---

[12] My first book on peacekeeping also focuses on the local level, arguing that success in peacekeeping is contingent on the UN's ability to learn from local actors (Howard 2008). In this book, I shift the focus from *how* to *what* the UN has learned about the sources of its power.

Second, when it comes to force, I argue that the essence of the problem is not one, single, dominant peacekeeping culture (comprised of common practices, principled ideas, and normative expectations). In fact, there is deep disagreement about the basic practices, uses, and purposes of force in peacekeeping. This disagreement lies at the heart of the UN's current inability to use the power of persuasion effectively in the "big four" (I dive into this problem in Chapter 4, in the Central African Republic). Autesserre's first book reflects the common and essential disagreement over whether peacekeepers should use force. After arguing that peacebuilders should listen to and involve local actors in order to better consolidate peace, Autesserre later proposes that the United Nations seek to "conduct real combat operations so that, for example, UN troops could hunt down spoilers" (2010, 270). In other words, Autesserre's points on the use of force here mirror not one monolithic peacekeeping culture but profound tension over the use of force. Like many scholars writing in the rational tradition, Autesserre suggests that increasing the UN's exercise of military force will produce better results. The empirical record, however, does not support this proposition.

Third, instead of taking a purely ethnographic approach, and although I use ethnographic methods in my field research, I am interested in establishing cause–effect relationships, focusing on the UN's sources of power – I do not examine all international interveners, opting instead to examine the largest and arguably the most influential: the United Nations. I also contend that, although obviously important, local ownership is not a silver bullet. Local ownership means "'control over policy creation' and implementation" (Autesserre 2014, 102, quoting Moore 2013, 121). Very often, local actors are not inclined toward peace, and thus their exclusive authorship and ownership would not produce peaceful results.

Despite Autesserre's undeniable charges that peacebuilders are often, to their detriment, deeply disconnected from the societies in which they work, there is also abundant evidence that the presence of peacekeepers correlates with important, positive developments in civil wars. I find convincing evidence that supports both the rationalist and the constructivist assessments of peacekeeping – that it has worked, and continues to *manage* violent conflict, even if many current practices are deeply flawed and self-defeating for achieving conflict *resolution*.[13]

---

[13] See Crocker, Hampson, and Aall (2007) on the differences between conflict management and conflict resolution.

I take issue, however, with the central proposed causal mechanism of military-based security guarantees, as well as with the notion that local ownership will result in peace. The UN does not provide compellence-based security guarantees, thus that cannot be the means by which peacekeepers achieve their goals. Additionally, local ownership, although obviously extremely important as an end goal, is not always the key variable in peacekeeping effectiveness. In many current conflicts, violent local actors already own political processes. UN peacekeepers and actual military forces intervene to try to change their behavior or enable other political actors to rise. Local ownership by peaceful actors is less a causal variable than a dependent variable or end goal. How, then, do peacekeepers produce results? If not through security guarantees or local ownership, what are the causal mechanisms that may lead to peace through peacekeeping?

The Means of Power in Peacekeeping

Power lies at the center of analysis in International Relations. The field is generally divided between three scholarly traditions, or "isms:" realism, liberalism, and constructivism. Realists and liberals, both working with rationalist assumptions, examine material means and instrumental action by employing cost-benefit analyses. Liberals often explore the effects of varying levels of economic interdependence and the role of international institutions in regulating state behavior (for key works in this tradition, see Keohane and Nye 1977 and Keohane and Martin 1995). Unlike liberals, realists investigate the types and effects of military power, but not when wielded by international organizations (key books in this tradition include Mearshiemer 2001; Waltz 1979; and Walt 1987).

Unlike the material bases of power that realists and liberals emphasize, constructivists tend to argue that power lies less in military or economic force than in the social world of ideas, culture, norms, and identity (Barnett and Duvall 2005; Finnemore and Sikkink 1998; Hurd 2007; Katzenstein 1996; Wendt 1999). Power is thus not something that is necessarily exercised by A "over" B; rather, the constructivist focus is often on B's abilities, and the ways in which A and B are co-constituted.[14]

---

[14] Peter Katzenstein and Lucia Seybert's work examines "protean power," which they define as "the effect of improvisational and innovative responses to uncertainty that arise from actors' creativity and agility in response to

This confluence of theoretical assumptions among the great "isms" in International Relations, as well as favored empirical areas of focus, mean that, as Barnett and Duvall muse, "there seems to be something about how global governance is understood, conceptually and empirically, that de-centers power as an analytical concept ... the tendency of the discipline to gravitate toward realism's view of power leads, ironically, to the underestimation of power in international organizations" (Barnett and Duvall 2005, 2).

Barnett and Duvall offer one of the few sustained, non-rationalist explorations of the role of power in international organizations, and in global governance more broadly. In eschewing the equation of power with military force, and in a variation of John Scott's formulation (2001, 1–2), they define power as "the production, in and through social relations, of effects that shape the capacities of actors to determine their own circumstances and fate" (Barnett and Duvall 2005, 3). In other words, their focus is largely on B's abilities and self-determination. Barnett and Duvall urge analysts to broaden the scope of the study of power to include not only compulsory power, as classically understood by Dahl and many other analysts, but also other dimensions of power such as "institutional power" – where, for example, states construct international institutions that benefit some actors more than others – and "structural" and "productive" power – wherein structural or discursive positions define the types of actors (in this study, the "peacekeepers" and the "peacekept") in ways that mean that neither actor exists without the other (i.e., actors are mutually constituted socially) and that often privilege one type of actor over another (Barnett and Duvall 2005, 12–22).

Although I appreciate Barnett and Duvall's deep theoretical dive into categorizing the ways in which power can manifest and operate, in this study, I seek to analyze mainly the *purposeful* exercise of power. Like Barnett and Duvall, I am interested in how international organizations exercise power and the unintentional, or unintended, effects. But unlike Barnett and Duvall, I am interested in devising a typology of classical "power over" relationships. I fully understand that the "peacekeepers" and the "peacekept" are both socially constructed and, importantly, that only the "peacekept" exist before, during, and

uncertainty" (2018, 4). This type of power is very difficult to study empirically because, by definition, it is shape-shifting and unbounded.

after the arrival and departure of peacekeepers: "A exists only by virtue of its relation to the structural position B" (Barnett and Duvall 2005, 18; citing Bhaskar 1979 and Isaac 1987). In other words, peacekeepers do not exist without the peacekept. Peacekeepers are dependent on the peacekept, whereas the peacekept are not equally and reciprocally dependent on peacekeepers. Although peacekeepers seek to exercise power over the peacekept, there are no peacekeepers independent of the people who participate in, or are victims of, wars. While this association characterizes many power relations (e.g., slave owner–slave), what is uncommon about the power relations exercised here is that the stated long-term goal of A (the peacekeepers) is *not* to gain more power over B (the peacekept), but rather to *increase* B's power.[15] It is important to recognize and explore this unusual final intent of the UN's exercise of power in peacekeeping.

Recall Dahl's classic definition of power: A has the ability to get B to do what s/he otherwise would not. Barnett and Duvall contend that this means that B does not want the same things as A. They assert that there must be a *conflict of desires* between A and B, that "A and B want different outcomes, and B loses" (2005, 13). Especially when we take into account the exercise and effects of both ideational and material resources in peacekeeping, I cannot assume that B necessarily loses or that A alone wins; the outcomes of power exercises are not always zero-sum (see also Baldwin 2016, 36, and Lukes 1974, 27). Changing behavior does not *necessarily* entail compulsion on the part of A or loss for B.

I make two other assumptions in this study. First, I assume, and find empirical support for the contention, that sometimes the peacekept have the ability to exert power over the peacekeepers – that B will resist A's goals, especially when the goals are unclear or hypocritical (i.e., when peacekeepers misuse the power of persuasion). When peacekeepers are imprecise in stating their goals and producing the means by which to achieve them, not surprisingly, they generate unintended results. Peacekeepers may, nevertheless, continue to perform the same acts (Autesserre 2010) while hoping for a better result (fitting the definition of irrational behavior).

---

[15] Note also, however, that although peacekeeping mandates dictate that peacekeepers must turn over power to locals, peacekeepers may, in fact, create unintentional dependencies where, for example, the state and citizens come to rely on the UN for security and other services.

Second, therefore, I cannot assume that the actors in this study behave rationally, though of course they would like to. Unclear goals, conflicting messages, bad behavior, and misunderstandings in peacekeeping often mean that peacekeeping fails and violence continues, or that we witness "post-conflict" violence (Autesserre 2010, Boyle 2014, Daly 2016). As I explain elsewhere, "failure is to be expected. If we define failure as a continuation or worsening of the internal conflict, then failure is the status quo ... if the status quo continues, then the UN, by almost any measure, fails" (Howard 2008, 3). In other words, the UN is often pre-positioned toward less-than-rational behavior and failure in its exercise of power to stop violence. Thus, I assume elements of both rational and constructivist scholarship to trace the processes by which UN peacekeepers achieve their goals.

My analysis of these processes entails establishing patterns of cause and effect. In other words, I adopt "modern" constructivist assumptions about social relations (Fearon and Wendt 2002; Nexon and Jackson 2009; Ruggie 1998, 35). I recognize that the three of primary forms of power – coercion, inducement, persuasion – align closely with notions of causality that are central to the three "isms" in IR – realism, liberalism, constructivism. Although such explanations are often pitted against one another, I contend that each holds causal weight. In sum, I bring both material and ideational forms of power together, engaging in a theoretical and empirical bridging exercise in order to investigate the forces that may produce more or less effective outcomes in peacekeeping.[16]

Power is notoriously challenging to capture causally. For decades, scholars have recognized that "power has many forms, such as wealth, armaments, civil authority, influence on opinion" (Russell 1938, 13–14). As Kenneth Boulding states: "because power is a multidimensional concept, it is difficult to quantify and measure" (1989, 20). According to Robert Dahl, "some 14,000 different types [of power] might be derived" (1957, 295–296). Baldwin and others posit that power is not something that someone can "possess," rather, it can only be detected after it has been exercised (2016, 30). The analysis of power is thus contingent on

---

[16] In the Weberian tradition, rather than separating the ideal and material, I bring them together (Weber 1978). Eschewing or blending the "isms" is becoming more common in international relations research. See, for example, Goddard and Nexon (2016), Lake (2011), Sil and Katzenstein (2010), Newman and Posner (2018).

a difficult counterfactual: "A relationship of power can never be known until after power is exercised" (Wohlforth 1993, 4; see also Gilpin 1975, 24; and Mearsheimer 2001, 57). The analysis of power has grown more sophisticated in recent decades, as scholars recognize that, because of international economic interdependence, "calculations of power are even more delicate and deceptive than in previous ages" (Hoffman 1975, 184). In our current age, where multilateral war is waged with the intent to empower B by building democratic and economically liberal domestic power structures, the analysis of power has become even more complex (Finnemore 2003; Paris 2004; Wendt 1999, 249–251).

It is, nevertheless, important for scholars to attempt to categorize and explain exercises of power. In this book, I present a typology of the essential forms of power that peacekeepers intend to exercise directly on the peacekept: persuasion, inducement, and coercion. As with any typology, sometimes the categories bleed into one another, but that does not negate the importance of striving for clarity.[17] I devote a chapter defining and delineating specific mechanisms of each type. I then demonstrate how UN peacekeepers effectively employed the type of power in a peacekeeping mission, contrasting with the undermining of each type in a within-case comparison in the Central African Republic.

Case Selection and Research Methods

This is not another book that evaluates overall success and failure rates in peacekeeping. Many works already perform this task, using both quantitative and qualitative methods. I accept both the positive findings in the rationalist literature as well as the negative findings in the constructivist analyses, as they both reveal important outcomes and practices in peacekeeping. Rather than contesting these findings, I instead contest the central hypothesized causal mechanism in the rationalist literature – the notion that peacekeeping is effective because peacekeepers provide security guarantees through compellent military force. I also question explanations posited by constructivists regarding the importance of local ownership as the key to peacekeeping success.

---

[17] See George and Bennett (2005) on typological theorizing, Bennett's (2013) further specification, and Weber (1978) on ideal types.

In the chapters that follow, I investigate the causal links between peacekeeping action and outcomes by devising a typology of how peacekeepers exercise intentional power. I do explore outcomes of both effective and ineffective uses of power in peacekeeping, but my aim is not to provide a comprehensive picture of variation in success/ failure. Rather, my central interest is on the causal variable side: to establish basic categories of the ways in which peacekeepers seek to keep the peace and some of the conditions under which exercises of power have proven effective. By understanding these categories and conditions, I clarify, both theoretically and for policy purposes, the differences between peacekeeping and military action.

Because my central aims concern typological theorizing and causality, I searched for cases that would provide the best examples of the ways in which peacekeepers *try* to exercise power in peacekeeping. We can only know the shape and outcomes of a power relation, and whether B changed behavior in the direction A desired, *after* an act of power has been committed. My case selection thus required variation on a number of different dimensions.[18] Each case in this study represents the effective application of an ideal type of power (the Central African Republic serves as both a positive case of effective coercion, and, eventually, a negative case of all three). Each case also marks a different milestone in the intentional practice of peacekeeping: the first traditional mission (Lebanon); the first successful multidimensional mission (Namibia); and the newest and most innovative of the ongoing "big four" multidimensional missions (the Central African Republic).

Although each case has unique qualities, and it is difficult to make generalizations based on a small sample of cases (Seawright and Gerring 2008, 295), I overcome these limitations by choosing cases that are also representative of many others. The causal mechanisms by which peacekeepers have kept the peace in Lebanon are similar to those of the other longstanding, traditional operations in Cyprus,

---

[18] Table 1.2 lists the current operations, and Table 1.1 the concluded, multidimensional operations. The UN has officially concluded 71 missions overall, but this number is deceiving, as many of those missions were small and brief: peacekeeping missions are not all like units. Moreover, since I am interested in relationships of causality rather than correlation, it makes sense to answer the question of how peacekeepers exercise power by using qualitative methods.

Western Sahara, and Kashmir. The sources of effectiveness in Namibia mirror those in the other successful, completed multidimensional missions such as in El Salvador, Mozambique, Eastern Slavonia, Timor Leste, Sierra Leone, and Liberia. In the ongoing, large and complex "big four" UN missions, in DR Congo, South Sudan, and Mali, the difficulties of effectively using force are similar to those in the Central African Republic.[19]

On the outcome or "dependent" variable side, I examine a variety of dimensions to assess both the outcomes of completed peacekeeping missions, as well as the effects of those that are currently in motion, noting that the ongoing missions change over time, and success/failure rates shift over the course of an operation. Of my three cases, two are ongoing (Lebanon and Central Africa) and thus are representative of the other twelve ongoing missions. Two are generally considered to be more successful (Namibia and Lebanon), while one is not enjoying that designation (the Central African Republic, although some aspects of this mission were, and might once again, prove effective). As I contended earlier, arguably the best way to evaluate success or failure is to wait until the operation has concluded. Given, however, the large number of ongoing missions, and the fact that the average peacekeeping operation lasts 28 years, with a median length of 19 years (Landgren 2018), researchers, peacekeepers, and the victims of civil wars do not have the luxury to wait. It is important to decipher how the UN wields power effectively *before* the missions have concluded. However, it is also crucial to recall and analyze the means by which UN peacekeepers have succeeded in the past.

From these three cases – which are at once unique and also representative of others – we may decipher several general trends and policy

---

[19] In my original research design, I intended to use the Force Intervention Brigade (FIB) in DR Congo as the case study for effective coercion, and the Central African Republic as a case of the effective use of all three forms of power. The FIB, however, has not managed to stem the violence or proliferation of armed groups in DR Congo. Moreover, since the departure of French forces from Central Africa in 2016 – and with them the essential function of a military-based security guarantee – Central Africa is looking more like DR Congo. It would have proven redundant to elaborate case studies of both. Moreover, the recent events in the Central African Republic provide a terrifying natural experiment in the effective use of compellence – in tandem with a well-functioning, multidimensional peacekeeping operation – and the results of removing the compellent, coercive power.

lessons. Namely, that compellent force is not really possible for UN peacekeepers. Entities other than the UN have proven far more effective at peace enforcement because, unlike peacekeepers, they were intentionally designed from their inception to possess an offensive force capacity. Moreover, the cases show that peacekeepers have exercised power effectively through the noncoercive means of inducement and persuasion. My overall focus is on comprehending what worked and showing the causal pathways by which peacekeeping proved effective in representative cases – cases that also illustrate each ideal type of power.

I build my argument by triangulating between many data streams, including elite interviews, off-record conversations with non-elites, my own observations of peacekeepers in action, primary sources gathered in the field and elsewhere, and secondary evaluations. I have been studying peacekeeping since I worked at the UN in the early 1990s. Since then, I have researched and taught courses on peacekeeping, providing me with more than two decades of unreplicable background knowledge and data on UN peacekeeping operations.

My primary source of direct information for this book stems from field research that I conducted in all three countries (as well as in DR Congo), mainly in the spring and summer of 2015. Since then, I have reinterviewed key figures in order to clarify and update some causal processes. As Layna Mosley explains, "interviews are an important, and often essential tool for making sense of political phenomena ... interviews can provide a basis for constructing more-general theories, or they can be used for testing the accuracy of theories; in both cases, interviews reveal causal mechanisms" (2013, 2; see also Kapiszewski, MacLean, and Read 2015, chapter 6).[20]

In the field, I engaged in several forms of interviewing: (1) formal, one-on-one interviews with key figures in peacekeeping, or "investigative interviewing"; (2) formal interviews for "concept clarification," especially on the meanings and forms of coercion; (3) "evaluation research" wherein I asked interviewees which actions of theirs they thought were most effective and why; and, finally, (4) "ethnographic interpretation," which enabled me to see and understand some of the

---

[20] MacLean, and Read (2015, 194, 197) contend that, as a research method, interviewing is expensive and inefficient. But it is unmatched in its capacity for tracing lines of cause and effect.

key practices, symbols, and actions of peacekeepers (Rubin and Rubin 2005, 1–15). Sometimes I found myself an "accidental ethnographer" (Fujii 2014), although intentional ethnography was also part of my design (Wood 2003, chapter 2).

This investigation tends toward the more positivist, as opposed to interpretivist, type of qualitative research. That said, even interpretivist ethnography does not necessarily rule out causal interference. As Lisa Wedeen explains, "interpretive social science does not have to forswear generalizations or causal explanations ... ethnographic methods can be used in the service of establishing them ... ethnography adds value to political analyses in part by providing insight into actors' lived experiences" (2010, 257, 261). In sum, I conducted more than 100 semi-structured interviews to ask direct, hypothesis-testing-type questions, while also asking open-ended questions, in order to hear directly from the peacekeepers and their leadership about how they were keeping the peace. For my ethnographic experience, I had the great fortune to be "embedded" on patrol and on base with peacekeepers in Lebanon, DR Congo, and the Central African Republic (for six weeks during the spring and summer of 2015), which enabled me to observe them keeping the peace firsthand.

For finding my interview subjects, I used the classic "snowball" technique, whereby the researcher asks each interviewee for suggestions of other people to interview. However, after 20 or so years of interviewing peacekeepers in the field, at UN headquarters, and in a variety of other places, I was also able to identify and interview precise interlocutors with specific information. For the ethnographic portions, since I was conducting research sometimes in active war zones, I was less able to pick and choose with which battalions I could spend time – I made general requests to observe a variety of different battalions (from countries still developing, as well as from advanced-industrial states; from those new to peacekeeping, as well as the more experienced), and the Department of Peacekeeping Operations, thankfully, obliged.

For each case I employ process tracing – a useful method for both theory development and testing (George and Bennett 2005, 214). I also delineate observable implications of the mechanisms behind each type of power. Observable implications are proposed observations the researcher expects to find if the theory or mechanism is operative (Collier, Brady, and Seawright 2010). As Brady and Collier explain, "qualitative research uses causal process observations to ... slowly but surely rule out alternative explanations until they come to one that stands up to scrutiny" (Collier and Brady 2004, 260). I also lay out conditions under which I expect to see the effective use of each mechanism.

In addition, when relevant, I assess peacekeeping effectiveness in each chapter, along with some of the essential measures that other researchers have used, depending on the availability of reliable data (see especially Diehl 1994 and Diehl and Druckman 2010). These include the following: (1) *Violent Deaths* – although the number of civilian, belligerent, and peacekeeper deaths fluctuates over time and numbers are not always accurate, an overview of these trends can help in assessing whether an operation has a violence-dampening effect. (2) *Human Development and Literacy Rates* – the United Nations Development Programme issues an annual Human Development Index score for each country as measured by life expectancy at birth, the average years of education, and the gross national income per capita. Whether human development scores rise or decrease over the course of a peacekeeping operation (and after) is a good proxy for understanding whether peacekeepers helped to provide basic order.[21] (3) *Conflict Containment* – containment may be gauged by changes in the number of armed groups and the extent of displaced persons over the course of a peacekeeping mission. (4) *Unintended Consequences* – although the previous three measures help to show whether peacekeepers are accomplishing what they intend, as scholars in the qualitative literature assert, sometimes the results of peacekeeper deployment are unintentional and negative, such as when they sexually abuse citizens or spread disease.[22] Unintended consequences can also, however, be positive, such as UNIFIL providing needed employment in southern Lebanon.

---

[21] I thank Dr. Renata Dwan, Chief of the UN's Policy and Best Practices Service, for proposing the idea of examining the general question of order rather than whether peacekeepers are implementing the more specific dimensions of each mandate.

[22] In terms of unintended consequences, one can conceive of sexual exploitation and abuse as both an unintended *outcome* of poor leadership and accountability structures, and a *cause* of distrust of peacekeepers by the peacekept (which can generate larger, negative inadvertent consequences and outcomes). We see such processes in the Central African Republic. The introduction of cholera to Haiti had similar causes and effects.

Table 1.3 *Overview of the Argument*

Type of Power	Tools/Mechanisms	Exemplified In
Persuasion	Mediation (Civilian and Military) Shaming Outreach and Public Information Symbolic Displays Education and Training	Namibia
Inducement	Aid, QIPs, and Trust Funds Sanctions, Market Restrictions Institution Building The Peacekeeping Economy	Lebanon
Coercion	Compellence Deterrence Defense Surveillance/Monitoring Arrest	Central African Republic

For each form of power and its attendant case study, I seek evidence of the main counter-hypothesis: the UN provides security guarantees through the use or threat of compellent military force. Constructivists do not formulate local ownership as a hypothesis, but I do explore whether and how involving locals can lead to more or less effectiveness. I also develop and test my own theory by laying out observable implications that confirm or disconfirm my propositions of the sources of power in peacekeeping. I contend that UN peacekeepers have been, and are currently, able to save lives because they exercise non-compellent means of power in three primary forms: coercion short of offensive military force, material inducements, and ideational persuasion. I also explore *unintended* exercises of power and their consequences. I demonstrate the plausible causal weight of each of these mechanisms in the three case studies (see Table 1.3).

Overview of Chapters

In Chapter 2, I explore the notion of persuasion. Persuasion is a social process of interaction wherein one entity changes the behavior of another, in the absence of material inducement or coercion. Persuasion in peacekeeping generally manifests in five forms. First, peacekeepers mediate on a daily basis, all the time – civilians and troops help to de-escalate low-level disputes, while higher-level military and political figures work diplomatically to avert crises. Mediation is the most common method that peacekeepers use when confronting rebels (United Nations 2014a). Second, when positive mediation techniques fall short, members of the leadership in peacekeeping may employ the psychological punishment of shaming. Third, peacekeepers engage in physical outreach to local populations by setting up offices and out-posts wherein peacekeepers and locals can interact; they also use public information as a way to convey messages. Fourth, as an extension of outreach and public information, peacekeepers employ symbolic displays to convey messages, such as wearing blue hats, driving in white cars, and issuing visual items like posters and billboards to convey their intentions. Finally, increasingly, peacekeepers persuade and seek to socialize through educational and training campaigns. I argue that effective persuasion is contingent on three factors: (1) having a clear and unified message, (2) understanding how mes-sages – both verbal and symbolic – might be received, and (3) behaving in line with the message. These factors are necessary for effective persuasion, but fulfilling each of the three does not ensure success.

All forms of power, even when employed expertly, do not necessar-ily change behavior as intended. In the case of Namibia, however, the UN's power of persuasion proved effective. The UN Transitional Administration (UNTAG) deployed in 1989 in an unstable and uncer-tain environment. The mission had nearly as many civilians as uni-formed troops; 40 percent of its personnel were women. The mission's leadership and staff took it upon themselves to interact closely and frequently with the leadership and people of Namibia – the outreach campaign was unparalleled. The mission was underfunded, and it did not have an enforcement mandate, thus it could not employ the levers of inducement and coercion of the more contemporary missions. But it did successfully employ persuasion.

By most social science indicators, one could expect Namibia to be in constant turmoil. It is the only country in the world that has endured genocide, multiple colonial rulers, apartheid, and regional and civil war; it is also endowed with abundant natural resources, and thus the country is susceptible to be "resource cursed." And yet, Namibia is faring well, due in part to an effective peacekeeping mission that exercised persuasion as its primary form of power.

In Chapter 3, I explore a second crucial way that UN peacekeepers exercise power, through inducement. Inducement involves material, but nonmilitary-based incentives to change behavior. It is a broad category, encompassing at least four basic mechanisms including (1) the carrots of aid and trust funds, (2) market restrictions in the form of weapons bans, mineral trade restrictions, and economic sanctions, (3) building institutions such as legal, municipal, and military, and finally, (4) the overarching peacekeeping economy that develops around large, longstanding international missions. The first three categories are intentional, the final is not.

I provide an in-depth look at inducement practices in Lebanon. Lebanon houses the UN's oldest, and one of the oldest, missions – the UN Troop Supervision Organization (UNTSO) and the UN Interim Force in Lebanon (UNIFIL). UNIFIL includes large numbers of peace-keepers in a small geographical area, and thousands of NATO-trained western troops, which would suggest that it provides compellence-based security guarantees. However, I argue that the UN peacekeepers' ability to deter violence stems not from compellent or deterrent military power but primarily from inducement (and also persuasion). Lebanon is the most developed country to house a current multidimensional mission and thus should prove a hard test case for inducement – material incentives should be more effective where scarcity dominates. And yet, inducement is arguably the basis of UNIFIL's ability to dampen – if not end – violent conflict in a volatile area.

The final form of power – coercion – is my focus in Chapter 4. Coercion concerns a strong actor influencing another's behavior by limiting choice. I devise a typology of coercion in peacekeeping by drawing on Thomas Shelling's seminal distinction between compel-lence and deterrence (1966), Robert Art's further elaboration of these differences (1980), and Michel Foucault's insights into surveillance as a form of coercive power (1977); I also add my own category of arrest. Compellence requires an offensive military capacity that peacekeepers do not possess. Deterrence, if military-based, requires a second-strike capacity – another element that is, by definition, not something that peacekeepers enjoy. Peacekeepers may, however, deter through inducement and persuasion. Defense has a much lower military bar – it is easier to fend off attack than to attack; peacekeepers defend themselves and civilians. Peacekeepers, like all military forces, seek to stem violent behavior through surveillance, often in the form of patrol. Finally, the deprivation of liberty through arrest is an important means by which peacekeepers exercise coercive power over the peacekept.

The Central African Republic is home to what promised to be the most innovative of the current large, multidimensional missions when it began in September 2014. After more than a dozen years of frustration in DR Congo, many highly motivated UN staff members sought to move to the incipient UN mission just north, in neighboring Central Africa. The United Nations Multidimensional Integrated Stabilization Mission in the Central African Republic (known by its French acronym, MINUSCA) deployed after French special forces halted the violence that had been raging for the previous two years. Together, the two interventions proved effective: violence against civilians abated, displaced people returned home, and the economy began to recover. The MINUSCA peacekeepers used the power of arrest as one of their main means of coercion, as well as inducement, enabling Central Africans to create, build, and manage their own development projects. Because the conflict in Central Africa stemmed more from local bands of impoverished fighters than from organized military forces, most of MINUSCA's military battalions were subsumed under police command. Moreover, unlike some missions, the United Nations' central means of inducement through development projects were integrated directly into the peacekeeping mission: the deputy Head of Mission is dual-hatted as the UN Development Programme's Resident Representative. These innovations spelled great promise for the UN and Central Africa in MINUSCA's first two years of operation. However, the sexual abuse perpetrated initially by French forces undermined the UN's – and all external actors' – capacity to persuade. Despite the successful election in February 2016 of a new president, the UN is no longer trusted. Rebel groups have splintered and assumed control over more than 80 percent of the country. The rush to elections as a means of involving local actors in governance has resulted in re-creating similar patterns of corruption and abuse that sparked the initial conflict. Innovation in compellence has been over-run by speedy re-localization, with the effect that half of the population remains in dire humanitarian need, and more Central African citizens are now displaced than ever before.

In the concluding chapter, I summarize my main findings and turn to practical recommendations. Many UN peacekeeping missions have succeeded in part because they were assisted, in an ad hoc fashion, by actual military troops. The international application of violence and nonviolence worked in tandem, and convinced rebels and governments to stop killing each other and civilians. I contend that lately, many scholars and practitioners alike have conflated peacekeeping with war fighting, to uncertain ends; increasingly, peacekeepers are getting killed, and the path to concluding the "big four" missions is not clear. A new international division of labor might alleviate the problems. When compellent force is necessary to coerce spoilers to stop fighting, or protect civilians under threat, it would be logical for the responder to have an actual, material, war-fighting capacity. Many single states, the African Union, and NATO hold such ability. UN peacekeepers do not possess a war-fighting capacity, nor should they. About two-thirds of the time, UN peacekeepers have proven successful at implementing multidimensional peacekeeping mandates – fulfilling the tasks of retraining troops and police, delivering humanitarian aid, establishing judicial and security institutions, rebuilding political and economic structures, overseeing elections, and then exiting the country – without resort to compellence.

Since the mid-2000s, however, shifts in peacekeeping mandates, structures, and training have led to confusion about the purposes of peacekeepers and their basic message. Peacekeeping – which by definition is impartial, consensual, and eschews the use of force – is being confused with its less-successful cousin, counterinsurgency. Counterinsurgents are partial (they take sides), thus they do not enjoy the consent of all parties, and they use compellent force as their main source of power. This uncertainty and mixed-messaging undermines peacekeepers' persuasive power. However, there are ways to improve peacekeeping, especially if we look to previous missions that have succeeded. In a world where people everywhere crave constructive political action, peacekeepers – wearing blue and driving in white vehicles – have satisfied that yearning in the past, and may once again. Where the UN best exercises its powers of persuasion, inducement, and coercion, peacekeeping has been, and might continue to be, effective.

2 | *Persuasion in Namibia*

We couldn't just register people to vote. We had to change the overall political atmosphere.

– H. E. Marti Ahtisaari, UN Special Representative for UNTAG[1]

Persuasion is the power of nonmaterial, "ideational" factors to change behavior.[2] The United Nations in general, and more specifically UN peacekeeping, employs persuasion to try to convince warring parties to stop fighting, and to consolidate peace, by engaging politically as opposed to violently. As Michael Barnett asserts, "The UN's power derives primarily from its ability to persuade rather than its ability to coerce" (1995, 429).

Persuasion in peacekeeping manifests in a wide variety of ways. I outline five types here and demonstrate how they functioned in the case of the UN Transition Assistance Group (UNTAG) in Namibia. First, in their daily actions, when they confront situations of conflict escalation, peacekeepers generally do not brandish their weapons but, rather, they *mediate*. Mediation occurs on all levels – high and low – and by different actors in peacekeeping missions, both civilian and military. Second, peacekeepers, especially at high political levels use *shame* (or the threat thereof) as a direct, negative, and nonmaterial means of changing behavior. Third, since the time of UNTAG in Namibia, many peacekeeping missions have placed great emphasis on *civilian outreach and information dissemination*, often centralized through a Department of Public Information and/or a political section (Oksamytna 2018, 93). Fourth, peacekeepers employ and embody a wide array of *symbolic displays* as forms of nonmaterial, persuasive power – from symbolic acts, like General Assembly votes, to visual

---

[1] Author interviews with Martti Ahtisaari, President of Finland, Kulturanta, Finland, 10–12 July 1998.

[2] "Ideations" include not only ideas but also norms, beliefs, symbols, and culture – the nonmaterial aspects of politics and society (Yee 1996).

displays such as signaling peaceful intent by driving in white vehicles. Finally, all multidimensional peacekeeping missions engage in *training*, which is a method of directly seeking to persuade participants to change behavior through a process of socialization. Training programs, however, are often short-term. On a deeper level, sometimes the UN has also engaged in longer-term *educational* initiatives. These five basic forms – mediation, shaming, outreach, symbolic displays, and training/education – are some of the key tools of persuasion in peacekeeping. They may not change an actor's identity, but we often witness behavior change.

Effective persuasion in peacekeeping is difficult to achieve because operations at once are multivocal *and* seek to influence a variety of different audiences. Although peacekeeping missions try to centralize communications through a Department of Public Information, *all* peacekeepers speak for, act on behalf of, and represent, the United Nations. From the head of the operation – the Special Representative of the Secretary-General (SRSG) – to the civilian staff, to the actual peacekeeping troops – who hail from dozens of different countries, speak different languages, and do not share common cultures or practices – all peacekeepers nevertheless seek to speak and act in unity. Often in these operations, however, the UN does not have one clear or consistent hierarchical chain of command, with the heads of different UN agencies (the United Nations Development Programme, the United Nations High Commissioner for Refugees, etc.) in the country, trying to coordinate but not consistently cooperating with one another. Thus the task of communicating with one voice in a peacekeeping operation is inherently difficult.

These challenges are compounded by the fact that peacekeepers seek to influence multiple audiences at once. As the UN's principles and guidelines on peacekeeping assert: "Key strategic [peacekeeping] goals are to maintain the cooperation of the parties to the peace process, manage expectations, garner support for the operations among the local population, and secure broad international support, especially among troop contributing countries and major donors" (United Nations 2008, 82). Although the task of persuasion is not simple – because of the sheer number of actors and targets – it is essential: "Effective [persuasion] is a political and operational necessity. Its overall objective in UN peacekeeping operations is to enhance the ability of the mission to carry out the mandate successfully" (United Nations 2008, 82).

Recall Dahl's conception of power as a dynamic relationship between A and B, where A influences B to behave as B would not otherwise. I contend that effective persuasion is contingent on three factors: (1) a clear, unified message on the part of A; (2) A demonstrates understanding, respect for, and learning from, B; and (3) A's message aligns with its behavior and symbols.

In this chapter, I define persuasion, and I explain five possible mechanisms in peacekeeping. I then devise a series of observable implications of, and conditions for, effective persuasion. Finally, I demonstrate an example of effective persuasion in a case study of the UN's peacekeeping operation in Namibia. UNTAG marked the UN's first successful multidimensional peacekeeping operation. Ending in March 1990, the mission both implemented its mandate and helped to create conditions for political democratization – and social and economic stability – in post-independence Namibia. Both Namibia and UNTAG are unique. Namibia is the only country in the world that has suffered the worst ills of the twentieth century – multiple colonial rulers, genocide at the hands of German colonists, 42 years of apartheid government, regional war, civil war, and it has natural resources – thus the country is prone to the resource curse. The parties in the conflict never signed a peace accord together. These factors combined would tend to predict continuous turmoil. And yet, Namibia today is stable and faring well.

UNTAG was also unlike other missions: it was the first of its kind, so there were no standard operating procedures for this type of complex peacekeeping; the civilian component was almost as large as that of the military; its staff was 40 percent female; the UN General Assembly was deeply supportive of the mission (the Security Council, less so, but still supportive); the SRSG had been planning for UNTAG for nearly a decade; and the mission purposefully sought ways to empower Namibians. From the first day, the operation faced a number of obstacles – including a massive, violent challenge – but the leadership and staff, working together and with Namibians, using primarily the power of persuasion, ended the fighting, brought home tens of thousands of refugees, enabled Namibians to hold their first free and fair elections, helped to establish constitutional rule, and concluded an effective mission. Although both Namibia and UNTAG are unique, that does not preclude the fact that mechanisms of persuasion have been, and may again be, employed effectively in other peacekeeping operations.

Definitions

I define persuasion as a social process of interaction wherein one entity changes behavior in another, in the absence of overt material inducement or coercion. This definition falls in line with those put forth by scholars in both cognitive psychology, and in the constructivist school of international relations. Scholars in both disciplines tend to cite social psychologist Richard Perloff's definition of persuasion as "an activity or process in which a communicator attempts to induce a change in the belief, attitude, or behavior of another ... through the transmission of a message in a context in which the persuadee has some degree of free choice" (Perloff 1993, 15; see also Checkel 2008, 3). Joe Nye, in his seminal book *Soft Power*, elaborates:

If I am persuaded to go along with your purposes without any explicit threat or exchange taking place – in short if my behavior is determined by an observable but intangible attraction – soft power is at work. Soft power uses a different type of currency (not force, not money) to engender cooperation – an attraction to shared values and the justness and duty of contributing to the achievement of those values. (Nye 2009, 7)

Although psychologists and political scientists may agree on a common definition of persuasion, the disciplines tend to view causal processes differently, and research topics are dissimilar. In psychology, "persuasion operates by influencing an actor's *cognitions*" (Walsh 2005, 3). Much of the seminal works in this domain apply less to political processes and more to business and advertising, where the focus is on the internal cognitive processes of individuals and individual behavior (Hovland et al. 1949; McGuire 1968; Zimbardo and Leippe 1991). In contrast, constructivists explicate processes beyond individual cognition, wherein persuasion (often initiated by "norm entrepreneurs") leads to a change in collective beliefs, which may engender change in identities, interests, norms, and values. These changes, in turn, may result in political and institutional change (Barnett 1998; Busby 2007 and 2010; Checkel 1999; Crawford 2002; Finnemore 1996a, 1996b, and 2003; Finnemore and Sikkink 1998; Haas 1990; Jackson 2006; Klotz 1995; McNamara 1998; Price 1991). Constructivists analyze ideational processes of political change in a number of domains such as human rights, the end of slavery, the taboo surrounding nuclear weapons, and the cult of the offensive in World War I (Kier 1997; Risse, Ropp, and Sikkink 1999; Tannenwald 1997).

Linking persuasion to warfare has a long history. The concept of "winning hearts and minds" emerged in the late 1880s among French colonists and was used to inform American strategy in Vietnam, Afghanistan, and Iraq (Eikenberry 2013; Porch 1986, 394). But this process of "winning," by definition, has to occur by choice and not by fear. For both psychologists and political scientists, if someone's behavior changes when they are facing the barrel of a gun, the behavior change cannot be attributable to the power of persuasion alone.

Mechanisms of Persuasion in Peacekeeping

Persuasion as a form of power is difficult to pin down, because it is nonmaterial in nature. Persuasion can also occur in a nearly infinite number of forms or tools, unlike coercion, which is more material, and thus more prone to the possibility of achieving scholarly consensus over basic mechanisms. However, it is possible to lay out some general types and conditions under which effective persuasion would be most likely. I contend that, in peacekeeping, there are at least five basic categories of persuasive power at work: mediation, shaming, outreach and public information, symbolic displays, and training/education. The types are interrelated, and often reinforce one another in practice, so teasing them apart empirically can be challenging, but still possible. In order for persuasion to be effective, I contend that three essential factors must be met: centralized messaging, a deep understanding of the peacekept, and aligning the basic messages of the peacekeeping mission with peacekeeper behavior. I address each type in the following sections, before turning to effectiveness conditions.

Mediation

Mediation encompasses a wide array of actions to bring two or more parties together. As Crocker, Hampson, and Aall explain: "Definitions of mediation are as various as mediators themselves. Most, however, include the idea of a process undertaken by an outside party to bring or maintain peace" (1999, 7). In the late 1980s, the Cold War deadlock in the United Nations Security Council and General Assembly subsided, which had rippling effects throughout the organization. At the request of the George H. W. Bush administration, the UN Security Council met in 1992 at the level of the Heads of State for the first time in history,

Table 2.1 *Mediators in Peacekeeping*

	Civilian	Military
High Level	SRSG, UN mediators, regional representatives, groups of friends	Force commander, Police commander
Lower Level	Civilian staff	Peacekeeping troops

during which the worlds' great powers decided to seek to end civil wars in mediated settlements.[3] Since that time, scholars have found abundant evidence that third-party mediation is positively correlated with lasting post-settlement peace in civil wars (Beber 2012; Bercovitch and DeRouen 2004; Kydd 2003; Melin and Svensson 2009; Regan and Aydin 2006). For states emerging from civil wars, international mediators convinced belligerents to moderate their stances, engage in dialogue, and negotiate political solutions to violent conflict (DeRouen and Bercovitch 2012; Sisk 1996). As Doyle and Sambanis assert: "While the UN is very poor at 'war,' imposing a settlement by force, it can be very good at peace, mediating and implementing a comprehensively negotiated peace" (2006, 5).

Over the course of a peacekeeping mission, mediation occurs at a variety of different levels, and is performed by different actors. These generally fall into four types: civilian and military, and high level and lower level (see Table 2.1).

The Special Representative of the Secretary General (SRSG), or another UN-designated mediator, is often the top political figure conducting higher-level mediations with government and rebel leaders; regional actors and international groups of friends also frequently engage (increasingly, we see a multitude of civilian actors trying to mediate). The Force Commander and Police Commander, who generally report to the SRSG, perform similar tasks with military and domestic police counterparts. As we will see in the case of Lebanon, high-level military mediation is a key function of UNIFIL and UNTSO. At lower levels in the organizational hierarchy, civilian staff seek to mediate local disputes between civilian actors, while UN military and police mediate among armed actors.

---

[3] See Boutros-Ghali (1992) "An Agenda for Peace."

Shaming

Of all psychological tools, mediators sometimes resort to the very specific, but often effective, persuasive tool of shaming. Shame and its study have been a source of fascination for influential thinkers throughout history, in multiple academic fields, from philosophy (Artistotle 2015), to biology (Darwin 1872), to anthropology (Benedict 1946). In recent international relations research, the study of emotion in general is ascendant (Ariffin, Coicaud, and Popovski 2016; Mercer 2010; Renshon 2017). Shame, in particular, has been singled out as a particularly important motivating source of behavior change in international politics. Scholars have studied the role of NGOs, IOs, and state-level actors' peer-shaming in areas such as climate change policy (Murdie and Urpelainen 2015; Taebi and Safari 2017), child abuse in armed conflict (Nyamutata 2013), financial markets regulation (Pfaeltzer 2014), and education and trade policy (Cabus and De Witte 2012; Kende 2018).

Most studies of shaming processes, however, focus on various aspects of human rights. Beginning with a seminal edited volume by Ropp, Risse, and Sikkink (1999), scholars have studied how international human rights norms arose, are applied, and manifest in policy changes (Ausderan 2014; Barry, Clay, and Flynn 2012; Burgoon, Ruggeri, Schudel, and Manikkalingam 2015; Esarey and DeMeritt 2017; Franklin 2008; Krain 2012; Meernik, Aloisi, Sowell, and Nichols 2012). Some studies question the efficacy of this type of change, highlighting problems of enforcement, hypocrisy, biases or unevenness in application, and inadequate accountability mechanisms (Boockmann and Dreher 2011; Cole 2012; Fariss 2014; Hafner-Burton 2008; Hendrix and Wong 2013; Hill, Moore, and Mukherjee 2013; Lebovic and Voeten 2006 and 2009). Many examine the progressions by which human rights norms are diffused and absorbed, in processes of socialization (Finnemore 1996a; Goodman and Jinks 2013; Greenhill 2010; Simmons 2009; Simmons, Dobbin, and Garett 2007).

As Barnett and Finnemore explain, "IOs often use various sorts of shaming techniques ... to get states and non-state actors to comply with existing or emergent international practices" (2005, 176). Changing behavior through shaming is often more effective when it is conducted by friends rather than by adversaries (Terman and Voeten 2018). In the case of UNTAG in Namibia, I examine processes of peer shaming between leaders in the UN Secretariat, the P-5, and South Africa. I note that the more the SRSG appeared cordial with the South Africans, the more they were willing to compromise. When they were not compliant, the SRSG called on other political authorities – UN Secretary-General Javier Pérez de Cuéllar and Prime Minister Margaret Thatcher of the United Kingdom – to shame South Africans and their surrogates in Namibia into sticking with the process.

Outreach and the Department of Public Information

Outreach is a concept that developed over time in religious communities as a way to connect the faithful with wider populations, often through providing services, in hopes of conversion (Patrick 2013; Wuthnow 2009). Thus the original notion is linked with inducement. In the United Nations, however, "outreach" is conceived as nonmaterial, and nonreligious.[4] The Outreach Division of the United Nations' Department of Public Information in New York "fosters dialogue with global constituencies such as academia, civil society, the entertainment industry, educators and students to encourage support for the ideals and activities of the United Nations" (United Nations 2018a). Outreach is a key component of the UN's legitimation strategy – the way in which the organization attempts to justify its actions by appealing to common norms (Goddard 2008, 121). In the UN system, outreach is often about attempted persuasion through delivering information. But sometimes it delves deeper.

If we conceive of war as largely a problem of private information (Fearon 1995), it follows that, by developing information-gathering and possibly intelligence capacities, the United Nations might better resolve conflicts (Norheim-Martinsen and Ravndal 2011). However, "the United Nations is neither technologically advanced nor psychologically equipped" for this type of endeavor (Dorn 2010, 1; see also Barry 2012). Although peacekeepers do surveil (as I explore further in Chapter 4), the use of information thus far in peacekeeping has been largely about conveying intent and seeking to control or offset damaging narratives through the UN's persuasive outreach, rather

---

[4] This nonmaterial conception is similar to that emerging among American armed forces, but coupling persuasion with compellence means compellence dominates. See Bishnoi (2006), de Dardel (2004), Kupchan (2010), Sprenger (2008), Williams (2018).

than gathering military intelligence in order to defeat an adversary. UN member states are wary of the UN developing an independent capacity to gather intelligence.

Members of the UN Secretariat have pushed to develop "public information campaigns by peacekeeping missions aimed at the local population" (Oksamytna 2018, 79). As Oksamytna explains, "Information plays an important role in volatile post-conflict environments and can both advance and endanger the peace process" (2018, 80).[5] The first peacekeeping mission to develop a public information capacity was UNTAG in Namibia (Lehmann 1999, 28). UNTAG was also the first mission to have a "visual identity ... UNTAG's slogans and symbols were printed on stationery, posters, decals, badges, bumper stickers, and T-shirts ... A 'particularly gifted Namibian artist' [created] linocuts of Namibian faces [to assemble] an electoral poster, which became 'everyone's image of UNTAG, and 'the best known thing'" (Oksamytna 2018, 92. See Photo 2, page 181). In recent years, public information in peacekeeping has taken on the more forward-leaning title of "strategic communications," but the practices remain largely similar, with the overriding purpose being "to promote consensus around a peace process" (United Nations 2008, 83; see also de Dardel 2004; and Price and Stremlau 2016).

Symbolic Displays

Symbolic displays are often employed as an integral component of outreach efforts. Symbols represent or characterize an entity or relationship. They are the vehicles through which societies make meaning and, eventually, culture (Bourdieu 1991; Gupta 2000; Kertzer 1988; Lakoff and Johnson 1980; Ross 2009). Social anthropologists study contests over symbols, their meaning, and how symbols may represent changing power relationships between individuals and groups (Bryan 2000, 7; Cohen 1974, 29). International relations scholars have explored the exercise of power and legitimacy through symbols of the United Nations Security Council (Claude 1966; Hurd 2002). As Hurd explains, "taking seriously the symbolic power of the Council

---

[5] For example, the absence of UN radio programming in Rwanda, coupled with the decision to allow the genocidaires to control the airwaves during the genocide, are some of the reasons why the UN may be considered complicit in the genocide (Straus 2008, 29, 240).

helps us to see the reasons behind certain otherwise inexplicable phenomena in international relations ... most political conflicts have symbolic payoffs at their root, which a concern only with studying material gains will inevitably misunderstand" (Hurd 2002, 35).

Anthropologists have extended this type of argument to explore the symbolic nature of peacekeeping. Richard Rubinstein explains the importance of paying careful attention to the symbols that peacekeepers employ: "interveners must attend to the symbols used in a site to convey meaning. These symbols may be words, pictures, activities, or objects that convey meanings conventionally recognized by group members. Symbols do not exist in isolation; rather, they are part of a symbolic system" (Rubinstein 2005, 533). The "root metaphor" of the United Nations is that of an actor of peace and multilateralism (Rubinstein 2005; Ruggie 1992). Peacekeepers are the most visible sign of these purposes. As Rubinstein exhorts: "It is essential to ensure that the symbolism and cultural practices incorporated into peacekeeping operations are supported by the meanings at the core of the root metaphor of a pacific world order, symbolized by the United Nations" (2005, 542; see also Autesserre 2010 and 2014).

In Namibia, the UN, performed symbolic acts of great importance, such as the UN General Assembly vote to recognize the South West African People's Organization (SWAPO) as the "authentic representative" of the Namibian people – and not South Africa (A/RES/3111, XXVIII, 12 December 1973). This symbolic act was purely nonmaterial but eventually had material consequences, paving the way to Namibian independence. In peacekeeping, peacekeepers themselves are symbols of peaceful, international solidarity. Peacekeepers also employ a wide variety of symbols – colors, signs, and slogans – to convey their character and purpose. Most notably, they wear blue hats and helmets, and drive in white vehicles marked with the large, black letters, "UN," to symbolize their pacific intent. The white four-by-four vehicle, however, does not always convey the message of peace, but rather sometimes aloofness and superiority (Autesserre 2010). Symbolic displays alone are not always self-explanatory and sometimes require verbal explanation through outreach and public information, or training programs.

Training and Education

As I demonstrate in this chapter, "outreach" in peacekeeping takes on many forms – from mere public information campaigns to deeper attempts at societal transformation through processes of socialization. Although most of the literature on states and socialization processes focuses on the elite level, in peacekeeping, the practices are often more localized. The most material manifestation of the UN's attempts at socialization comes in the form of training and educational programs.

Currently, the UN undertakes training programs in all of its multidimensional missions, as part of its regular practices. From meditation techniques, to political party formation, to human rights norms, to gender sensitivity, to elections monitoring, all missions seek to change behavior through training as a form of persuasive power. This does not mean, however, that training is always efficient or effective (Oksamytna 2018, 80; Solli, de Carvalho, de Coning, and Pedersen 2011).

Training programs arose first in the UN missions in Namibia and Cambodia, focusing on elections preparation, human rights monitoring and reforming national police forces. In Namibia, in a creative innovation, a Dutch police battalion began training Namibian police in democratic policing practices. This training was enabled in part by language affinities (Dutch is close to Afrikaans, the language of most Namibian police at the time). The Dutch battalion was then transferred to the UN's mission in Cambodia, where language and cultural differences precluded effective training (none of the Dutch officers spoke Khmer). This example of effective and ineffective training opens a window on the general conditions under which persuasion may, or may not, prove successful.

Conditions for Effective Persuasion

The literature on persuasion is vast and multidisciplinary. It addresses a wide variety of ways in which actors seek to influence each other using nonmaterial means. However, the literature does converge on some general findings that are relevant for understanding the conditions under which persuasion in peacekeeping may be effective. These include: (1) asserting one, coherent message, (2) understanding and respecting the target of the message, and (3) aligning behavior and actions with the message or ideas being presented. I address each in turn, followed by a discussion of the observable implications of persuasion in peacekeeping.

Messaging and Communicating

First, in terms of messaging and communicating, many scholars point to shared values in a community as an essential precondition for effective persuasion (Habermas 1981; Risse 2000). Writing in the Habermasian tradition, Thomas Risse discusses this precondition as the sharing of a "common lifeworld," where collective interpretations are facilitated by a common language, history, or culture. Although commonality has often proven helpful in peacekeeping, such as in the example of language affinities, this commonality is not always possible because of the multinational character of peacekeeping. Part of the intent of peacekeepers, however, is to *create* commonality and community, amongst both themselves and the peacekept.

In peacekeeping, a prior condition for effective persuasion is not necessarily that all members of A share a common lifeworld, but they must come to a consensus on a clear and unified message. The traditional and early multidimensional peacekeeping missions enjoyed nearly unanimous consent within the United Nations system about peacekeeping doctrine and the overall message that peacekeepers were deployed "to help everyone, and harm no one." Peacekeepers would occasionally wield their weapons, but only in self-defence. Of late, however, this central message is confused. Peacekeepers are now being implored to "change their mindset," and to be proactive about the use of force (Cruz, Phillips, and Cusimano 2017). The attempt at peacekeeper mind-set change is also manifest in the "Kigali" principles, where troop-contributing countries have been asked to pledge that their peacekeepers will take the initiative in using force to protect civilians (High Level Conference on the Protection of Civilians 2015). Thus far, only about one-third of troop- and police- contributing countries have agreed to sign onto the Kigali principles (Global Center for the Responsibility to Protect 2018). In other words, today, there is deep disagreement about the basic mind-set and message of peacekeeping: is it about using proactive force, or eschewing the use of force, in favor of relying on other means of power to change behavior? I return to this debate in this book's concluding chapter. In the case of Namibia, however, messaging was generally unified and clear. Peacekeepers also exhibited curiosity about, and respect for, Namibians.

Understanding and Respecting B

The power of persuasion in peacekeeping rests not only on having a unified message but also on listening to, understanding, and respecting the target audience, which fosters willingness to receive the message.

The notion of respect for the target audience has been well documented in psychology-based studies of consumer behavior (Perloff 2014; Zimbardo and Leippe 1991). Nye agrees: "All power depends on context – who related to whom under what circumstances – but soft power depends more than hard power upon the existence of willing interpreters and receivers" (2004, 16). Willingness is predicated on establishing a relationship of respect. The people on the receiving end of any message are not simply empty vessels to be filled or manipulated. In order to effectively persuade, peacekeepers must understand the context in which they are deployed and how they are being received, and must constantly update and renew their relations with the citizens of the country (Autesserre 2010; Rubinstein 2005).

In Namibia, peacekeepers – especially the sizeable civilian staff – were instructed to interact directly with Namibians on an everyday basis, as a way to gain mutual trust and confidence, exchange information, and ultimately assist in a peaceful transition. In recent years, the fear of peacekeeper sexual abuse and exploitation has motivated leaders in peacekeeping missions to distance their troops from locals, and to avoid "fraternization." However, as I contend later, frequent, low-level interaction is one of the main ways in which peacekeepers persuade. Persuasion relies on listening to and learning from the peace-kept. It also relies on practicing what one preaches.

Aligning Message and Behavior

Aligning message with behavior is a necessary factor for effective persuasion. As Nye explains about soft power in general: "the resources that produce soft power arise ... in the examples it sets by its internal practices and policies, and in the way it handles its relations with others" (Nye 2009, 8). The constructivist literature on discursive causality generally centers on positive cases, where ideas and accompanying arguments provide the ideational impetus for institutional, normative, and even sometimes cultural change (Bukovansky 2002; Clunan 2009; Crawford 2002; Jackson 2006; Risse 2000). Sometimes the mechanism works more through "naming and shaming" (Barnett and Finnemore 2004). The empirical landscape of peacekeeping provides fertile ground to demonstrate where, when, and why attempts at ideational change occasionally succeed, but also where, when, and why they fall short. In contrast to the early "ideations" work, constructivism has taken a "practice" and "habit" turn in recent years – particularly to examine phenomena that appear to follow neither a logic of consequences or appropriateness (Adler 1997; Checkel 1998; Hopf 2010; Howard 2015b; March and Olsen 1998; Pouliot 2008).

In this book, I draw on both strands in the literature – discursive causality as well as practices – to show how attempts at communicative action can clash with peacekeeping practices. Sometimes a clash between the UN's objectives and actions can lead to learning and effective organizational change (Campbell 2018; Howard 2008). Dissonance between word and action, however, can also lead to significant problems, such as when peacekeepers proactively use their weapons, or in the domain of sexual abuse and exploitation. The problems of sexual abuse and exploitation represent the deepest disconnect between word and deed in peacekeeping today. Sexually abusing the very people whom peacekeepers were sent to protect fundamentally undermines peacekeeping's – and the whole UN system's – ability to employ the power of persuasion. I will return to these issues in Chapter 4, on coercion, examining the case of UN peacekeeping and French stabilization forces in the Central African Republic. In sum, peacekeepers employ a variety of suasion tools, including mediation, shaming, outreach, symbolic displays, and training/education. How might we observe these processes at work?

Observable Implications of Effective Persuasion

Nye contends that soft power cannot regularly be observed in specific actions: "attraction often has a diffuse effect, creating general influence rather than producing easily observable specific action ... Nonetheless, the indirect effects of attraction and a diffuse influence can make a significant difference in obtaining favorable outcomes" (Nye 2009, 16). If we are thinking of soft power primarily as attraction, then it may indeed be difficult to trace causal processes. But Nye also sees persuasion as a more direct component of soft power; this direct dimension is easier to trace causally. I contend that in peacekeeping, there are several observable implications that may indicate effective persuasion:

1. The communicator issues a unified message that "attempts to induce a change in the belief, attitude, or behavior of another" (Perloff 1993, 15).

2. The communicator (A) may employ one or more tools of persuasion: mediation, shaming, outreach, symbolic displays, and training/education.
3. The persuadee (B) has some free choice.
4. A exhibits understanding of, and respect for, B.
5. A aligns behavior and action.
6. B changes behavior.
7. B may or may not vocalize that s/he changed behavior because of A's ideas.

In my case studies, in the course of tracing the key causal factors in this complex process, I searched for evidence of these observables. I note, however, that even if UN peacekeepers satisfy all of these conditions, because persuasion is inherently about choice, the peacekept might not choose to go along.

In sum, I argue that the ability to persuade in peacekeeping is observable, and that persuasion – primarily through the mechanisms of mediation, shaming, symbolic displays, outreach, and training/education – is an important source of power in UN peacekeeping. A key prior condition for effective persuasion is broad agreement within the UN about the central ideas, principles, and normative expectations about the content of what peacekeepers ought to communicate to belligerents and local populations. Without agreement about the fundamental message, it is not possible for others to receive the message or be persuaded by it. Peacekeepers must also demonstrate a genuine willingness to understand and respect the expectations, norms, and culture of the peacekept, even if unfamiliar, which fosters willingness to receive the message. Finally, the shared ideas, principles, and norms must align with peacekeepers' behavior and practices. When peacekeeping practices contradict the communicative action of peacekeepers, there is little chance of persuasion.

I demonstrate in Namibia that the UN's ideas and norms of peacekeeping were, for the most part, clear and unified, and aligned with the actions of peacekeepers; the messages were also delivered in a respectful manner and based on a deep understanding of the specific circumstances in pre-independence Namibia. Through the tools of mediation, shaming, symbolic displays, outreach, and education/training, the staff of UNTAG effectively exercised the power of persuasion. In contrast, as I show in Chapter 4, since 2016, the basic message of the peacekeepers in the Central African Republic has been unclear (are they deployed in Central Africa to fight or not?). Peacekeepers have committed sexual abuse, thus severely undermining trust. As evidenced in growing death and displacement numbers in general, and the Sukula battle in the spring of 2018 in particular, UN peacekeepers appear to have lost their capacity to persuade. Such a loss did not occur in Namibia.

Namibia

Namibia is a sparsely populated but large country, measuring about one and one-half times the size of France.[6] It has two immense deserts encroaching on much of the land – the Namib in the west and the Kalahari in the east. Namibia is also home to abundant diamond, uranium, zinc, and other mineral reserves, as well as natural gas. There are about one dozen ethnic and linguistic groups; the Ovambo make up about 50 percent of the population (Central Intelligence Agency 2017). Upwards of 90 percent of Namibians regularly attend church, and they belong to more than one dozen different faiths. Lutheranism – introduced by Finnish missionaries in the 1870s – holds a plurality in this dimension. In 1990, the population stood at about 1.5 million. Today it is about 2.5 million; population growth has slowed in recent years (Central Intelligence Agency 2017).

Background

Namibia is unlike any other country in the world, in that it has endured nearly every major sociopolitical malignancy conceived in recent history. In the late 1700s, the United Kingdom colonized parts of the country, but then Germany seized most of it as "German South West Africa." In retribution for resistance from the minority Herero and Nama, German colonists committed genocide against the two ethnic groups in the early 1900s.[7] As Dr. Peter Katjavivi, founding vice-chancellor of the University of Namibia, explains of German

---

[6] Parts of this section are from Howard (2002).

[7] Germans systematically killed approximately 65,000 Herero (about 80 percent of the group) and about 50 percent of the Nama – about 10,000 people (Amukugo 1993, 131; Caroll 1967; Madley 2005). It was in Namibia that Germans first experimented in eradicating populations they did not like.

colonialism: "First, land was taken from the Namibian people and made available to German settlers. Second, traditional structures were destroyed. Third, Namibians were used as forced laborers on the now white-owned land and the new mines and early industries ... no education was provided for Namibians by the German colonial regime" (1988, 11). After Germany's defeat in World War II, Namibia was slated to fall under UN Trusteeship, but South Africa claimed the territory as "South West Africa," refusing to relinquish control. In 1948, South Africa formalized its *apartheid* system of institutionalized racial segregation in Namibia.

SWAPO

Starting in the late 1950s, Namibian elites (often in exile) sought peaceful means to self-rule through UN recognition, but by the mid-1960s, it was clear that South Africa and its supporters would not permit such a transition (Katjavivi 1988, 34–58). The leading Namibian independence movement, the South West African Peoples' Organization (SWAPO), turned, as many independence movements of the time did, to armed struggle. The war in Namibia progressed over time from a guerilla war of independence to a civil war, as South Africa increasingly developed indigenous Namibian forces to fight SWAPO. But the war was also part of a larger, decades-long regional struggle, with separate but at times interrelated fighting in Angola, Mozambique, Namibia, South Africa, and Zimbabwe (Mandela 2004; Nujoma 2001). Thus, from 1966 to 1989, Namibia succumbed to simultaneous independence, regional, and civil wars (Dreyer 1994; Katjavivi 1988).

Around the time of the crumbling of Portuguese colonial rule in Angola and Mozambique in 1974 and in the lead-up to Zimbabwean independence (which eventually arrived in 1979), most Namibians thought their time for liberation had come. A 1978 "settlement proposal," approved in UN Security Council Resolution 435, outlined the basic principles of a UN-assisted Namibian transition to independence. But international disputes rooted in the Cold War prevented the start of the plan's implementation for more than a decade. The rough international political division over Namibia was between, on one side, South Africa; the Namibian "internal parties," especially the Democratic Turnhalle Alliance (DTA); and, at times, the Western Contact Group.[8] On the other side stood SWAPO, the majority of states in the UN General Assembly, the Non-Aligned Movement, the Organization for African Unity, and the frontline states.[9]

The DTA, SWATF, SWAPOL, and Koevoet

The conservative, multiracial DTA is the second-largest political party in Namibia, and one that is still struggling to rid itself of its identity as the "colonial collaborator" (Dreyer 1994, 109). Part of the DTA's political platform during the 1980s included the claim that the party would protect Namibia from the spread of socialism as promulgated by SWAPO. The DTA enjoyed significant financial support from South Africa during the 1970s and 1980s. Another important aspect of South Africa's strategy to maintain its sway over Namibia was to develop indigenous military and militarized police forces to fight SWAPO and its People's Liberation Army of Namibia (PLAN). Under the 1980 legis-lative proclamation AG 8, Namibians of fighting age were forcibly conscripted into the South West African Territorial Force (SWATF), which the South African Defense Forces (SADF) designed to fight alongside themselves, against SWAPO/PLAN, mainly in the north.[10] By 1986, "officially, 35,000 [SADF] troops were stationed in Namibia, with unofficial estimates indicating the much higher number of 80,000" (Dreyer 1994, 161). Joining the SADF, by 1989, the SWATF had grown to more than 30,000 troops, about half of whom were nonwhite Namibians.

In addition, 7,000–10,000 Namibians (Cliffe 1994, 33) were hired into well-paying "counterinsurgency" units, under command of the South West African Police (SWAPOL). The most infamous was the Koevoet or "crowbar" unit. The vast majority of Koevoet troops – upwards of 90 percent – were ethnic Ovambos, with an all-white command (Hearn 1999, 79). Notorious for their brutal and

---

[8] The "Western Contact Group" was set up in 1977 to aid in the mediation process. Its members were the United States, the United Kingdom, France, West Germany, and Canada.

[9] The frontline states included Tanzania, Zambia, Angola, Mozambique, Botswana, Zimbabwe, and Nigeria.

[10] This rule provoked massive protests within Namibia, and a 5,000-person refugee exodus. See Official Gazette Extraordinary of South West Africa 1980.

indiscriminate use of force – especially against SWAPO supporters who were also primarily Ovambo – some analysts contend that the Koevoet were responsible for the majority of civilian deaths during the 1980s (Leys 1989; Wren 1989). Describing themselves as the "exterminators," the Koevoet's preferred vehicles were menacing "Casspir" and "Wolf" armed personnel carriers mounted with 0.50-caliber machine guns (Hearn 1999, 80). The Koevoet were supposed to be disbanded before the start of UNTAG, but instead, according to official reports, 1,200 ex-Koevoet were transferred into SWAPOL; unofficial reports indicated more than twice that number (Hearn 1999, 80). Ties between the Koevoet and the Democratic Turnhalle Alliance (DTA) were deep, with Koevoet members visibly wearing DTA T-shirts during the transition period from 1989 to 1990 (Hearn 1999, 82–93). Also during the transition, SWAPOL, which included hundreds if not thousands of Koevoet, was the *only* entity that held the official monopoly over the use of force in Namibia (Hearn 1999, 78). During the 1980s, the war of liberation from South Africa took on more of the quality of a civil war, with Namibian political groups and military forces fighting each other for control of the state.[11] The battle, however, was not simply one of brute coercive capacity, but also of ideas and access to education.

Education

During the 1970s and 1980s, in part because SWAPO and its PLAN were so overpowered by South Africa and forces loyal to it in Namibia, leaders of the Namibian independence movement sought non-coercive forms of international support. In 1973, the UN General Assembly voted to recognize SWAPO as the "sole and authentic" representative of the Namibian people. Beyond this symbolic display, at the same time, Namibian students in exile at the University of Western Cape in South Africa banded together to form the Namibian Student Organization (NAMSO) to fight Bantu education and inequality and to establish English (not Afrikaans) as the medium for instruction in schools (Amukugo 1993, 118–119). As the NAMSO students explained, Bantu education "is the foundation of racism and group

---

[11] The buildup of these forces meant that more than half of those fighting SWAPO were indigenous Namibians – a potentially dangerous circumstance that was overlooked in the peace deals of the late 1980s because the external mediators, at South Africa's request, refused to allow SWAPO to negotiate on its own behalf.

identity; it is there to prepare black students for a third-class citizenship. It is a propaganda machinery of apartheid, dehumanization, and discrimination" (Rogerson 1980, 678).

NAMSO's efforts began to bear institutional fruit when Irish human rights activist and UN Commissioner for Namibia (and eventual Nobel Peace Prize winner), Sean MacBride took up the cause of creating a United Nations Institute for Namibia. In the fall of 1974, the UN Security Council and General Assembly approved the start of this unusual institute, to be housed in Zambia (with funding from the UN, bilateral government assistance, and the Ford Foundation). As President Kenneth Kaunda explained: "This is the first time in history of a non-self-governing country that the international community has taken the initiative before liberation of preparing the infrastructure and administration that will be required as soon as freedom is achieved" (Rogerson 1980, 676). The Institute initially housed six academic departments – in law, economics, agricultural management, etc. – that were geared toward preparing a civil service that would govern Namibia. The Institute was founded on three principles that could be held as an example for all "intermestic" projects such as peacekeeping:

(1) That as far as possible it should project the views of Namibians, and be administered in such a manner as to further their interests; (2) that being established outside Namibia, but within the continent, it should reflect an African outlook; and (3) that as the progeny of the world community, it should also be international in scope. (Rogerson 1980, 676)[12]

Thus, from early on, education played an important role in Namibian and UN efforts to see out a peaceful end to the conflict, but the conflict dragged on.

Linkage

The central cause of delayed Namibian independence was the American-, South African- and British-agreed "linkage" policy. In neighboring Angola, 50,000 Cuban troops were fighting alongside the Marxist-sympathetic Angolan government. According to the linkage plan, the Cuban troops had to withdraw before Namibia could be granted

[12] Shortly after Namibian independence in March 1990, the UN Institute for Namibia moved to Windhoek and became the University of Namibia.

independence. In late 1988, the war in Angola reached a military stale-mate, after South African and Angolan rebel forces were defeated during the Battle of Cuito Cuanevale. The large costs to South Africa for supporting the military operations in Angola and Namibia, coupled with anti-apartheid international economic sanctions and the growing anti-apartheid mobilization of church groups, students, and workers in Namibia and South Africa, led the South African government to back down on its military campaigns (Price 1991, 277; Wood 2003). These events, as well as the ouster of the P. W. Botha administration, the release of Nelson Mandela from prison on Robben Island, and Soviet sugges-tions to stop the armed struggle, all culminated in an opening in the Namibian negotiations.

South Africa insisted on excluding SWAPO from all official deliber-ations, a demand to which its main supporters on the Security Council – the United States and the United Kingdom – assented. Sub-sequently, the Protocols of Geneva and Brazzaville and the Tripartite Accord were all signed in 1988 by the governments of Angola, Cuba, and South Africa, under the mediation of American diplomat and scholar Chester Crocker (S/20566, 4 April 1989; S/20346, 22 December 1988). These agreements stipulated the withdrawal of South African and Cuban troops from Angola in exchange for Namibian independ-ence, but they did not specify the mechanics of political transition in Namibia. Namibia was an afterthought, mentioned only in passing. Given SWAPO's exclusion from the process and the deepening civil war in Namibia, more mediation and eventual "multidimensional" peacekeeping proved necessary.

To that end, since South Africa refused to legitimate SWAPO by signing an agreement directly with the party, UN Secretary-General Pérez de Cuéllar pieced together a ceasefire declaration between SWAPO and South Africa by asking each party to sign identical letters to him pledging to abide by Security Council Resolution 435, and the date of 1 April 1989 for the ceasefire. Thus, by implication, UNTAG was to begin operations on that day.

The formal ceasefire and implementation start date was set for 1 April 1989. But the debates in the Security Council and the General Assembly dragged on to 1 March, which meant that UNTAG would not be fully operational until well into May 1989. The western powers argued that the main problem – Cuban troop withdrawal from Angola – had been solved (Crocker 1992, 484). Therefore, UNTAG's budget should be cut severely – they recommended halving the

UNTAG military component from the original estimate of more than 7,500 troops.[13] In contrast, the nonaligned countries contended that the situation on the ground in Namibia had changed for the worse, in that there were many more South African–trained and sympathetic police and Security Forces fighting against SWAPO in a civil war. They argued that this new ground situation necessitated *more* of an UNTAG presence rather than less (Pérez de Cuéllar 1997, 308). The Secretariat, represented by UN Secretary-General Pérez de Cuéllar, split the difference. It recommended that troop levels be kept at the original number in reserve but that only 4,650 be deployed.

The budget for the operation was cut from approximately $700 million to $416 million, but none of the implementation tasks, as detailed in the next section, were removed (United Nations 1996, 228). By 1 April, the official start of the ceasefire, UNTAG only had some 300 military observers on the ground, and hardly any office space for its staff. This inadequate presence worked to precipitate the violent clashes of early April, which almost led to complete failure just as the mission was beginning.

Death and Displacement

Most of the killing in Namibia took place during the period of delayed independence. Unlike today's civil wars, where civilians are often directly targeted, most deaths in Namibia were military. In all, approximately 11,291 of SWAPO's People's Liberation Army (PLAN) fighters, 2,000 civilians, and 715 South African–sponsored security forces were killed in the Namibian battles. In terms of displacement, somewhere between 44,000 and 90,000 Namibians were made refugees out of a pre-independence population of 1.4 million (Brown 1995, 37; Ntchatcho 1993, 65; Steenkamp 1989, 185). During UNTAG, all of the refugees returned, and most of the killing ceased, but not during the first week or so of the mission.

Mandate

Confusingly, the UNTAG mandate stems from many sources: (1) the Contact Group's Settlement Proposal of 10 April 1978 (S/12636,

---

[13] As one scholar explains, the United States had "a regional strategy and was not explicitly concerned with internal conflicts" (Weiland and Braham 1994, 78).

10 April 1978); (2) the Secretary-General's report of 29 August 1978 (S/12827, 29 August 1978); (3) Security Council Resolution 435 of 29 September 1978 (with an update four years later on constitutional principles); the three agreements between Angola, Cuba, and South Africa of 1988–1989 (Protocol of Brazzaville 13 December; 1988 S/20566, 4 April 1989; S/20346, 22 December 1988); and, finally, Security Council Resolution 632 of 16 February 1989.

This unusual, multipronged mandating process requires a bit of explanation. Unlike at the end of most wars, Namibia never had formal peace negotiations because the South Africans, who to the very end, refused to speak directly with SWAPO representatives as equals, even though, in 1971, the UN General Assembly voted to recognize SWAPO as "the sole and authentic" voice of the Namibian people. Therefore, the process was anything but straightforward or easy.

First, the members of the Western Contact Group – the United States, the United Kingdom, France, West Germany, and Canada – devised a "Settlement Proposal," which called for free and fair elections to pave the way for a transition to Namibian independence. The proposal included the mandate for the Secretary-General to appoint a Special Representative, who "will have to satisfy himself at each stage as to the fairness and appropriateness of all measures affecting the political process at all levels of administration before such measures take effect. Moreover, the Special Representative may himself make proposals in regard to any aspect of the political process" (S/12636, 10 April 1978, para. 5). This proposal placed the Special Representative at the center of all operational decision-making. Finnish diplomat Martti Ahtisaari was chosen for the position in 1978, after his appointment as the UN General Assembly's Commissioner for Namibia starting the year before. Ahtisaari had previously held diplomatic posts in Africa, serving as Finnish Ambassador to Tanzania, with accreditation to Zambia, Mozambique, and Somalia. Ahtisaari would eventually become the UN Under Secretary-General for Administration before serving as UN Special Representative in Namibia, and later, the President of Finland.[14]

---

[14] Ahtisaari has since played important roles in peace negotiations across the world, including in Bosnia, Aceh, Iraq, Central Asia, and Kosovo. In 2008, he won the Nobel Peace Prize for his work.

The Settlement Proposal included a very specific timetable for the steps necessary to pave the way for elections, with explicit tasks that the UN, the South African government, and SWAPO were to fulfill. The elections were to create an independent Namibian Constituent Assembly, which would draw up a constitution immediately after being elected, and govern as the independent Namibian "National Assembly" from then on. All adult Namibians would be eligible to express political views, form political parties, and vote by secret ballot without fear of discrimination. Before the election campaigns, discriminatory or restrictive laws were to be repealed, refugees welcomed back into the country, hostile acts were to cease, and political prisoners were to be released. An independent jurist would be appointed to oversee matters concerning the release of political prisoners and detainees.

Although the above provisions concerning the elections were basically clear, some uncertainties remained, many of which were resolved five months later in the Secretary-General's report S/12827 of 29 August 1978. For example, Secretary-General Javier Pérez de Cuéllar requested specific numbers of forces based on estimates of the numbers of South African forces in the country. He united the civilian and military components of UNTAG, and put them under the civilian command of Special Representative Ahtisaari. He also broadly defined the military component's ability to use force in self-defense, including "resistance to attempts to prevent it from discharging its duties under the mandate of the Security Council," although the Security Council mandated the mission under Chapter VI of the UN charter, which enables the "pacific settlement" of disputes, and not Chapter VII, which stipulates "enforcement" measures. Pérez de Cuéllar estimated the exit date for this unusual peacekeeping mission to occur one year from the start date (S/12827, 29 August 1978, part II, para. 20).

The Secretary-General's report, however, did not address a number of issues including: the start date of the operation; how and whether SWAPO would be restricted to base; the process of disarmament; police, judicial, and constitutional reform; reform of the civil service; economic reform, including the question of land redistribution; the specifics of financing the operation; and the extent to which the UN would be "controlling" or merely "supervising" the elections. These uncertainties, while potentially hindering the operation, actually helped SRSG Ahtisaari define the mission based on the realities of

1989 when the operation began, rather than 1978, when the mandate was initially drafted.

Finally, Security Council Resolution 435 of 29 September 1978, a rather brief document, accepted the settlement proposal and the Secretary-General reports, reiterated the objective of the withdrawal of South Africa's "illegal administration" of Namibia, welcomed SWAPO's readiness to sign a ceasefire, called on South Africa to sign, and later included an annex on broad constitutional principles. Other than the constitutional principles, it did not attempt to address the thorny issues listed above.

The 435 vote was not unanimous. In a mild diplomatic counter to the western initiative, the USSR and Czechoslovakia abstained while China did not participate in the vote. As the Soviet Ambassador to the UN at the time, Anatolyi Adamishin, explains: "We [Soviets] did not hate 435, we only considered it unbalanced... Our African friends asked us not to veto it because it was better than nothing. So we agreed. Later our friends reproached us, requesting that we do something about it because it gave too many advantages to South Africa. But by then it was too late" (Weiland and Braham 1994, 21).

But the resolution also gave many advantages to SWAPO, namely internationally-supported majority rule and independence through free and fair elections. Although it appeared that conditions were ripe for 435's implementation, both sides remained resistant to setting a cease-fire date, believing each was being pressured by its allies to concede too much. The fighting endured another ten years.

In 1988, as the Cold War was winding down, all sides appeared ready to restart negotiations. After the Angolan battlefield stalemate in Cuito Cuanevale, Angola, Cuba, and South Africa, under the mediation of Chester Crocker, signed the Protocols of Geneva and Brazzaville, and the Tripartite agreement. These accords set dates for Cuban and SADF troop withdrawal from Angola, UN verification of the withdrawals, SWAPO deployment to north of the 16th parallel in Angola, and a "Joint Commission" between Angola, Cuba, and South Africa (with the US and USSR as observers) as "a forum for discussion and resolution of issues regarding the interpretation and implementation of the tripartite agreement" (S/20566, 4 April 1989; S/20346, 22 December 1988). These agreements mentioned Namibia only in passing, but they paved the way for the Security Council to agree to allow UNTAG to begin, finally, on 1 April 1989 (S/RES/632, 16 February 1989).

The Namibian peace process was unusual because the people who were actually fighting and killing each other during the 1980s (the PLAN vs. the SWATF, SWAPOL, and Koevoet) never once sat down with their civilian leaders to hammer out their own accord. There was no written domestic agreement between SWAPO and the DTA. Neither was there an international accord between South Africa and SWAPO, because of the South African leadership's refusal to speak directly with the group. Nevertheless, UNTAG had a mandate, under Chapter VI of the UN charter, to try to make sure the peace would hold, using only the power of persuasion.

Putting all of the pieces together, UNTAG was mandated to (1) oversee a ceasefire, which included confining all troops to base, overseeing the withdrawal of South African Defense Forces, and monitoring, demobilizing, and reconstituting the military and police forces; (2) oversee the repeal of all discriminatory legislation; (3) facilitate the return of refugees in time for the elections; (4) and oversee free and fair elections for a Constituent Assembly, which would then draft a new constitution. In order to accomplish these goals, UNTAG offices would have four central components: civilian/political offices (including a civilian police component), a military division, a refugee return program, and an elections preparation division.[15] Each of these components confronted crises or shifting circumstances, and learned to employ different forms of power – mainly persuasive – in order to achieve their ends.

The Crisis of 1 April 1989

UNTAG's first task was simply to set up its offices, but this proved extremely difficult. On 1 April 1989, UNTAG's staff were supposed to begin monitoring the ceasefire and the start of the political transition. But instead, the violence re-ignited in a haze of misunderstanding, mistrust, and bad information.

---

[15] A separate component of the operation was the office of the "Independent Jurist." This office was to offer legal advice to the Special Representative when needed and oversee the release of Namibian political prisoners and detainees in South Africa and elsewhere. In the 1970s and 1980s, some 2,000 SWAPO members were allegedly detained by their fellow comrades under suspicion of spying on behalf of South Africa. In 1989, members of UNTAG visited all reported sites of SWAPO detention of Namibians and found them to be empty. However, the problems of SWAPO detaining its own remains a sore political issue even today (Groth 1995; Saul and Leys 2003).

For nearly one year, in preparation for this day, the SADF stationed in Namibia, along with SWATF indigenous troops, had been confining themselves to their bases, under the authority of South African Administrator-General of South West Africa, Louis Pienaar. Throughout the transition period, South Africa and its partners in Namibia – SWATF, Koevoet, and SWAPOL – effectively held the monopoly over the use of force, with Pienaar at the top, but SWAPO, most Namibians, and the majority of states in UN General Assembly, did not recognize this monopoly as legitimate. SWAPO's PLAN forces were positioned in both mobile and stationary bases, mainly in Angola.

In the morning of 1 April, some 300–500 PLAN fighters emerged on the Namibian border with Angola. SWAPOL/Koevoet and SWATF forces began to fire at the PLAN, believing their intentions to be aggressive. SWAPO responded by sending more PLAN reinforcements southward, from Angola, to aid their fellow PLAN fighters in Namibia. Pienaar requested that the UN permit South African Defense Forces – thousands of whom had already been restricted to base – to be released to fight in the emerging battle. The SADF declared that their troops on the battlefield were outnumbered, that SWAPO was acting in

1946 South Africa refuses to relinquish control.
1974 Institute for Namibia established in Lusaka, Zambia.
1976 UN General Assembly recognizes South West Africa People's Organization (SWAPO) as the sole and authentic representative of the Namibian people.
1978 Canada, France, the Federal Republic of Germany, the United Kingdom, and the United States submit the proposal for settling the question of Namibia to the UN Security Council. The Council legalizes the plan in S/RES 435.
1980 South Africa formally accepts the plan but does not stop fighting.
1980 AG 8. Young Namibians forcibly conscripted into the SWATF.
1988 Tripartite agreement signed by Angola, Cuba, and South Africa to end the regional war, including the withdrawal of 50,000 Cuban troops fighting alongside the government in Angola, against South African and troops in Angola.
1989 April 1, UNTAG set to begin its transitional authority; fighting breaks out between PLAN on the one side, and SADF, SWATF, and Koevoet on the other.
1989 April 9, Mt. Etjo Agreement.
1989 July Elections Code of Conduct signed by all major parties.
1989 September 12, Anton Lubowski killed.
1989 November 1, South African Foreign Minister Pik Botha claims PLAN forces preparing to invade from Angola.
1989 November 7–11, Elections, to choose the 72 delegates to the Constituent Assembly.
1989 November 22, South Africa's remaining troops depart Namibia.
1990 February 9, Constitution adopted.
1990 February 16, the Constituent Assembly elects SWAPO leader Sam Nujoma as President of the Republic for a five-year term.
1990 March 21, UNTAG closes its offices; Namibia is officially independent.

Figure 2.1 Namibia Timeline

violation of the peace accords, and that SWAPO's PLAN must be countered with force. (Figure 2.1 on page 58 summarizes the major events.)

Mechanisms of Power in UNTAG

UN Special Representative Martti Ahtisaari had arrived in Namibia before 1 April 1989, but he was unequipped materially to take control of the situation. A mere 300 UNTAG military observers had arrived several days earlier, but they were not prepared even to observe the ceasefire violation, much less try to counter it with any sort of military compellence or security guarantee. UNTAG's political offices were not established. Misinformation abounded. Ahtisaari had no carrots to induce the parties to go along with the UN's transitional assistance. The only way out was for Ahtisaari to use his diplomatic powers of persuasion. Above all, Ahtisaari needed to find a way to convince South Africa to continue with the UN-led transition plans.

At the behest of the South African government, Ahtisaari convinced Secretary-General Pérez de Cuéllar to allow some SADF and SWATF troops to leave their bases to counter the purported military attack being waged by PLAN fighters. After nine days of fighting, more than 300 PLAN fighters and civilians, and 13 SADF soldiers, had perished. After these events, South Africa and SWAPO had reason to pull out of the hard-won agreements, as both had violated them. The causes of the fighting and UNTAG's inauspicious start were numerous, but because there were no impartial observers or surveillance mechanisms in place to determine conclusively who was at fault, the episode remains mired in difference of opinion. What was clear was that it looked as though UNTAG might fail even before it began.

Persuasion: High-Level Mediation and Shaming

As the fighting subsided, high-level negotiations ensued, with South Africa emboldened by SWAPO's apparent blunder and the UN's response to allow some SADF to re-mobilize. On 9 April 1989, on Mt. Etjo, several miles to the north of the capital Windhoek, Angolan, Cuban, and South African representatives met with members of the UN (with US and USSR representatives observing), to reconfirm their commitment to the peace agreement. Representatives of the United Nations knew that the SWAPO debacle would be a perfect excuse for the South Africans to revoke their adherence to 435, ask the UN to leave, and proceed with South African plans for Namibian "independence." A South African-controlled process would not be democratic, and would enable a power shift to the white minority and other groups in Namibia who were sympathetic to racist South African rule. The South Africans, however, remained at the bargaining table, signaling to Special Representative Ahtisaari that they were serious about adhering to the internationally legitimate plan for independence. Gentle shaming by a friend in the form of diplomatic pressure from Prime Minister Thatcher during a visit to Pretoria in early April, played an important role in convincing the South Africans to uphold the UN framework.[16]

On the other side, political leaders from the non-aligned states and the Organization of African Unity, previously strong backers of the operation, accused Ahtisaari of excessive sympathy toward the South Africans (Goulding 2003, 166). Secretary-General Pérez de Cuéllar and Marrack Goulding – head of the UN's Department for Political Operations, where peacekeeping was housed at the time – received considerable criticism in New York for not acting sufficiently impartially, and not adequately representing the interests of SWAPO, given SWAPO's disadvantaged negotiating position. Pérez de Cuéllar and Goulding thus proposed that a Deputy Special Representative from one of the frontline states be added to UNTAG in the field. In a matter of weeks, Joseph Legwaila of neighboring Botswana joined the mission, and remained at Ahtisaari's side throughout (see Photo 1, p. 180).[17]

In the end, although SWAPO was not a signatory to the ceasefire declaration, its leaders accepted it. The agreement called for PLAN troops to gather at specific "assembly points" in Namibia, where they would immediately be escorted to camps north of the 16th parallel in Angola by UNTAG and South African Administrator-General observers.[18] With SWAPO forces withdrawn for the transition, and South

---

[16] Author interviews with Martti Ahtisaari, President of Finland, Kulturanta, Finland, 10–12 July 1998; and Carl von Hirschberg, retired Ambassador of South Africa and former Deputy to the South African Administrator-General, Finland, 11 July 1998.

[17] Author interview with Sir Marrack Goulding, telephone, 1 July 1999.

[18] In all, only several hundred PLAN fighters at most ever made it to the assembly points in Namibia, while 5,000 were confined to base in Angola (Dreyer 1994, 191).

African forces and their allies in Namibia demobilizing, the stage was set to begin the practical tasks of peace implementation.

High-level political negotiations and external diplomatic pressure as shaming resolved the 1 April crisis. Bringing a representative from a peaceful and prospering neighboring state into the heart of the mission served as something of a form of "localizing" ownership. But in no way did the UN provide security guarantees as a way for both sides to stand down; the SADF, SWATF, and SWAPOL/Koevoet remained the dominant military forces throughout.

In retrospect, Ahtisaari holds that he was not particularly concerned that the UNTAG military component was not on the ground to stand between the two sides during the 1 April crisis. UNTAG was not organized to perform such a task, and the seemingly pro-South African move to allow SADF forces to leave their bases helped to convince South Africa that the UN was more even-handed in its outlook than generally assumed by South African-sympathetic whites. As a consequence, the South Africans eventually became more willing to compromise with UNTAG and, eventually, with SWAPO.[19]

Ahtissari and his staff employed mediation and shaming throughout the mission. At times the levers of mediation took on nearly-institutional forms. For example, the Security Council granted Ahtisaari the authority to override AG decisions that contradicted any of the pre-transition agreements, since each step in the independence process "had to be fulfilled to the satisfaction of the Special Representative" (S/15287, 12 July 1982). As Donald McHenry, the US Ambassador, explained: "we gave [Ahtisaari] an 'atomic bomb'" (Weiland and Braham 1994, 15). But this "bomb" was based on ideas and not material in nature. The Administrator-General (AG) Louis A. Pienaar's office still functioned as the main legal authority in the country. Pienaar also, of course, held the reins over the South African-sympathetic military forces.

The Administrator-General's office sought to thwart UNTAG's operations in a variety of ways. For example, the "Status of Forces Agreement" between South Africa and the UN set out the legal and logistical conditions under which the UN could function (S/29412/Add.1, 16 March 1989). Despite careful advanced planning between the two delegations, South Africa often breached the agreement. UNTAG personnel were often caught up in bureaucratic hassles such

---

[19] Author interviews with Ahtisaari; see also Thornberry (2004, 111).

as being presented with unauthorized customs duties and taxes, and problems securing diplomatic pouches (Unpublished UN Report #1, 1). When such problems could not be solved within Namibia, Ahtisaari would call officials in South Africa and UN headquarters, threatening Pienaar and his administration with political sanction and/or bad press; usually the shaming techniques were effective, and the Administrator-General's office would acquiesce.

In another important example of high-level mediation and shaming, several days before the November elections, South African Foreign Minister Pik Botha held a press conference announcing falsely that SWAPO forces had again amassed on the Angolan side of the border, and were preparing to invade Namibia. CIVPOL, along with the UNTAG military, and district and regional centers, quickly determined that the reports were false, and widely publicized South Africa's duplicity. Also in response, the Security Council issued a statement "deploring South Africa's false alarm of 1 November, and calling on South Africa to desist from any such further actions" (United Nations 1989). Unlike the similar-sounding alarm of 1 April 1989, this time UNTAG had outreach and information mechanisms in place to establish the veracity of the reports, and preempt a possible armed clash through persuasive means.

Persuasion: Outreach and Public Information

After the crisis of 1 April, UNTAG deployed to a country that was plagued by three interrelated problems. First, Namibia had been at war for decades, and deep mistrust and fear pervaded the social atmosphere. Leaders of the main political parties, along with their followers, had often never spoken directly with their adversaries. Second, disinformation in the lead-up to the elections abounded, since the South African Administrator General controlled the South West African Broadcasting Corporation (SWABC), most importantly, the radio airwaves. Third, over the course of the 1980s, and accelerating in the lead-up to UNTAG's deployment, the main police force in Namibia, the "SWAPOL" had become militarized. Members of the notoriously violent counterinsurgency police called the "Koevoet" had integrated in large numbers into SWAPOL (instead of being disbanded, as the South Africans had promised). In 1989–1990, this militarized SWAPOL was "the only security force officially operating in Namibia" (Hearn 1999, 78). Unlike the UN, it held the official monopoly over the use of force in the territory; UNTAG had only persuasive means to counter them. The UNTAG leadership and staff devised creative ways to overcome each of these obstacles, using different aspects of the power of persuasion. An unpublished UN report on Namibia explains,

> While the central feature of UNTAG's overall mandate was the supervision of free and fair elections for a Constituent Assembly in a transition to independence acceptable to the whole international community, the SRSG [Ahtisaari] had decided that such free and fair elections could take place only if no less than a major change in the overall atmosphere of the country had first taken place; so that the Namibian people could feel free, and sufficiently informed, to express genuine choice as to their future. (Unpublished UN Report #2, para. 30)

For 10 years, Ahtisaari had been pushing for "a massive active intervention by UNTAG to change the political climate in the country" (Unpublished UN Report #2, para. 12). In order to achieve success, racial tensions and military and police violence would have to be curbed through creative means. It was envisioned that UNTAG would

> Interpose itself as a source of authentic and objective information in a country which had been starved of this for many years ... UNTAG would have, as a condition precedent to its success, to ensure that its legitimacy and authenticity were accepted throughout the country. The establishment of UNTAG's legitimacy, in turn, depended upon the perception of its effectiveness in dealing with the problems confronting the implementation, and upon its reputation for objectivity and integrity. Thus a closely integrated and coordinated operation was required. (Unpublished UN Report #2, para. 13)

The first step was to establish UNTAG's physical presence throughout Namibia, coordinated and administered through the Office of the Special Representative of the Secretary-General (OSRSG), in conjunction with a new, in-mission Department of Public Information.[20] The original plan called for nine district centers in the north, but early in the operation it became clear the number would not suffice in this populous, war-torn region; UNTAG opened another three (Unpublished Report #2, para. 42). In all, the UN set up 32 district and 10 regional centers throughout the vast territory.

The OSRSG was responsible for the political direction and overall coordination of the operation.[21] Each morning, representatives of

---

[20] The Director of the OSRSG was Cedric Thornberry. See Thornberry (2004).
[21] Where previous peacekeeping operations had employed two political officers, this operation had 100.

different UNTAG components would meet to share information and discuss strategies. The first meeting of the day was between the main heads of UNTAG – the Special Representative, his deputy, the Force Commander, the Commissioner of the Police, and the Director of the OSRSG. They would discuss top-level political concerns and developments of the last 24 hours. The second was a lower-level "co-ordination meeting," where Liaison Officers (with the UNTAG Centres, governmental representatives, and observer missions) would brief the UNTAG press spokesman and military, police, and civilian heads. In these ways, the UNTAG leadership sought to unify their efforts so as to speak and act with one voice. In other words, the members of UNTAG worked to speak with one voice and deliver a unified and clear message of peaceful transition through free and fair elections.

This unified effort had deep institutional roots. Before UNTAG began, Ahtisaari served as the UN's Under Secretary-General for Administration. He thus had knowledge of and access to some of the most talented UN staffers. Almost all UNTAG staff volunteered for a rotation in UNTAG. Since 1978, Ahtisaari had in mind specific individuals to fill key positions and was able to recruit others over the course of the 10-year delay in implementation. Ahtisaari was also very conscious of the importance of recruiting and promoting women so that different perspectives on gender relations and how to resolve conflict could be integrated into the mission's everyday practices. As Louise Olsson describes, "many of the women in the civilian UNTAG staff took it upon themselves to adapt their work to meet the local needs of both women and men" (2001, 97). Approximately 40 percent of operation's staff were women, with many women in key decision-making positions (Thornberry 2004, 63). Moreover, since the troops numbers in the military division had been cut nearly in half (to 4,500), after tripling UNTAG's civilian police troops (conceived as part of the civilian operations) to 1,500, in conjunction with 2,000 civilian electoral observers and 1,000 civilian staff, UNTAG had a decidedly civilian makeup and character. This civilian character enabled UNTAG to align messaging and behavior.

In order to establish UNTAG as a legitimate authority with all Namibians, Ahtisaari's strategy was to have the staff of the 42 district and regional offices interact as much as possible with the local population. They were to strive for "moral" rather than "executive" authority by helping to create "a new atmosphere and climate of reconciliation"

(Ahtisaari, in Weiland and Braham 1994, 67; Thornberry 2004, 376). The district and regional centers were often referred to as the "eyes, ears and voice" of UNTAG. "Staff were provided with broad guidelines, rather than detailed recipes, on how to execute their functions ... [they] were in constant contact with the local population and thus had instant feedback on their own performance permitting adjustment as necessary" (Unpublished UN Report #2, paras. 75–77). In addition, UNTAG devised a decentralized system of interpreters, whereby staff were allowed to seek out and hire interpreters on the spot as needed. The combination of well-structured, widely disbursed offices with flexible guidelines provided an efficient and effective means of exercising the power of persuasion through outreach. In other words, the mission actively sought to understand and communicate directly with its target audience.

One of Ahtisaari's most important methods for "changing the atmosphere" was to raise public consciousness of what UNTAG was doing and why. He sought "to build up and rely upon a moral authority rather than direct executive or enforcement powers" (Unpublished UN Report #2, para. 81). In order to accomplish these aims, he created a Department of Public Information as an integral component of his office and operations (Lehmann 1999, 30; Thornberry 2004, 187–188). A mandate for this program was not specified in any of the settlement documents, but Ahtisaari realized that in order to persuade effectively, he would need such a program (Lehmann 1999, 28–50).

The Namibian population, after years of abusive rule and Bantu education, was poorly educated and informed, and prone to rumor and exaggeration. For example, some white Namibians feared that UNTAG would take over the administration of the territory, redistribute land, and destroy their businesses and communities. Some members of all races were under the impression that UNTAG was a political party. Many were also fearful of voting, as there were rumors not only that the ballot would not be secret, but also that one's hand could be permanently marked or even cut off when it came near the ballot box.[22]

---

[22] Author interview, Nangolo Mbumba, Minister of Finance, Windhoek Namibia, 23 July 1998. After voting, election observers did stamp people's hands with indelible ink, visible only under ultraviolet light, in order to prevent people from voting twice. It did not help that one of the UNTAG voting rights posters featured a hand that was not obviously attached to an arm.

In order to counter misinformation and disinformation, UNTAG staff resorted to diverse and creative methods. For example, staff would attend church services and afterward discuss their operations with thousands of Namibians on a weekly basis.[23] They would also meet with community leaders, unionists, student groups, political groups, traditional groups, veterinarian associations, and farmers' unions (Wren 1990). Many of these meetings would last up to four or more hours. The staff's tenacity paid off, as "reports of intimidation decreased, numbers of peaceful political rallies (almost all were monitored by the civilian staff) increased, and dialogue, at all levels, commenced" (Unpublished UN Report #2, para. 70).

Ahtisaari and his staff also sought frequent contact with local and international radio, television, and newspapers by holding press conferences every day. But the South West African Broadcasting Corporation (SWABC) continued to operate as a source of disinformation. Rather than shutting down the SWABC, UNTAG used SWABC facilities to counteract disinformation on SWABC's own airwaves. Starting in June, UNTAG began running two radio programs each day during the peak listening hours in English, Afrikaans, and 13 other Namibian languages. In all, UNTAG produced 202 radio programs and 32 television programs, usually concerning different aspects of the mechanics of the democratization process.[24]

Persuasion: Symbolic Displays

A concrete manifestation of UNTAG's outreach and public information efforts came in the form of material items as symbolic displays. Staff printed T-shirts, pins, and posters to relay their messages,

---

[23] Approximately 90 percent of Namibians are Christian, and many attend church regularly.

[24] The return of tens of thousands of Namibian refugees and exiles was an important requirement for holding free and fair elections. UNTAG was not directly responsible for fulfilling this portion of the mandate. Instead, the UN High Commission for Refugees (UNHCR) oversaw this dimension, working closely with other UN agencies (IOM, UNICEF, WHO, FAO), and, most importantly, the Council of Churches in Namibia. The Council of Churches and UNHCR recruited thousands of local volunteers to work in the reception camps and mission stations. In the end, the UNHCR handled papers for the voluntary return of 42,736 returnees in less than one year (Ntchatcho 1993, 62; Unpublished UN Report #2, para. 99).

producing and distributing approximately 600,000 visual articles. Many items included slogans such as "Namibia: Free and Fair Elections," "Your Vote Is Secret," and "It's Your Chance to Choose for Namibia" (see Photo 2, p. 181). More detailed messages, sometimes conveyed through skits and short performances, explained what political parties were, how to create and join them, the rights of all citizens in a free and democratic society, how citizens should expect to be treated by a legitimate police force, how to register complaints, and step-by-step procedures for voter registration and voting.

Another important symbolic display featured the Special Representative traveling and working alongside his deputy. DSRSG Legwaila had been friends with the SWAPO leadership for decades, and was well-known throughout Namibia. He and Ahtisaari "would travel all over the country together. It was a confidence building measure, when all people of Namibia saw me with him [Ahtisaari] they were reassured" (Legwila, quoted in Hearn 1999, 127). In other words, Ahtisaari and Legwaila presented their relationship as a symbol of potential future interracial cooperation (see Photo 1, page 180).

UNTAG also enjoyed important symbolic displays of international consensus. For example, the initial General Assembly vote in 1971 to recognize SWAPO as the authentic voice of Namibians and the establishment of the UN Institute for Namibia proved important persuasive symbols of the justness of Namibian independence. Moreover, more than 120 UN member states sent representatives to work in UNTAG – a previously unheard of symbol of international unity (Lehmann 1999, 28).

The most operative forms of power in UNTAG proved to be various mechanisms of persuasion. The mission, however, did employ some aspects of *inducement* (as a means of DDR), and *coercion* (mostly in the form of surveillance). I address each of those aspects of power next, before returning toward the end of this chapter to address additional forms of persuasion employed in the final stages of the mission.

Inducement in DDR

The UNTAG military component was not large, but it had three main tasks: (1) restricting to base and monitoring SADF and PLAN disarmament, (2) monitoring SADF withdrawal from Namibia, and (3) demobilizing the Namibian regular and territorial units that fought against SWAPO (mainly the SWATF and SWAPOL), dismantling their offices, and collecting and guarding their weapons.[25] At the time of the ceasefire, there were approximately 32,500 non-SWAPO forces to disarm and demobilize, only about half of whom could be withdrawn from Namibia to South Africa. There are no reliable estimates of how many SWAPO forces were in the country, as they were mainly guerrilla troops and moved in and out of the civilian populations essentially without detection. UNTAG's military component was small. There was no way it could coerce its way through demobilization, disarmament, and reintegration (DDR). Instead, financial inducement and some surveillance proved the main mechanisms of power in DDR.

After the 1 April debacle, high-level political agreement about military force demobilization and disarmament meant that these processes proceeded fairly smoothly. What proved more difficult, however, was dealing with SWATF demobilization.

Often SWATF troops came from less-developed communities, and would rather have remained employed, even under a racist force, in order to earn a salary. Continued pay – even without service – was offered as a carrot to allow demobilized troops time to find new employment in Namibia. But as Harlech-Jones explains:

When the payment of salaries to former permanent soldiers for the SWATF ceased in February 1990, almost ten thousand more men joined the ranks of unemployed and unremunerated Namibians. Many thousands of Namibians had been taught to fight and kill in the South African Army, in the SWATF, and in SWAPO's PLAN. But few had gained skills that could secure their prosperity in peacetime. (Harlech-Jones 1997, 32)

UNTAG was too short an operation to retrain demobilized forces for other employment.

After the end of UNTAG, the UNDP and other UN agencies established offices in former UNTAG space and continued development assistance where the new Namibian government thought appropriate (United Nations 1990, 45). After independence, the main carrot for continuing not to fight was the possibility of being integrated into the

---

[25] Four subsidiary tasks included: (1) transferring SADF civilian functions (in communications, schools, and hospitals) to parts of UNTAG, and then to the new Namibian government; (2) providing communications, security, and logistics for the UNTAG civilian and military components; (3) monitoring borders; and (4) ensuring the security of returning refugees and exiles.

new Namibian National Defense Force. About half of the former combatants were eventually employed this way. Former PLAN and SWATF forces were integrated in equal numbers into the new Namibian military. In general, however, inducement was not an important source of power in this small-budgeted peacekeeping mission.

Coercion: Surveillance in Policing

Similarly, because the mission did not have great material resources at its disposal, coercion was not a major source of power. Of all the mechanisms of coercion, surveillance was the only one employed in UNTAG, especially to condition the behavior of the local police. Most of Namibian society had a deep mistrust of the police, and the leaders of UNTAG wanted to make sure that its mission would not be associated with the repressive force. As Leys explains, from 1978 onwards, "the militarization of Namibian society had one clear effect on policing: it finally ended any pretense that the police upheld the rule of law" (Leys and Saul 1995, 135). By 1989, the oppressive counter-insurgency Koevoet members numbered about one-third of the national police, or about 3,000 of the 8,250 SWAPOL (Unpublished UN Report #2, para. 158).

UNTAG also was to have "no direct responsibility for maintaining law and order in Namibia" (Unpublished UN Report #2, para. 140). UNTAG did not seek to acquire these responsibilities because, as Ahtisaari reasoned, most of the UNTAG police troops were not familiar enough with Namibian law or society. Instead, the local police demonstrated to the UN police how they operated and what they thought was appropriate. In turn, UN CIVPOL watched the local police, accompanied them on patrols, stationed themselves in all police outposts, watched, took notes, investigated abuses, and reported to the Special Representative.

CIVPOL did not have a training mission, but its leaders did seek to impart the principles of "even-handed," "non-discriminatory," and democratic policing to their SWAPOL counterparts, primarily through the reporting and investigations mechanisms (Unpublished UN Report #2, para. 136). CIVPOL was to play a "civilian," "political," and "psychological" role (Unpublished UN Report #2, 58). For this reason, although the Namibian police were highly militarized, CIVPOLs were placed under control of the civilian Special Representative, not the military division. They were to have "a high level of contact and interaction with the general public" (Unpublished UN Report #2, para. 141). This placement was meant to signal that the UN's policing mission was primarily not one of compellence or arrest, but rather civilian and persuasive. As for their psychological role, CIVPOLs were to "maximize the visibility of the UN in Namibia. Local people needed to trust that the presence of the UN police would guarantee their freedom of political movement" (Unpublished UN Report #2, para. 142).

In 1978, the Secretary-General had requested 360 police monitors for approximately 3,000 Namibian police. But by the mid-1980s, the number of police in Namibia had risen sharply to over 8,000 (Jaster 1990, 41, 75). In addition to the increase in numbers, at the time that the settlement proposal was drafted, the elite and brutal Koevoet was not in existence.

Given the change in the situation on the ground, the Special Representative, with the support of the Secretary-General, and the nonaligned and Soviet Bloc states on the Security Council, sought to augment UNTAG's civilian police numbers. In January 1989 the number was increased to 500.[26] In the wake of the 1 April events and the supposedly brief redeployment of some of the Koevoet, the number was further increased by 1,000.[27] And again, after persistent police "intimidation and abuse," especially in the north, another 500 CIVPOLs were added in September, for a total of 2,000, by the time of the elections.[28] Governments of 34 UN member states loaned their civilian police to the mission. In terms of physical spaces, 49 stations were set up by September; 30 of these were in the northern region. Often the CIVPOLs were housed near or with the UNTAG district and regional centers and shared some equipment with the military division.

CIVPOL troops would monitor SWAPOL by accompanying them on foot and vehicle patrols, monitoring them during political gatherings, reading their paperwork, and observing their behavior in police stations. It was important that CIVPOLs remain identifiably distinct from SWAPOL, thus they traveled in separate white vehicles, flew the UN flag, and wore distinctive blue clothing. The CIVPOL troops sought to interact with SWAPOL, and to report any abuse of power

---

[26] S/20412, 23 January 1989 in response to S/RES/629, 16 January 1989.
[27] S/20658, 26 May 1989, and S/RES/640, 9 August 1989.
[28] S/20872, 28 September 1989, and S/RES/643, 31 October 1989.

first to the UNTAG Station Commanders, District Commanders, the Police Advisor, or finally all the way up the chain of command to the Special Representative.[29] The primary methods of conditioning behavior were through surveillance and, to a certain extent, shaming. After the CIVPOL observed and reported abuses, SWAPOL officers would be warned by their superiors, sometimes even by officials in South Africa, to desist from wrongdoing or non-compliance with CIVPOL. At one point, the Special Representative had a SWAPOL commander fired, but in general the threat of, or actual, firing was reserved only as a last resort.

In order to deepen CIVPOL's surveillance capacity, Special Representative Ahtisaari and Police Advisor Fanning created two new divisions within the CIVPOL. The first was an "Investigations Unit" to "gather information required by the OSRSG on the progress of sensitive cases" (Unpublished UN Report #2, para. 191). The other was the "Forward Investigation and Co-ordination Centre," which gathered information on potential disruptions in the independence process in the north, reported on rumors, and sought ways to counter them through outreach mechanisms (Unpublished UN Report #2, 74, para. 192).

Given the novelty of their task, the quick expansion of the CIVPOL force, and the diverse cultures represented in the CIVPOL, there were some significant problems within the operation. For example, approximately one-third of CIVPOL did not have driving skills, there was only one vehicle for every three officers, few vehicles were equipped with communication devices, the radio system for the force was not fully operational until late in the summer, there was often not enough housing for the increasing numbers of CIVPOLs, and many did not speak compatible languages with each other or with the local population. The working language was often Dutch, since many CIVPOL members were Dutch, and Afrikaans and Dutch are fairly mutually intelligible, allowing SWAPOL and CIVPOL at least a minimum level of communication.[30]

---

[29] SWAPOL attempted to thwart CIVPOL's activities by using a wide variety of tactics. For example, SWAPOL would hide information, would not provide accurate patrol schedules or rosters, and would play "cat and mouse" games such as driving over terrain that they knew CIVPOL vehicles could not handle.

[30] English was also widely spoken within UNTAG, and increasingly so in Namibia. English is now the national language of Namibia.

Aside from the internal difficulties and problems with the SWAPOL regular police, CIVPOL also experienced significant resistance from the Koevoet. The only two Security Council resolutions passed during the UNTAG operation related directly to efforts to stem Koevoet "para-military" and "counterinsurgency" activity (S/RES/640, 29 August 1989; S/RES/643, 31 October 1989). UNTAG was subject to consider-able misinformation about the Koevoet units and deception on the part of the offices of the South African Administrator-General. Koevoet was supposed to have been confined to base or disbanded by December 1988. However, as the Secretary-General's report to the Security Council of 6 October 1989 states:

Although ostensibly members of SWAPOL, many of the ex-Koevoet person-nel continued to operate in the same manner as they had before the disband-ment of Koevoet. This included the use of armored personnel carriers known as "Casspirs" mounted with heavy machine guns. UNTAG received many complaints of intimidation and other unacceptable conduct by ex-Koevoet personnel, and UNTAG police monitors were on a number of occasions themselves witnesses of such behavior. (S/20883, 6 October 1989)

In response to Koevoet abuses, Ahtiassari suggested creating a "Task Force on Koevoet," and Secretary-General Pérez de Cuéllar and the Security Council approved it. The force was a combined CIVPOL and military effort, which surveilled, gathered information about Koevoet members and activities, and reported up the chain of command.

The UNTAG leadership searched for ways to undermine Koevoet decisively. Some members of the mission suggested using the power of arrest: that all Koevoet be incarcerated. Ahtisaari maintained that to do so could potentially give Koevoet members a sense of grievance, while giving them space and time to organize, which could cause problems upon their eventual release. Ahtisaari predicted that simply allowing them to disband in a new, independent Namibia would diminish the group's coherence and that they would simply dissipate over time (Weiland and Braham 1994, 114). Ahtisaari also organized a public symbolic display to reinforce the notion that the group was disbanding by organizing an official, "demobilization parade" on 30 October 1989 – just in time for the start of voting on 7 November.[31]

---

[31] But of course the problems with Koevoet did not end there. Throughout the election period there were reports of intimidation by "DTA supporters" who

Persuasion: Training in Policing

The symbolic parade was not the only persuasive method of dealing with the question of policing. Before and after the elections, UNTAG members devised a police retraining program for a new Namibian police force. The newly constituted police force was to be based on the British model of "policing by consent," where such principles as a more bureaucratic approach to upholding the rule of law, policing with minimal force, fair treatment, and service were central. But even under the climate of good will in the post-election period, this transition was extremely difficult.

The problems stemmed from lack of funds and means to retrain or otherwise employ former police and combatants. The UN's four-week training course reportedly graduated less than 200 police (Leys and Saul 1995, 138). Other training courses organized through the UN Institute for Namibia in Zambia saw a bit more success in training approximately one thousand ex-PLAN and SWAPO members. They, along with several thousand others, were integrated into the Namibian Police, the Ministerial "Home" Guard, the Border Guard, Protection Officers, as well as the new National Defense Force. After the UNTAG operation ended in March 1990, about 500 former CIVPOL and military forces stayed in Namibia on bilateral arrangements with the new Namibian government to continue to assist the new government with the creation and training of the Namibian Police. Within two years, UNTAG had essentially changed society's relation to the police – people no longer feared the police. There remain, however, criticisms of incompetence and corruption.

Persuasion: Mediation, Outreach, Symbols, and Training for the Elections

Turning back to the pre-election period, creating the conditions for and managing the elections were arguably the UN's most important contributions in helping Namibia transition to peace and independent rule. The central persuasive mechanism in this process was an unusual invention: an elections code of conduct. Namibians had never before

were former members of the Koevoet. After the elections, the ex-Koevoet were widely vilified and they did not regroup in any significant way.

experienced free and fair elections. In the first few months of register-
ing voters and creating political parties, UNTAG centers were
reporting widespread intimidation, harassment, and violent crimes
committed by all sides, but mainly by DTA supporters. The turbulence
was proving so destabilizing that the UN Secretary-General himself
decided to visit Namibia to see if he could employ his persuasive
powers of mediation.

In July 1989, UN Secretary-General Pérez de Cuéllar convened a
meeting in Windhoek with all political parties contesting the upcoming
elections. Because SWAPO had been excluded from the peace talks, it
was the first time in history that all major actors had come together in a
single room in public. Pérez de Cuéllar suggested some key, mechanical
manifestations of political rights and responsibilities. For example: no
political leaders should allow their supporters to carry weapons during
political rallies; rallies should not be held physically close to one
another, at the same time; and heads of parties should meet in person
to negotiate differences. Ahtisaari then worked to incorporate these
ideas into a more formal "code." The UNTAG spokesman, Fred
Eckhard, described how Ahtisaari "put on the table a draft set of
principles, a kind of code of ethics, you know, we won't shoot each
other's candidates, we won't disrupt each other's rallies, we won't tear
down each other's electoral posters, that kind of thing – we'll refrain
from inflammatory rhetoric in our campaign activities" (quoted in
Hearn 1999, 129). The political parties each had time to revise the
code and approve each other's revisions. They agreed to sign it together,
in a symbolic public display of progress toward democratization.

But several months later, on 12 September 1989, Anton Lubowski,
the most prominent white member of the SWAPO leadership, was shot
to death in front of his house. As an internal UN report describes:
"Events at that stage were felt to be on a knife-edge ... [Ahtisaari]
decided that the Code would be used and publicized as a means of
broadening and strengthening the central political consensus which
was beginning to develop, and to isolate extremists at all parts of the
spectrum" (Unpublished UN Report #1, para. 95).

From then on, UNTAG members broadcast the Code widely on the
radio, and in posters. In the regional and district centers, UNTAG staff
would hold "fortnightly meetings with the political parties of their
region where usually 5–6 major parties turned up ... the party leaders
[would] talk to each other and discuss their problems" (Churches

Information and Monitoring Service 1990, 199). When verbal disputes or violence broke out, UNTAG staff "got the sides talking together very quickly. Talking together, working through the disputes" (Hearn 1999, 131). Staff would then encourage the parties to develop public statements condemning the violence (Hearn 1999, 132).

If UNTAG offices were unable to resolve conflicts locally, they would report problems and abuses of the Code to the CIVPOL investigating divisions or a new Commission for the Prevention and Combating of Intimidation and Electoral Malpractice, otherwise known as the "O'Linn Commission."[32] The O'Linn Commission investigated complaints and brought cases to trial.

Meanwhile, UNTAG offices in different regions adapted the Code of Conduct to fit the circumstances. In Damaraland, for example, a relatively quiet region, the UNTAG Regional Director and political party representatives held weekly meetings where they discussed "problems and solved them on the spot" quickly and without much trouble (Hearn 1999, 131). In more contentious areas, such as in the township of Katatura near the capital Windhoek, after an outbreak of violence, UNTAG civilian staff held meetings where, "DTA and SWAPO ... agreed on eight additional points within the Code of Conduct," such as all areas of the township would be made accessible to all parties; leaders would not be insulted at rallies; and no rallies would take place late at night or without prior public notice (Hearn 1999, 131).

At the highest levels, representatives of both SWAPO and the DTA recognized the benefits of the Code. A prominent business person and SWAPO leader described, "In the absence of rules to guide the opposing political parties, the political situation would be become uncontrollable ... ultimately the benefits of the Code flowed to the public, as the followers of the different political parties were disciplined by their political leaders, who increasingly adhered to the code" (Hearn 1999, 133). Similarly, Dirk Mudge, the head of DTA stated: "I think [the Code] was a good thing. The parties did not always adhere to that but at least is was an effort and I think it was a necessary effort to come to agreement" (Hearn 1999, 132). A senior UNTAG member further explained, "Unlike most elections, violence decreased over time, from a

---

[32] Named after its chairman, Bryan O'Linn, then an acting Judge of the High Court. This commission also worked with the Churches Information and Monitoring Services, which compiled hundreds of election-related abuses. Author interview with Bryan O'Linn, Windhoek Namibia, 29 July 1998.

high level during the summer preceding the formal campaign to negligible significance immediately before the balloting" (Paul Szaz quoted in Weiland and Braham 1994, 150).

Elections were held from 7 to 11 November 1989. With 97 percent voter turnout, of the 72 seats in the Constituent Assembly, SWAPO won 41 and the DTA 21. The remaining 10 seats were divided among five smaller parties. Given that the adoption of a constitution required a two-thirds majority, SWAPO and the DTA would either have to cooperate with each other or abandon the constitutional process. SWAPO immediately documented its primary ideas and, to their surprise, the DTA accepted the SWAPO proposal as the working draft Constitution.

The Constitution was adopted on 9 February 1990 – 80 days after the convening of the Constituent Assembly. While not a requirement, the Constitution was formulated and adopted by consensus. A top SWAPO member explained:

Our Constitution is the product of serious internal political negotiations. We debated every aspect until we reached a consensus ... we never had to vote on a single issue even though we were a collection of political parties from across the spectrum – a racist party at one extreme and SWAPO at the other ... Our constitution is at once our victory, our shield, and our guide for the future. (Weiland and Braham 1994, 171–172)

The document is based in large part on the 1948 Universal Declaration of Human Rights, making it exceptionally broad-minded when it comes to human rights. The constitution remains a negotiated document, founded in an atmosphere of "give and take," which has set the tone for the future of Namibia.

Three negative unintended consequences from this time, however, continue to plague Namibia. The first is that the Constitution stipulated that no ancestral land claims would be honored. This provision has generated continued land alienation and poverty among the large portions of the population that rely on subsistence farming to survive (Bauer 1998). New legislation to regulate the problems with land reform has been slow to develop.

The second essential problem concerns the civil service. Civil servants under the South African–controlled administration were for the most part allowed to keep their positions while the new government built up its own parallel structures. This process has been criticized both for creating too large a state, and as "an overdrawn policy of national reconciliation" (Weiland and Braham 1994, 176). But as the Deputy Minister of Trade Wilfried Emvula declared: "Better to live with a bloated civil service than a civil war."[33]

A third problem is the concentration of power in the hands of one party: SWAPO. The international preference and support for SWAPO were necessary conditions for achieving Namibian independence, but it has meant that SWAPO retains control over politics and economics in Namibia, veering toward a "competitive authoritarian" regime (Bauer and Taylor 2011, chapter 8; Levitsky and Way 2010).

Conclusion

Although there are some lasting unintended negative consequences stemming from the time of UNTAG in Namibia, most of its legacies are positive. In the years since the end of UNTAG, Namibia has remained at peace. There is no ongoing military confrontation, nor is the level of crime or private violence high. According to Freedom House ratings (on a 1–7-point scale, one being the most positive), Namibia moved from a 6 in 1972 to a 2 in 1990. It has remained there since. Namibia ranks among the countries of "Medium Human Development," in a category with, for example, Morocco, India, and Pakistan, and ahead of most other countries in Africa (Human Development Report 2016, 200). It is also considered to be an upper-middle-income country, even though half of the population is technically unemployed and/or engaging in subsistence farming (CIA 2017). The literacy rate is 83 percent (CIA 2017), up from 38 percent at the time of UNTAG – a remarkable climb in one generation.

There have been several national and local elections since the one overseen by the UN. Namibia's economy has been growing steadily, with occasional contractions. Diamond mining and offshore gas exploitation have expanded. The population now stands at about 2.5 million, and GDP per capita (purchasing power parity) is nearly $10,000, which is relatively high but masks significant inequalities. Namibia remains economically dependent on South Africa and economically stratified internally, between a growing rich nonwhite and

---

[33] Author interview with Wilfried Emvula, Deputy Minister of Trade and Finance, Windhoek, Namibia, 28 July 1998.

white class, and a large, poor black underclass. Thus, while the political forms of apartheid have been outlawed, economic divisions persist.

The nature of the problems during the transition in Namibia was somewhat different from some of the others today but not necessarily easier: violence, dislocation, and racial segregation raged for many decades. For 70 years, the territory was the subject of violent controversy, during which time no one – internally or externally – was able to fix the problems.

The essence of the UN's strategy to bring about change in state–society relations was to use the power of persuasion – in the forms of mediation, shaming, outreach and public information, symbolic displays, and training. I find evidence that the UN's ideas and norms of peacekeeping were, for the most part, clear and unified, its messages were delivered in a respectful manner and based on a deep understanding of the specific circumstances in pre-independence Namibia, and the ideals set forth by UNTAG aligned with the actions of peacekeepers. It also helped that for nearly one decade before UNTAG, the UN and Namibian exiles had been educating Namibians to take over the essential civil service tasks of running an independent state.

Namibians have had remarkable political successes, many of which stem from the first elections and constitution drafting, facilitated by the United Nations. In the words of Namibia's current President, Hage Geingob, "UN diplomacy in Namibia played a major role in the independence process. Namibia today is the child of international solidarity. It's because of the UN connection that we've been so successful."[34]

UNTAG faced several crises, including the SWAPO debacle on 1 April, the resurgence of the Koevoet, the killing of Anton Lubowski, and the desperate South African challenge on 1 November, but each of these crises were quickly and adequately defused through persuasive means. The mission did not possess the capacity to supply security guarantees. The abusive South West African Police and South Africa Defense Forces maintained a monopoly over the use of force throughout the transition period, even though this monopoly was not perceived as legitimate by most Namibians.

In the case of UNTAG, the positions of all major political parties were integrated at all phases of planning and execution (unlike during

[34] Author interview, Windhoek Namibia, 30 July 1998.

the peace process, when SWAPO was formally excluded from all high-level talks). Local ownership was the overriding goal of the mission. Local ownership was not a means to an end, but incorporating Namibian perspectives and learning from Namibians certainly were.

The mission had a unified message, exhibited respect for and understanding of Namibian culture and politics, and aligned peacekeeper message, action, and behavior. The mission's use of persuasive means to change behavior set an example for ongoing political processes in Namibia. Many of the innovative strategies devised in the Namibian context – such as civilian police monitoring and training, the information program, regional and district centers, and the electoral code of conduct – would later be replicated in other parts of the world. However, some of the central elements that made for UNTAG's success have been lost over time. The mission had more civilians, more women, and more commitment to democratic principles – both internally and as part of its messaging – than any of the current missions today.

I contend that an important source of the current foundering of peacekeeping missions – especially the "big five" – stem not from a singular peacebuilding culture, but rather from a deep and pervasive disagreement about the ideational roots of peacekeeping, namely its doctrine and purpose. This disagreement lies at the heart of the UN's current difficulty in effectively using its primary source of power – persuasion.

3 | *Inducement in Lebanon*

UNIFIL is the largest formal-sector employer in southern Lebanon.
That is why people go along with the UN here.
  – Dr. Tarek Mitri, Director of the Issam Fares Institute for Public
  Policy and International Affairs at the American University of Beirut,
  former Minister, and former UN Special Representative in Libya[1]

The most obvious bases of power in peacekeeping stem from
persuasion and coercion; however, UN peacekeepers also employ a
variety of carrots, market restrictions, and institution-building efforts
to achieve their ends. In other words, they exercise power through
inducement. Inducement entails material and institutional incentives to
change a person's behavior (Acemoğlu and Robinson 2012; Krasno,
Daniel, and Hayes 2003; North 1990; Pierson 2004; Thelen, Steimno,
and Longstreth 1992). In the context of peacekeeping, focusing on
material incentives, Fortna explains, "if a civil war faction and its constituents benefit from the projects undertaken directly by peacekeepers,
or indirectly by NGOs and development agencies because the mission is
there, this can give peacekeepers substantial leverage over would-be
'spoilers.' … Leaders who benefit economically because of peacekeepers'
presence will have less incentive to resume war if doing so will chase the
mission away" (Fortna 2008, 92). They will also have less incentive to
continue fighting if institutions that may regulate disputes are in place.

Although peacekeepers regularly employ inducements, as it
has been conceived thus far, official peacekeeping doctrine largely
sidesteps targeting the political economy of conflict. In *An Agenda
for Peace* – the paper that originally defined the concepts of post–
Cold War peacekeeping, peacebuilding, and peace enforcement – UN
Secretary-General Boutros Boutros-Ghali implored members of the
UN to "identify and support structures which will tend to strengthen

---

[1] Author interview, Beirut, Lebanon, 13 March 2015.

and solidify the peace in order to avoid a relapse into conflict" (1992, 29). He did not mention the political economy of postwar societies, but many scholars and practitioners have interpreted peacebuilding as referring to the economic dimension of securing peace. As peace mediator and diplomat Alvaro de Soto lamented, since the early 1990s, "key multilateral players [made] little or no effort to adjust their [economic] priorities or practices so as to synchronize them with the fundamentally political objective that [peacebuilding] was meant to enshrine ... far from midwifing cogent policy and strategy, post-conflict peacebuilding was orphaned in infancy" (Berdal and Zaum 2013, xix).

Beyond targeting economic inducements and restrictions, multi-dimensional peacekeeping missions also often seek to restore state authority – through building local administrative, electoral, and security institutions – as key mechanisms of peacebuilding. Just as security vacuums produce incentives for spiraling conflicts, so do administrative vacuums. Peacekeeping missions endeavor to create or rebuild institutions that induce peaceful behavior. In this chapter, I explore some of the UN's tools of inducement (as well as persuasion) in Lebanon. Lebanon is home to the oldest peacekeeping mission – the United Nations Truce Supervision Organization (UNTSO) – which dates back to 1948. It remains a traditional, unarmed observer mission staffed by dozens of highly skilled officers who serve, in part, as the "eyes and ears" of the larger, parallel, UNIFIL mission. UNTSO's Observer Group-Lebanon officers embody the idea of the persuasive means of power, employing mediation, symbolic displays, and outreach to bolster local cooperation and peaceful coexistence.

The United Nations Interim Force in Lebanon (UNIFIL) deployed in 1978, in the midst of the Lebanese civil war, with a mandate to calm the unrecognized border between Israel and Lebanon. Its mandates and practices have changed in line with the larger trends in peacekeeping and the global war on terrorism (Makdisi 2014). Since the Israeli invasion of 2006, different troop contributors, often from Western Europe, have sought to augment UNIFIL's coercive capacity and actions, but those attempts have generally been rebuffed by locals in southern Lebanon. In this region, the UN does not provide security guarantees because it cannot compel compliance. Israel and Hezbollah possess arsenals that could destroy those of the UN many times over. But at the same time, UNIFIL has proven effective at reducing conflict primarily by inducing cooperation.

In terms of local ownership, the UN frequently interacts with and employs local actors in its operations – local input is a key component of UNIFIL's ability to function. UNTSO and UNIFIL have existed for more than 70 and 40 years, respectively, and as a result have become intertwined with the social, political, and economic fabric of southern Lebanon. Locals do not "own" these missions, however, because they remain largely international, and their conclusion is nowhere in sight. Full local ownership (and the conclusion of the missions) will only happen when Israel and Lebanon (and Hezbollah) agree to a peace settlement. Such an event is not foreseeable in the near term.

Instead of providing security guarantees, or transitioning to full local ownership, I argue that the UN bends behavior toward peace primarily through inducement. Persuasion and some aspects of coercion are also employed, but not to the same effect. Peacekeepers in Lebanon exercise persuasion by successfully mediating disputes and training local actors; no major actors in either Israel or Lebanon, however, have changed their beliefs such that they are prepared to conclude a peace deal with the other side. As of 2006, an updated mandate "authorizes UNIFIL to take all necessary action" to keep the peace, but of all the types of coercion, it almost exclusively exercises surveillance. Inducement is the operative form of the UN's power in this mission, both intentionally and unintentionally.

First, intentionally, UNIFIL peacekeepers in southern Lebanon offer a variety of different assistance programs. Although not specifically mandated by the Security Council to do so, each peacekeeping battalion supplies various types of material inducements to local south Lebanese communities, which endear the battalions to locals. The UN and associated agencies also provide substantial development assistance to the south, where the state has not collected taxes for decades. Additionally, UNIFIL peacekeepers help to build municipal governing and electoral institutions and, importantly, the Lebanese Armed Forces, which serve to induce peaceful relations both within Lebanon and between Lebanon and Israel.

Second and less intentional is the fact that the UN has become the region's largest formal-sector employer, rendering it the engine of the region's economy. Many families rely on the UN for their financial survival, which undergirds the UN's missions with an unexpected and under-acknowledged source of power. Economic dominance is not part of the UNIFIL mandate, but many scholars and political actors in Lebanon note these points as crucial for understanding how UNIFIL operates. In sum, inducement is the main mechanism of UN power in Lebanon.

Types of Inducement

Despite the advent of the peacebuilding commission in 2005, coordination in the realm of the UN's mechanisms of inducement remains an elusive pursuit. As Mats Berdal and Hannah Davies explain, "the UN 'system' is not a system in the true sense of the word, composed as it is of a myriad of specialized agencies, programs and funds that operate in a semi-autonomous fashion" (2013, 112). The semiautonomy of the UNDP, and the complete autonomy of what were originally the UN's international financial institutions – the IMF and the World Bank – along with that of single-state bilateral aid as well as regional economic communities, muddies the exercise of economic power that might be associated with the UN and its peacekeeping efforts. Because the landscape of economic inducement is so diverse, I do not attempt to capture all of it here.[2] But I do explore what I contend are the four basic types of inducements practiced in current peacekeeping operations. The first three are intentional; the fourth is not. Types of inducement may include: (1) providing carrots and other incentives such as Quick Impact Projects (QIPs, usually at the battalion level), trust funds (often geared toward DDR), and development and humanitarian aid; (2) sanctions or market restrictions (such as on weapons trade and conflict minerals); (3) the creation or rebuilding of state institutions (often electoral, municipal, legal, and security sector); and (4) local employment and the unintentional peacekeeping economy. I explore each in turn.

Quick Impact Projects, Humanitarian and Development Aid, and Trust Funds for DDR

UN peacekeepers and other well-intentioned external actors in conflict zones (such as other international organizations, single states, regional economic unions, and NGOs) often provide funds – carrots – for projects they think will help bring peace. In peacekeeping today, there are three main areas of such inducements: (1) QIPs; (2) targeted trust

---

[2] I have, however, engaged in such an exercise previously. See Howard (2014).

funds, often geared toward DDR; and (3) broader efforts to deliver humanitarian and development aid.

QIPs are intended as somewhat modest tools that might induce support among local communities where international forces are deployed. The instrument was first used in the early 1990s by the UNHCR to describe "small-scale, low cost projects designed to assist reintegration of returnees and displaced persons in Nicaragua" (UNHCR 2004, v). These projects came to prominence in the early 2000s, with the Brahimi Report on UN peacekeeping in 2000 mentioning them as useful, and then in US/NATO military initiatives in Afghanistan beginning in 2003. Under the "hearts and minds" philosophy of counterinsurgency, military forces reasoned that in order to achieve their objectives, they should help rebuild communities devastated by conflict. By providing services, peacekeepers and international military forces might reinforce their legitimacy in the eyes of local populations.[3]

Although the QIPs approach has been criticized when exercised by NATO forces in Afghanistan, assessments of negative or positive impacts of QIPs are rare and inconclusive (Lepin 2015). In peacekeeping, individual battalions in most complex UN peacekeeping operations engage in financial inducements (i.e. QIPs) in a limited and often ad hoc fashion with the goal of ingratiating themselves to local people. Proponents of QIPs contend that these projects increase the population's willingness to accept a foreign presence and, by extension, efforts at maintaining peace. Short-term QIPs are usually not part of any formal peace agreements or peacekeeping mandates, and yet they are integral to what many peacekeepers do on a daily basis.

Inducement in peacekeeping works in a variety of unexpected ways, often at the micro level. I have encountered UN peacekeepers providing dental, medical, and veterinary services; building schools; building parks and soccer fields; teaching martial arts and yoga; providing escort for women and children as they walk to school or to gather

[3] US and NATO forces in Afghanistan began to implement development and humanitarian projects through the Provincial Reconstruction Team (PRT) initiatives (Dziedzic and Seidl 2005). The use of PRTs and QIPs was quite controversial and widely criticized by existing humanitarian and development organizations that feared their neutrality would be undermined if aid became associated with the political objectives of foreign military interventions.

firewood; providing solar-powered street lights on dangerous corners; helping to reconstruct houses of worship; paving roads; providing garbage trucks; restoring sewage lines; and building recreation centers where kids may play and receive homework assistance after school in a safe and secure environment. Sometimes these projects can temporarily stoke intercommunal tensions, as when peacekeepers from wealthier nations provide nicer or better services only in their area of operation, depriving neighboring villages of the benefits. In southern Lebanon, UN force commanders have sought ways to even out what could otherwise exacerbate relative deprivation or local inequalities.

QIPs are geared toward improving local relations between peace-keepers and civilians in the communities they serve. In contrast, DDR, is about integrating troops back into societies. The "first generation" concept of DDR developed in Namibia, in the late 1980s, and then advanced further in the mid-1990s, when the UN peacekeeping mission in Mozambique devised an innovative trust fund and "weapons buy-back" program for reintegrating former combatants and reigning-in their weapons. Since then, DDR has "assumed a kind of orthodoxy in the peace, security and development communities, especially amongst representatives of the United Nations agencies, the World Bank and a number of bilateral aid agencies" (Muggah and O'Donnell 2015). The original concept of DDR was that external funds would be used to enable troops – especially senior officers – to be cantoned for a time, their weapons removed and hierarchical chains of command dismantled (by mutual agreement, without resort to coercion). In exchange for participation, troops would be offered retraining for a new career, receive pension benefits, and/or join a new, postwar national military.

In the early to mid-2000s, DDR programs expanded significantly to include a much broader, institutional focus on "security sector reform" (United Nations Department of Peacekeeping Operations 2010). These "second generation" programs attempt to reshape the security land-scape where there is no peace accord, or other preconditions for "first generation" DDR (Muggah and O'Donnell 2015). Although the first generation of DDR programs, for the most part, succeeded in imple-menting mandates, the second-generation programs have had less clear effects (Humphreys and Weinstein 2007; Seethaler 2016). Reintegra-tion remains a challenge in societies where there is no peace accord, and where economies are unable to absorb former combatants into meaningful employment (Perazzone 2017).[4]

Nevertheless, DDR and related programs persist. They are sometimes funded through UN peacekeeping missions or bilaterally, but most often by the UNDP or the World Bank. Trust funds are the largest and most common funding mechanisms that enable DDR. Such funds have been established on an ad hoc basis, for a wide variety of programs in different conflicts. Although there is evidence that DDR and related activities can be effective, because medium- and long-term funding sources are unstable, this mechanism of inducement remains often used, but not necessarily reliable, for long-term integration. In Lebanon (as elsewhere), the UN has had trouble disarming rebel groups such as Hezbollah, but it has effectively worked to help build the institution of the Lebanese Armed Forces.

Unlike the small and local scale of QIPs or the trust funds targeting DDR, humanitarian and development assistance are often massive and multi-faceted enterprises (Barnett 2011; Ferguson 1990). Humanitarian assistance during violent conflict comes in three basic forms: medical, food, and shelter. Many organizations in and around the UN system – UNHCR, WFP, the International Red Cross and Red Crescent, Doctors Without Borders, Catholic Relief Services, etc. – offer this aid with the minimal intention of saving lives (and not necessarily creating peace). Similarly, development aid is only tangentially linked to averting or decreasing violence, but humanitarian and development assistance are often used by or alongside peacekeeping missions. Development aid also comes in myriad forms – bilateral and multilateral, public, private, and non-governmental. In the UN system, development is largely the purview of the UN Development Programme (UNDP). In developing countries – most of which are not at war – UNDP offices tend to be co-housed and coordinated with other UN programs, funds, and agencies that also engage in humanitarian assistance (the World Health Organization, the World Food Programme, UNICEF, etc.). If the country descends into violent conflict and UN peacekeepers deploy, in the newer "integrated missions," the UN's development and humanitarian efforts shift from being coordinated through the UNDP to the peacekeeping mission.

---

[4] Because there is little funding for analysis of DDR, it has been difficult to assess its effects on a broad scale (Seethaler 2016).

The effectiveness of development aid is highly disputed by scholars and practitioners, whereas humanitarian aid is less so. Some studies find that, unlike humanitarian assistance, unfettered and unconditional aid can perpetuate dependency, hinder economic growth, and increase corruption and poverty (Moyo 2009). In the specific context of civil wars, aid has varying results – some countries are able to establish peace and reconstruct states and economies using foreign aid, but many others fail (Girod 2015; Narang 2014; Qian 2015). In peace-keeping, humanitarian assistance can mean the difference between life and death for millions of people; development assistance, however, has less clear results (Gisselquist 2017a, 2017b).

In sum, peacekeepers and other well-intentioned international actors provide a wide variety of incentives to induce societies to stem violence and move toward peace – from small QIPs, to trust funds for DDR programs, to humanitarian relief, to large-scale development projects. In the context of conflict zones, all of these efforts involve the provision of goods and services, some of which are intended to change behavior. In contrast, other inducement programs are designed to work through the opposite means: to restrict or remove things, in order to induce peace.

Market Restrictions on Minerals, Weapons Embargos, and Economic Sanctions

Unlike the provision of economic carrots, market restrictions deployed by international actors are more targeted and typically pegged directly to conflict reduction. There are at least three basic types: (1) restrictions in conflict mineral trade, (2) weapons trade embargos, and (3) economic sanctions. I address each in turn.

Violent conflict and natural resources are linked in many ways (Ross 2004). Areas with important mineral resources and weak governance structures have higher levels of violence than others (Berman, Couttenier, Rohner, and Thoenig 2017). Diamonds in particular are often associated with violent conflict (Ross 2004). In 2000, the UN General Assembly voted to establish the Kimberley Process, whereby rough diamonds would have to be certified non-conflict-related in order to reach the international market. The certification scheme had important, although imperfect, conflict-dampening effects in Angola, Liberia, and Sierra Leone (Grant 2012, Hughes 2006). Similarly, the 2010

Dodd-Frank legislation in the American Congress held great promise for restricting trade in conflict minerals in the Democratic Republic of the Congo, as a way to dampen violence (Raj 2011). The bill prohibited any US-registered or listed corporation from procuring four minerals – tantalum, tin, gold, and tungsten – from areas of armed conflict (some of these minerals are essential for manufacturing components for cell phones and related technologies). Although the legislation was not without its problems (Schwartz 2015; Seay 2012), it did induce even non-US companies and neighboring states to maintain "clean" supply chains (Ochoa and Keenan 2011).[5] Corporate social responsibility programs have also worked to dampen trade in conflict minerals (Young 2015).

Similar to restricting conflict-related natural resources (which makes it more difficult for combatants to buy weapons), other programs and international agreements seek to directly restrict the weapons themselves. The Geneva Conventions and a variety of other international treaties forbid or restrict the use of chemical, biological, and nuclear weapons (also known as weapons of mass destruction). Barrel bombs, cluster munitions, and landmines are also restricted under international law for their indiscriminate nature (ICRC). In conflict zones where they are deployed, peacekeepers seek to stem trade in illicit weapons. They also sometimes benefit from Security Council sanctions against general weapons trade (such as in the Central African Republic). In Lebanon, UNIFIL is supposed to prohibit the transfer of new weapons to the south. In addition, the Lebanese Armed Forces, along with all of Israel's neighbors, are effectively restricted by Israel from purchasing weapons that might overshadow Israel's "qualitative military edge" (Wunderle and Briere 2008).

Programs and agreements to restrict the trade of valuable minerals and weapons are very specific and targeted. In contrast, economic sanctions in the past were often applied broadly and tended to harm populations (Elliot 1998; Haass and O'Sullivan 2000; Hultman and Peksen 2017; Pape 1997). Targeted, multilateral sanctions appear to have a higher effectiveness rate, but even these are questionable for conflict reduction (Strandow 2006). Scholars have found that, in contrast with economic sanctions, arms embargoes are positively

---

[5] In 2017, the Trump administration moved to undo the legislation. The European Union and China have taken up the cause.

associated with better outcomes such as shorter and less intense conflicts (Hultman and Peksen 2017; Strandow 2006). In UN peace-keeping, market restrictions generally work in parallel with peacekeepers. Although the two may help each other, and peacekeepers may be asked to monitor weapons embargos, often the two tools are not hierarchically coordinated or otherwise directly linked.

Building or Restoring State Institutions

Whereas market restrictions and financial inducements are concrete, material means of directing behavior change, institutional reforms are a somewhat less tangible, although still crucial, means of inducement. Institutions are enduring patterns of behavior among people. Some scholars understand them as any habitual interactions (such as the handshake). But most commonly, scholars and practitioners alike understand institutions to have more concrete forms, manifesting as laws and formal organizations such as militaries, stock markets, or parliaments (Hall 1986; Hall and Taylor 1996; March and Olsen 1998; Powell and DiMaggio 1991; Skocpol 1979).

Some scholars forward "rationalist" arguments about the ways in which institutions channel cost–benefit calculations for individual behavior, and how, since institutions embody actors' preferences, "con-tests over preferred policies necessarily spill over into contests about institutions" (Milner 1997, 123; see also Oye 1993; Weingast 2002). In contrast, "sociological institutionalists" forward constructivist argu-ments about the foundational dynamics of norm creation and diffusion, and how they manifest in institutional forms (Finnemore 1998a; Fligstein 1990; Katzenstein 1996). "Historical institutionalism" bridges the gap between the two traditions, examining "critical junctures" when individuals with new ideas sought to overturn or reorganize crucial state and international institutions, setting a country on a new path or enduring institutional pattern (Hall 1986; Skocpol 1979; Steinmo 1993).

All peacekeeping missions seek to change institutions that enable violent conflict and to create locally owned, legitimate institutions that will regulate future disputes in peaceful ways. In other words, one could argue that peacekeepers seek to put into practice all three strains in the scholarly literature. They strive to create a critical juncture in a nation's history – one that turns individuals in a society away from the path of war and toward the norms of a more just, democratic, prosperous, and peaceful future. More concretely, peacekeeping missions are mandated by the UN Security Council to reform or create basic state institutions. Numerous UNSC resolutions have stipulated that peacekeepers "extend state authority" in a variety of ways, from establishing the rule of law, to security sector reform, to building electoral infrastructure, to trying to develop the physical and legitimate authority of municipal and statewide governing structures.

Creating and reforming institutions combines aspects of both persuasion and coercion. Persuasive arguments provide the ideational underpinning for institutions and, thus, the reformulation of interests (McNamara 1998; Nye 2004). The threat of coercion is sometimes the means by which states and others gain compliance (Martin 1992). In the middle terrain, after institutions have been created and they are functioning, institutions induce individuals to behave in certain ways. Institutional inducement relies less on actual carrots and more on patterned expectations of behavior, as well as costs – both ideational and material – associated with deviating or defying the institution.

In Lebanon, since the withdrawal of the Israeli occupation in 2000, UN peacekeepers have been charged with "bringing the state back" to southern Lebanon (Newby 2018, 114; S/RES/1559, 2 September 2004). Peacekeepers are also mandated to build the capacity of the national military – the Lebanese Armed Forces. These state- and military-building functions are common to most multidimensional peacekeeping missions today. In Lebanon thus far, as I demonstrate next, these attempts are not producing results that might lead to the quick conclusion of the mission, but have nevertheless proven fairly effective at maintaining peace in the region.

The Peacekeeping Economy and Local Employment

When a peacekeeping mission deploys, especially a large one, it brings with it rippling, mostly unintended, economic effects. Peacekeepers – both civilian and military – require lodging, food, transportation, and a social life. All of these demands must be met in a country or region that is fragile economically, because it is not at peace. Scholars, especially writing in the critical/constructivist tradition, term the economies that develop around peacekeepers as the "peacekeeping economy" (Jennings and Bøås 2015). The designation "refers to economic activity that either would not occur, or would occur at a much lower scale and pay-rate, without the international presence" (Jennings and Bøås

2015, 282). Many studies of the economic impact of peacekeepers focus on the negative distortions when international staff introduce new flows of cash and accompanying disruptive practices such as the international sex trade to local markets (Jennings 2015; Jennings and Bøås 2015; Rohland and Cliffe 2002; Rolandsen 2015). They also highlight the arrogance and detachment of relatively wealthy, even if well intentioned, international interveners (Autesserre 2014).

Local spending by international staff spurs economic activity, but the negative side effects are manifold as people with local expertise are hired by the UN or other organizations, depriving domestic governments and institutions the personnel they need to thrive. Local labor markets are distorted by the high wages paid to mission-affiliated local hires. Peacekeeping and large peacebuilding missions also create "bubble markets" and spur inflation. More broadly, the local economy becomes increasingly dependent on the presence of the UN mission, stifling local economic self-sufficiency and independence (Bove and Elia 2017; Jennings 2015; Tejpar 2009). Thus the peacekeeping economy has many negative unintended consequences.

But peacekeeping economies may also work to bring war-torn economies into international markets. They contribute to job creation and formalization in a variety of new fields (Tejpar 2009). The arrival of numerous, relatively wealthy international personnel often stimulates local investment and agricultural production (Tejpar 2009). Most importantly, some scholars find that the reduction in violence brought about through the presence of peacekeepers has substantial positive economic effects (Carnahan, Durch, and Gilmore 2006 and 2007). I argue here that the UN's massive and long-term presence in southern Lebanon has downsides, namely that the economy has become dependent on the international presence. But the international presence has also had an overall positive unintended economic effect. As the largest employer in the south, in a place where for decades the Lebanese state and businesses have been unable to function because of domination by Israel, the PLO, or Hezbollah, the UN has maintained the support of many southern Lebanese primarily through inducement.

Observable Implications of Effectiveness in Inducement

In sum, I conceive of inducement as a broad category, and one that is mainly material (although ideas do creep in, especially during the formational stage of institution building). Peacekeepers seek to induce the peacekept by providing and withholding material incentives, through QIPs, DDR trust funds, development aid, market restrictions, and sanctions. They also seek to induce new patterns of individual and societal behavior through creating or reforming key state institutions. These three types of inducement are intentional. The arrival of peacekeepers also ushers in a "peacekeeping economy" with a variety of unintended effects, both positive and negative.

The conditions under which each form of inducement might prove to be more or less effective are too varied and underdeveloped in the existing literature to be able to specify in a systematic way here. However, the conditions for effective persuasion can assist in conceptualizing the domains of inducement, especially the first two. Certainly coordinating and achieving international agreement on providing steady and reliable funding sources, as well as agreement on market restrictions, are prior conditions for effective inducement. So too are understanding the interests of the targets of inducement programs and how such programs might be received. I formulate observable implications of effective inducement as follows:

1. Peacekeepers provide material goods and services, aid, and funds for activities such as DDR, with the goal of inducing the consent of the local population to go along with peace efforts.
2. Peacekeepers restrict markets with the goal of enabling peace.
3. Peacekeepers assist in creating or reforming domestic institutions to regulate behavior toward peaceful interaction.
4. Peacekeepers coordinate their efforts among themselves, align it with a political or persuasive strategy, and incorporate the interests of the peacekept in programming.
5. Peacekeepers offer employment through a "peacekeeping economy."
6. Local citizens and elites voice approval of peacekeepers' activities.
7. Belligerents change behavior as peacekeepers request, manifesting in a reduction of violence.
8. If, instead, we find well-intentioned programs producing little or even adverse results, or the unintentional "peacekeeping economy" distorts markets in adverse ways, we can say that inducement is being employed but not achieving intended effects.

In the remainder of this chapter, I provide some background information about conflict in Lebanon. I then lay out the mandates of UNTSO and UNIFIL and assess their varying effectiveness rates.

I explain these outcomes by examining how the UN exercises power – through persuasion, coercion, and inducement. I also weigh evidence of possible security guarantees as an alternative hypothesis that might account for the varying effectiveness rates. I also explore how the missions incorporate locals and local perspectives into the operations. In sum, I argue that inducement in a variety of forms – namely in the provision of goods, employment, and institution building – is the operative source of the UN's power to achieve conflict *management* in Lebanon; conflict *resolution*, however, remains elusive.

Lebanon

Lebanon is the smallest country in continental Asia, measuring a little smaller in size than the American state of Connecticut. Its deep literary culture, Mediterranean beaches, skiable mountains, and varied land-scape have proven significant tourist attractions over the course of its history. Lebanon does not possess much in the way of natural resources, but it is home to the fertile Beqaa Valley and the important water source of the Litani River; Lebanon is also a regional center for finance and trade. Bordered by Syria, Israel, and the Mediterranean Sea, Lebanon fell under Ottoman rule for 400 years until the end of World War I, when it shifted to colonial French rule. In 1926, the French ushered in a "confessional" constitution, recognizing sect – Christian, Druze, Shiite or Sunni – over individual rights, and weighted in favor of Maronite Christians; a French high commissioner held final authority. Upon independence in 1943, Lebanon retained a religious-based, ethnocratic governing structure (Howard 2012). Confessional deadlock often reigns, and has spilled into outright violence in civil wars in 1958 (which ended quickly after the arrival of American marines) and from 1975 to 1990.

Background

Since independence, parts of Lebanon have often been occupied by its neighbors for decades: Syria from 1976 to 2005 (under the guise of regional peacekeeping) and Israel from 1978 to 2000. Israel has invaded and bombed Lebanon several times since the 1970s, seeking to damage or destroy the Palestinian Liberation Organization (PLO) and, more recently, the militant group Hezbollah. The most recent war was in the spring of 2006, which killed more than 1,200 Lebanese and more than 60 Israelis, and destroyed significant parts of Lebanon's infrastructure. Just as Lebanon was recovering, in 2011, civil war broke out in neighboring Syria, and has occasionally spilled over the border. Of some six million people residing in Lebanon, more than one million are Syrian refugees (by official counts), and another half million are Palestinian refugees (both groups are of mixed confessions, but mainly Sunni Arab; Central Intelligence Agency 2018). Thus a substantial part of Lebanon's population is currently comprised of refugees. Despite these significant challenges, Lebanon ranks among the "high human development" countries, ahead of most others in the Middle East.

Lebanon has also been home to UN peacekeeping operations since the birth of its neighbor to the south, Israel, in 1948. The very first peacekeeping operation, the United Nations Truce Supervision Organization (UNTSO), deployed to Jerusalem and four other countries around Israel/Palestine, including Lebanon, in order to monitor the armistice agreements of the time. UNTSO today continues its small-scale, unarmed patrols along the still un-agreed border between Lebanon (which does not recognize Israel), and Israel (which is surrounded by unfriendly neighbors, although it has made peace with Egypt and Jordan). Because Lebanon does not recognize Israel, the two states do not have an official border. Instead, there is a UN-designated "Blue Line" that separates the two.

In 1978, during what turned out to be the early years of the Lebanese civil war, the UN deployed a second peacekeeping mission as a more robust means of preventing the PLO and Israelis from augmenting the internal fighting in Lebanon. At the time, southern Lebanon was essentially ungoverned (Newby 2018, 59). There was little if any electricity or infrastructure. The Lebanese Armed Forces had not been present in this sparsely populated, mainly farming territory, since 1968. Thirty-six or 37 different militia groups were competing to control the small space (James 1983, 615; Newby 2018, 62, 125). The groups eventually coalesced around three central actors in the south: (1) the Palestinian (often Sunni) militias, especially the PLO; (2) the Israeli-backed (Christian) South Lebanese Army (SLA); and (3) the Shiite resistance – first Amal, then later Hezbollah.

In June of 1982, Israel, with the assent of the Reagan administration, sought to expel the PLO from Lebanon by force. As the Palestinian resistance to Israel waned, Hezbollah – the Shiite nationalist, Iranian- and Syrian-supported Lebanese political party and military actor – grew. One of Hezbollah's central purposes is armed resistance to Israel and the West. The United States and Israel consider Hezbollah to be a terrorist organization, and will not engage in direct negotiations with the movement. In 2006, Hezbollah successfully repelled the IDF's territorial advance – for the first time in Lebanese history. Because of this event, many Lebanese are thankful for Hezbollah, even though the movement is not appreciated by a significant portion of Lebanese (of all faiths, or no faith), who are more oriented toward progressing toward a modern, rather than traditional, society. As Lebanon and Israel continue their antagonistic relationship, UNIFIL and UNTSO persist.

These two peacekeeping missions, more than 70 and 40 years old, respectively, have changed alongside these fluctuations in fighting and external influence. In the following sections, I explore their mandates, their effectiveness, and their sources of power. I turn first, briefly, to UNTSO. UNTSO is much smaller, both in the number of troops and in the scope of its mandate, so it does not require more than a short exploration of its mandate, effects, and power of persuasion. The remaining parts of this chapter, however, focus on UNIFIL, with an in-depth look at its mandate, effectiveness, and mechanisms of power. Although UNIFIL has not completely stopped the fighting, most obser- vers contend that the mission has helped to keep it at bay. I contend that UNIFIL (and UNTSO) do not supply security guarantees through com- pellent military power, nor is local ownership over the operations in sight. But they do exercise power through persuasion; some coercion in the form of surveillance and monitoring; and, for UNIFIL, importantly, inducement. I argue that, in the end, although it is not officially written into the mandate, inducement is the UN's main means of power in UNIFIL, whereas UNTSO's ability to influence is based in persuasion.

UNTSO: Mandate, Effects, and Persuasion

UNTSO deployed in 1948 with a mandate to use unarmed military observers to "call upon the parties" to cease hostilities (for, at the time, 4 weeks), refrain from military mobilization and training, refrain from importing and exporting military matériel, protect holy places in the city of Jerusalem, and assist the United Nations Mediator in Palestine (United Nations 1948, paras. 1, 4, 5, 6). UNTSO members were tasked with monitoring compliance. If the parties did not agree or comply, the resolution explicitly includes the threat of Security Council action under Chapter VII of the UN Chapter – but not that UNTSO would carry out such action (United Nations 1948, para. 11).

Seventy years later, UNTSO remains in operation, and its largest contingent is deployed in southern Lebanon (UN Observer Group-Lebanon). UNTSO personnel embody important symbolic displays of peaceful coexistence. Dual-national teams patrol on foot, unarmed, in soft-skinned, white UN vehicles. The purpose of two-member (minimum), dual-national patrol is to bolster impartiality – when UNTSO military officers witness a controversial incident, nationals from both governments must agree on the facts before reporting. Members of UNTSO must have achieved officer ranking in their national militaries; thus, most observers are deeply experienced.

For decades, because of Israeli government restrictions, members of UNTSO were housed across the "Blue Line" in Israel, working in southern Lebanon during the day, until the Israeli withdrawal from Lebanon in 2000. Today, unlike most peacekeepers in uniform, UNTSO troops do not consistently live on UN bases. UNTSO observers tend to live in typical Lebanese houses and apartment buildings, shop at local markets, dine in local cafes and restaurants, and sometimes marry people from Lebanese villages (there have been no reports of sexual abuse or exploitation). As the head of UNTSO explained to me: "We're in the market every day to buy our food – we cook ourselves – we have to know locals. We walk to the souk. We eat in local places. People know us. We're stationed here for much longer than 6-month rotations."[6] Although small in number – there are only several dozen of them – after several generations of deployment and interaction, UNTSO has become part of the fabric of life in southern Lebanon.

On their daily patrols, UNTSO representatives engage in outreach by talking with elders, politicians, religious and business leaders, and various community members. Middle East peace efforts have come and gone over the last 70 years, while UNTSO has remained "a vital mechanism for regional moderation, particularly by providing the means by which otherwise implacable enemies communicate with each other ... For decades, the only consistent way that Israel

---

[6] Author interview with Ruth Putze, Chief of Observer Group Lebanon (UNTSO), Marjayoun, Lebanon, 11 March 2015.

communicated with Egypt, Jordan, Lebanon and Syria, and vice-versa, was through UNTSO channels" (Theobald 2015, 121, 130). This open line of communication endures today. UNTSO officers are unarmed; thus they have zero pretense of providing any sort of compellent security guarantee. They interact frequently with locals, although locals do not "own" these operations. "The UNTSO experience illustrates the importance of peace observers who help temper conflict and facilitate communication between the Arab states and Israel" (Theobald 2015, 131). Their main mechanisms of encouraging de-escalation and peace derive from symbolic displays, outreach, facilitating communication, and mediation. In other words, the source of their power lies in persuasion.

UNIFIL

Whereas UNTSO patrols are unarmed and serve the purpose of facilitating communication and peace through persuasion, the mission exists alongside another UN peacekeeping operation, UNIFIL. For the first 30 years of Israel's statehood, its main adversarial relationships were with other neighboring states, and *not* Lebanon. However, this equation changed when Palestinian fighters and civilians were moved out of Jordan and into Lebanon, in the early 1970s. In 1975, the civil war in Lebanon was sparked when, as retribution for an attack on a nearby church, Christian Phalangist fighters struck a bus in Beirut, killing 27 passengers, mainly Palestinians. Three years later, in the midst of the Lebanese civil war, Palestinian fighters staged an attack on Israel, killing 37 civilians and wounding 76. In reprisal, Israel attacked Lebanon in March 1978, for the first of several times over the next decades, occupying the country up to the important water source, the Litani River.[7]

Mandate

In 1978, the Government of Lebanon was unable to counter either Israel or the Palestinians on its own, and it turned to the United

---

[7] The Israelis occupied all of Southern Lebanon *except* the area around the coastal town of Tyre (which is also called Sour), the Palestinians' "logistical and command center" (Goksel 2007, 55).

Nations and the United States. American President Jimmy Carter was preparing to mediate the Camp David accords between Israel and Egypt, and needed to halt the fighting in Lebanon as quickly as possible. He called on his Secretary of State Cyrus Vance to inform the UN Secretary General that "the United States saw no other solution to the crisis in Southern Lebanon than a UN force" (Skogmo 1989, 8). The US-sponsored peacekeeping resolution mandated UNIFIL for three basic purposes: "confirming the withdrawal of Israeli forces; restoring international peace and security; and assisting the Government of Lebanon in ensuring the return of its effective authority in the area" (S/RES/425, 19 March 1978). UNIFIL's mandate has undergone three changes over the years – the most recent in 2006 being the most significant.

First, in 1982, while the Lebanese civil war raged, Israel launched a successful invasion to expel the PLO from Lebanon. In the aftermath, the UN Security Council added *humanitarian assistance* to the UNIFIL mandate in light of significant devastation in southern Lebanon (S/RES 511, June 1982). Troop numbers waxed and waned over the years but often held at roughly 6,000 uniformed personnel (Makdisi 2014, 24). In order to sustain its victory against the PLO, Israel occupied parts of southern Lebanon for a total of 22 years.

Second, after the Israeli withdrawal in 2000, and in the wake of the attacks of 11 September 2001, the United States and France sponsored a somewhat confusing mandate augmentation. UN Security Council Resolution 1559 of 2 September 2004, "calls upon all remaining foreign forces to withdraw from Lebanon" and "for the disbanding and disarmament of all Lebanese and non-Lebanese militias." However, the resolution is not clear on the methods or funding for disbanding and disarmament, or which groups count as a "militia." Hezbollah does not consider itself, nor is it considered by others in Lebanon, to be a "militia," but rather a "resistance" and a political party with representation in parliament.[8] Hezbollah was excluded from the negotiations. As one analyst explains, "After long negotiations with and within contributing countries, the mandate does not

---

[8] CNN 2005. Hezbollah Disarmament Unclear. 7 May. http://edition.cnn.com/
2005/WORLD/meast/05/06/lebanon.report/. Note also that The UN's "Special Envoy" appointed to oversee the resolution's implementation, puzzlingly, reports through the Department of Political Affairs, not the Department of Peacekeeping Operations (Allee 2009, 93).

[ask UNIFIL to] … directly disarm Hezbollah but only support the LAF in doing so through assistance on the ground and by training personnel" (Elron 2007, 35). Thus, the UNIFIL mandate was augmented somewhat, with some confusion about what, exactly, it was being directed to perform. This "hastily-agreed" Security Council Resolution, which seemed to frame Hezbollah as "merely a proxy 'militia'" was not appreciated in the south (Makdisi 2017, 153). UNIFIL came to be seen as taking a "pro-Western, pro-Israeli stance on the conflict" (Kassem 2017, 472). The following year, UNIFIL was downsized to about 2,000 troops. Then things changed dramatically in the summer of 2006.

The third and final mandate change occurred in June of 2006. Six years after Israel's unilateral withdrawal from southern Lebanon, Hezbollah (with help from Hamas) captured two Israeli soldiers and killed three others as a way to show that they could disrupt, and thus should not be excluded from, any peace negotiations or political processes. In response, Israel waged a punishing campaign in Lebanon (and in the Hamas-controlled Gaza strip).

Several actors in the region sought Security Council condemnation of Israel's operation, but the United States vetoed a proposed resolution (S/PV.5488). After tough negotiations, the Security Council unanimously agreed to Resolution 1701 of August 11, 2006. While a lot of the language repeats that of the initial 1978 resolution for UNIFIL, the new one also uses the language of all contemporary Chapter VII civil war mandates:

Determining that the situation in Lebanon constitutes a threat to international peace and security, … [the Council] authorizes UNIFIL to take *all necessary action* in areas of deployment of its forces and as it deems within its capabilities, to ensure that its area of operations is not utilized for hostile activities of any kind, to resist attempts by forceful means to prevent it from discharging its duties under the mandate of the Security Council, and to protect United Nations personnel, facilities, installations and equipment, ensure the security and freedom of movement of United Nations personnel, humanitarian workers and, without prejudice to the responsibility of the Government of Lebanon, to protect civilians under imminent threat of physical violence. (S/RES/1701, introduction and para. 12)

In other words, Lebanon received an interstate mandate during its civil war in 1978, and a civil war mandate after the civil war had ended and during a cross-border war with Israel.[9] The resolution uses the language of a typical Chapter VII peace enforcement mandate; however, in a face-saving gesture to the Government of Lebanon, the Council did not specifically designate the new mandate under Chapter VII of the UN Charter. The Council also "in contrast with other UN operations, did not advance any sort of political peace process, a fundamental limitation that it has thus far been unable to address" (Gowan and Novosseloff 2010; author's translation from the original French). The Council also authorized the deployment of a vast number of troops – 15,000, mainly from NATO countries – for a territory measuring less than one-half the size of the small US state of Connecticut (S/RES/1701, para. 11). UNIFIL, as always, would maintain its headquarters in the Mediterranean town of Naqoura, in addition to, currently, 55 fixed positions.

In sum, initially, UNIFIL was narrowly supported by members of the UN Security Council and enjoyed only tepid backing from Arab states, the PLO, and Israel (Skogmo 1989, 7–10). Over time, however, it became "regarded as a valuable, indeed an essential, element of peace and stability in this extremely sensitive area, even by those who were once its main detractors" (Urquhart 1989, viii). Although the 2004 mandate alterations were not well received or clear, the mandate augmentation in 2006 had wide buy-in from all parties (Novosseloff 2015b, 769–770). To what extent has UNIFIL fulfilled its mandates? How have basic indicators of life (death, displacement, and the HDI), as well as conflict containment, changed over the course of UNIFIL's deployment?

Effectiveness

It is impossible to argue decisively that UNIFIL has been either a success or a failure. On the whole, the evidence indicates important positive effects, but with significant caveats. To recap some important background, UNIFIL deployed into a southern Lebanon characterized by full-on civil war being fought by more than three dozen militias, with little state presence or infrastructure. UNIFIL's spokesperson for more than two decades, Timur Goksel, explains how difficult it seemed

---

[9] UN peacekeeping mandates often reflect trends in international politics as much as, or sometimes more than, the particular conflict in question.

to fulfill the 1978 mandate: "So UNIFIL was throw into this environment where there was no state, where you had all these Palestinian groups, you had the Israelis, you had their SLA proxies ... there was a triple war going on ... the civil war 'south Lebanon version,' the civil war 'Beirut version,' and the cross-border Palestinian-Israeli war" (Goksel 2007, 56).

UNIFIL was intended as a quick operation: the word "interim" was inserted in its title precisely "to indicate the UN's understanding that UNIFIL was a short-term expedient; officials were afraid that a long-term presence would suck UNIFIL into the Lebanon quagmire with diminishing returns by way of contributing to peace" (James 1990, 618). However, given that 2018 marked its 40th anniversary, this mission has been anything but interim.

The initial mandate of UNIFIL entailed three tasks: (1) overseeing the withdrawal of Israeli forces, (2) restoring peace and security, and (3) assisting in the restoration of effective Lebanese authority. The 1982 mandate expansion included humanitarian assistance. The 2004 mandate to disarm militias was imprecise and largely ignored. The final, much larger mandate augmentation introduced the language of peace enforcement and taking "all necessary action" (S/RES/1701, 2006). I assess the extent to which UNIFIL implemented each of these responsibilities.

UNIFIL's first task in 1978 was to oversee the withdrawal of Israeli forces from southern Lebanon. This occurred 22 years later, in 2000, and not without significant difficulties along the way. When the Israeli Defense Forces (IDF) initially exited Lebanon in June 1978, they turned over control not to UNIFIL, but to their proxy forces, the Southern Lebanese Army (SLA), a Christian-led militia active in the civil war, who denied UNIFIL access to their territory (Makdisi 2014, 30). In addition, since Israel never occupied the Palestinian-held pocket of territory around Tyre, the Palestinians claimed that they had a right to control the area. Thus, "UNIFIL had no possibility of controlling infiltrations from the Palestinian positions north of the Litani through this area [Tyre]" (Novosseloff 2015a, 251). Moreover, because of Israeli support for the SLA and its control over the swath of territory along the border with Israel, "UNIFIL could not control Israeli incursions into Southern Lebanon" (Skogmo 1989, 22). Mona Ghali explains further:

The IDF assumed that UNIFIL would clear the entire area of Palestinians, and the failure of the force to deter Palestinian forays into northern Israel was used to justify Israel's continuing presence in the South. PLO Chairman Arafat, on the other hand, maintained that the 1969 Cairo Agreement legitimized the Palestinian presence in southern Lebanon. He claimed that the UN force should therefore not restrict Palestinian movement (Ghali 1993, 188; see also Brynen 1989).

Throughout much of its mandate, "UNIFIL could never effect an interpositional buffer zone, the operational mechanism deemed essential to the success of most traditional peacekeeping missions" (Hillen 1998, 132; see also Weinberger 1983). UNIFIL was only able to occupy 45 percent of the territory previously occupied by the IDF until Israel's withdrawal in 2000 (Hillen 1998, 13). Ultimately, however, Israel was able to withdraw because of UNIFIL's presence: "the IDF would not have left if a UN force had not been there" (Allee 2009, 102).[10] Thus the first component of UNIFIL's mandate – overseeing Israeli troop withdrawal – has been fulfilled.[11]

UNIFIL's second major task was to "restore peace and security." However, given the initial constraints imposed by the belligerents, not only did UNIFIL not have access to the entire territory, but it was also obligated to deploy in isolated detachments, which meant that, especially in the early years, many peacekeepers were "subject to constant harassment, virtual states of siege, and attack" (Hillen 1998, 134). The mission "faced constant attacks on its personnel, bases, and equipment, as well as restrictions of freedom of movement and communication" (Newby 2018, 61). As a result, UNIFIL lost 36 members in its first four years of operation in direct attacks and mine explosions (James 1983, 623). In other words, UNIFIL troops could not ensure peace and security for themselves, much less for the Lebanese and Israelis.

In June of 1982, Israeli Defense Forces overran UNIFIL positions, rendering what interpositional capacity they may have had completely inoperable. UNIFIL simply could not control the territory or keep the peace. In August, the United States, France, the United Kingdom, and Italy installed a Multinational Force (without authorization from the UN Security Council) as an "interposition" force with a genuine military enforcement capacity, although these troops were also not

---

[10] Author interview Dr. Tarek Mitri, director of the Issam Fares Institute for Public Policy and International Affairs at the American University of Beirut and former Minister of Culture, Minister of State, and Minister of Information for the Government of Lebanon, Beirut, Lebanon, 13 March 2015.

[11] The Shebaa Farms, however, are still contested.

successful at stopping the violence.[12] The civil war raged another eight years. According to the scholar Karim Makdisi, "the last remnant of the PLO was expelled from Lebanon in 1983," leaving something of a security vacuum in southern Lebanon, which allowed Hezbollah to form and grow. In all, UNIFIL did not "manage to forestall any of the five Israeli invasions or the twenty-two-year Israeli occupation" (Newby 2018, 5).

Writing in the early 1990s, Paul Diehl summed up UNIFIL's record to that point:

There is perhaps no other peacekeeping mission that has failed so consistently to limit armed conflict. Perhaps the only positive sign has been that violence in the areas fully controlled by UNIFIL has been less than in areas under partial occupation by one antagonist or another. In addition, UNIFIL has stopped thousands of Palestinian infiltration attempts, although it has been unable to stop perhaps at least as many more. Furthermore, it is apparently the view of many UN members and analysts that the situation would be even worse without UNIFIL; thus, despite all the problems, the UNIFIL mandate has been consistently renewed at regular intervals. (1994, 58)

Later, during the time from Israel's withdrawal in 2000 through 2005, there were "no serious breaches of the ceasefire in populated areas" (Makdisi 2017, 156). The 2006 invasion, however, was devastating. Paul Salem describes the destruction wrought by Israel on all of Lebanon, in its attempt to obliterate the Hezbollah threat:

Lebanon, particularly the Shiite areas in southern Lebanon and the southern suburbs of Beirut, paid an enormous human and economic price. Some 1,200 civilians (almost a third of them children) died, 4,000 were wounded, and a million people [about one-quarter of the population] were displaced. Some 130,000 housing units, thousands of small businesses, hundreds of roads, 300 factories, 80 bridges, dozens of schools and hospitals, and the country's electricity network were destroyed or damaged. This was the costliest Arab-Israeli war in Lebanon's history ... Economic losses were initially estimated at around $7 billion, or 30 percent of GDP. (2006, 18)

Although the fighting in Lebanon was horrific, there were fears at the time of much worse. There was a distinct possibility of all-out

---

[12] Indeed, the Sabra and Shatila massacres of Palestinians occurred while thousands of western troops were on watch. The MNF eventually departed Lebanon in 1984, after the barracks bombing that killed 241 American and 58 French troops (McDermott and Skjelsbaek 1991).

regional war, pitting Saudi Arabia (a long-time supporter of the government of Lebanon) versus Iran (Hazbollah's main supporter), versus Israel. The International Crisis Group warned,

Step by rapid step, the stakes and nature of the conflict have shifted: Israel increasingly sees it as a battle for its and the region's future; Hezbollah – torn between its identity as a Lebanese/Shiite movement and a messianic Arab-Islamist one – has increasingly slipped into the latter. On both sides, a tactical fight is metamorphosing into an existential war (2006, 4).

The war, however, did not transform into a full-scale regional war as feared. Instead, it lasted 34 days, and concluded with the broadly accepted Security Council Resolution 1705, augmenting UNIFIL's role in maintaining the peace.

Although Israel's intention in 2006 was to isolate and drive out Hezbollah from Lebanon, as it largely accomplished with the PLO in 1982, the plan backfired: "they hit the Shia hard, trying to force their migration out of Lebanon, and to create sectarian tensions. But what was amazing was that most people took in the displaced, even in Christian areas."[13] In other words, this massive show of Israeli force had the opposite effect of what was intended: Hezbollah became viewed as a strong defender of Lebanon, even by its domestic enemies.[14]

In sum, UNIFIL has been "useful in maintaining local and regional stability" (Novosseloff 2015a, 255). Another scholar asserts, "It can be said with certainty that without UNIFIL's on-the-scene impartial assessment of incidents and liaison to contain them, any number of the violations of the ceasefire ... would have escalated," as, indeed, they have between Israel and Palestinians in the Gaza Strip, where the UN does not have a peacekeeping presence (Allee 2009, 102). Israel and Lebanon have agreed to a cessation of hostilities (S/2015/147,

[13] Author interview with Dr. Karim Makdisi, Associate Professor, American University of Beirut, Beirut, Lebanon, 7 March 2015.
[14] Subsequently, Hezbollah has gained 11 out of 30 seats in Parliament's national unity cabinet. It now holds veto power over all proceedings. In a 2009 agreement with Prime Minister Saad Hariri, Hezbollah was allowed to keep its weapons arsenal. Hezbollah is the most consolidated political party in Lebanon and provides basic state services in much of the Shiite-majority parts of Lebanon (Cammett 2014; Kaplan 2010). In a recent agreement with its political opponents in the majority (the 14 March coalition), Hezbollah is now working in tandem with the Lebanese Armed Forces to ward off a possible future attack from Israel (Nasrallah speech, 27 March 2017).

28 February 2015), but there has been "no movement toward a permanent ceasefire" much less a peace accord (S/2015/475, 25 June 2015, para. 2).[15]

Despite the many years of violence in southern Lebanon, there are three clear indicators from "natural experiments" that the presence of UN troops has had a positive effect. First, even in the early years, although UNIFIL was unable to control rocket fire outside of its areas of deployment, in the areas where it was operational, "UNIFIL's record was almost amazingly good at halting nearly all attacks" (Skogmo 1989, 56). Second, conflict among southern Lebanese would regularly arise when troops were rotated: "the initial phase is critical. This is the period often accompanied by increased violence, during which local militias try to challenge the incoming troops and watch to see who blinks … units where rotation is not staggered tend to perform less effectively in this initial period" (Ghali 1993, 191). The increased violence stems from new UN troops that have not yet established "contacts with the local belligerents" (Hillen 1998, 123).

Third, in 2006, Israel's most destructive invasion came when UNIFIL troops were at their lowest numbers in history. The period since UNIFIL's augmentation has been the most stable in South Lebanon's recent history, despite occasional spill over from the devastating war in neighboring Syria (Newby 2018, 67).

In sum, over time, violence has arisen in areas where UNIFIL is not deployed, when there are changes in troop rotations, and/or when UNIFIL is low in numbers. UNIFIL "has created a predictable security environment that has helped to normalize peace for local citizens" (Newby 2018, 24). Thus, although UNIFIL has not definitively fulfilled its second task of restoring "peace and security," it has undoubtedly had a positive effect.

UNIFIL's third assignment entailed assisting the Government of Lebanon in "restoring effective Lebanese authority" south of the Litani River. Through much of UNIFIL's deployment, most of Lebanon north of the Litani River came under Syrian armed control, under the guise of

---

[15] Since the war in neighboring Syria broke out in 2011, Lebanon has endured "shelling, shooting and aerial incursions into Lebanese border areas from the Syrian Arab Republic" (S/2015/475, 25 June 2015, para. 62). The Lebanese Armed Forces have proven fairly successful at deterring these attacks and preventing deeper infiltration by Al Nusra or ISIS into Lebanon (S/2015/475, 25 June 2015, para. 30).

Arab League "peacekeeping" (Barnett 1998, 74–76).[16] Thus while Syria, Israel, and the PLO used the territory of Lebanon in their regional struggle, the people of Lebanon, and its government, suffered. The standoff between external forces meant that "the notion of building a 'strong state' with a well-equipped army capable of protecting its citizens from foreign forces was unthinkable" (Makdisi 2014, 28). The government of Lebanon "more than any other party welcomed the deployment of UNIFIL, which in its view could serve as an international" mechanism of support (Makdisi 2014, 28). Another analyst, writing in an earlier time period, offers a slightly different angle: "UNIFIL continues to remain deployed in southern Lebanon largely because the government of Lebanon does not appear capable of assuming these responsibilities from UNIFIL" (Hillen 1998, 136).

The Lebanese civil war ended in 1989 with the Taif Accords; however, given the rise of Hezbollah in the south and the uneasy peace between Christian militias and other groups, the government has only recently begun to exert its authority south of the Litani. For example, as the UNIFIL spokesperson explained to me, "In 2011, we brought the Lebanese Prime Minister to visit southern Lebanon for his first visit."[17] The current UNIFIL Force Commander, Major-General Beary, explains further: "UNIFIL will continue to work with Ministries as well as local leaders in extending their full authority in UNIFIL area of operations. It is important for the Government of Lebanon to continue to take advantage of this unprecedented calm that south Lebanon has enjoyed for more than 10 years."[18] While UNIFIL and many others have been encouraging the Government of Lebanon to exert its authority, this is not an easy task, given the deep dysfunction within the Lebanese political system and state. For example, for nearly

---

[16] In 1978, the Arab League created the Arab Deterrent Force in Lebanon as a way to prevent Israel from taking over more of the country. This force was staffed mainly by Syrian troops and was allied with the PLO and the Lebanese National Movement comprised mainly of leftists and nationalists. On the other side stood the right-wing Christian Lebanese Front, which was supported by Israel. In other words, Israel and Syria opposed each other by supporting different sides in Lebanon.

[17] Author interview with UNIFIL Spokesperson Andrea Teneti, Naquora, Lebanon, 12 March 2015. See also https://unifil.unmissions.org/prime-minister-mikati-visits-unifil-hails-its-contribution-peace-and-stability-south-lebanon.

[18] UNIFIL Force Commander Major-General Beary meets newly appointed Lebanese Prime Minister Saad Hariri. UNIFIL News, 10 January 2017.

two years before October 2016, Lebanon did not even have a president. As one expert laments, "President or no, Lebanon has had no effective governance for decades," whether north or south of the Litani River (Issa 2016). UNIFIL has "worked to bring state institutions back into the area, which in turn has brought greater stability and encouraged economic activity" (Newby 2018, 24). In sum, the third component of UNIFIL's mandate – the task of restoring Lebanese state authority to the south – has not yet come to fruition, but it is in process.

Vanessa Newby, a scholar with deep knowledge of Lebanon, summarizes UNIFIL's effectiveness:

UNIFIL has prevented accidental outbreaks of armed confrontation from escalating into war. It has reduced the overt presence of Hezbollah and has provided an environment conducive to economic development … if UNIFIL were not present, South Lebanon would be more vulnerable to conflict … in the absence of a political solution between the Lebanese and Israeli governments, UNIFIL has carved out an important role for itself … [It has built] positive local relationships … were UNIFIL not present, it is very possible [that a wider] war may have broken out (Newby 2018, 5).

UNIFIL has proven effective at reducing violence and restoring peace and security in areas where it is deployed. It assisted in the eventual withdrawal of the IDF after 22 years of occupation. The objective of restoring state authority to the south is ongoing, but it has not been fully achieved. Although most militias are no longer active, many remain armed, and Hezbollah's growth – as both a political and armed actor – continues to threaten Israel (and possibly

1948 UNTSO observers deploy in Egypt, Israel, Jordan, Lebanon, and Syria
1975 Civil war begins in Lebanon
1976 Syria deploys troops to Lebanon
1978 Israel invades Lebanon, UNIFIL deploys
1982 Second Israeli invasion
1983 Attacks on American and French troops in Multinational Force, MNF withdraws in 1984
1985 Israel pulls back to self-declared security zone in south
1990 Taif Accords, Lebanese civil war ends
1996 Israel bombs Hezbollah positions in southern Lebanon
2000 Israel withdraws from southern Lebanon
2005 Prime Minister Rafik Hariri assassinated; anti-Syrian rallies; Syrian troops withdraw
2006 In response to Hezbollah's growth and aggression, Israel bombs throughout Lebanon for 34 days; Lebanese Armed Forces deploy to the south for the first time in decades; UNIFIL's mandate is augmented
2007 Five Spanish UN peacekeepers killed
2011 Civil war in Syria breaks out

Figure 3.1 Lebanon Timeline

the state of Lebanon). Since 2006, southern Lebanon has grown economically and has enjoyed a period of peace. However, the ultimate
goal of conflict resolution between Israel, Hezbollah, and Lebanon –
which has never been a part of UNIFIL's mandate – remains elusive.
(Figure 3.1 on page 107 summarizes the major events).

Mechanisms of Power in UNIFIL

UNIFIL has served as a "deterrent and a physical obstacle to the transformation of southern Lebanon into Israeli-occupied territory, or a possible *de facto* annexation as Israel's 'North Bank'" (Thakur 1987, 69). In
other words, things could have been worse without UNIFIL's presence.
Thakur indicates that UNIFIL serves as a deterrent, but how does this
deterrent effect work in practice? What were and are UNIFIL's means of
power? In 2006, it became conceivable that, with 15,000 troops hailing
mainly from NATO countries, the mission could ensure international
peace and security and protect civilians through military compellence.
However, as I argue in the following sections, compellence is not a viable
feature of UNIFIL's power. Rather, we see evidence of fairly effective
patrolling (surveillance), military diplomacy, and deterrence mainly
through inducement. UNIFIL does not provide security guarantees based
in compellence, and local ownership remains elusive.

Coercion: Surveillance/Observation, Not Compellence or Security Guarantees

From its start, UNIFIL did not possess a compellent military capacity.
Although the Government of Lebanon had requested UN troops, none
of the parties in the south were willing to accept a large force: "There
was no thought of putting together a large military force bent on
coercing the belligerents into an accepted pattern of behavior" (Hillen
1998, 118; see also James 1983). UNIFIL was never deployed as an
interposition force. Although the UNIFIL mandate indicated that UN
troops were supposed to restore peace and security in the south,
"coercion is not an available option for UNIFIL" (Newby 2018,
166). Currently, nearly 11,000 troops from 40 different countries serve
in UNIFIL.[19] The overall number and composition has fluctuated over

[19] www.un.org/en/peacekeeping/contributors/2017/apr17_5.pdf.

time, with the largest surge coming after the Israel invasion of 2006. In December 2006, the four top troop contributors were Italy, France, Spain, and Germany, with 900 or more troops from each (Novosseloff 2015b, 769). Although many troops hail from NATO member countries, three factors continue to weigh against UNIFIL's material capacity to use force: (1) troop positions in isolated detachments, (2) reliance on light weapons, and (3) UNIFIL force and command structures.

First, in terms of deployment, like most peacekeeping missions, troop bases and positions do not serve to dominate or control the entire territory of operations through compellence. Troops are sometimes positioned in isolation from one another. As I explained earlier, UNIFIL was never deployed as a coherent interpositional force. As one American military analyst lamented: "To continue operations in such an incoherently occupied zone of operations was beyond the pale of military logic" (Hillen 1998, 135). That is because peacekeeping does not function by a compellent, military logic.

Second, UNIFIL troops deployed only with light weapons; although in 2006 some battalions arrived with heavier weapons, they quickly reverted back to the norm. Longtime UNIFIL spokesperson Timur Goksel exclaimed: "So this is where you send these nice UN soldiers with their light rifles and tell them not only to survive, but to fight these characters when necessary, with absolutely no support from anybody" (2007, 56). In other words, UNIFIL peacekeepers possess weapons that might help with their own defense but do not provide the capacity to compel behavior.

Third, UNIFIL's force and command structures likewise preclude the use of compellence. Contingents "come and go" on their own schedules, which makes for haphazard personal turnover and "force turbulence ... [personnel shifts are] inconsistent, unsynchronized, and uncoordinated" (Hillen 1998, 126). Troop contingents rotate every four or six months – or once per year – regardless, contingents are not in the country long, and "once troops have reached a stage where they can be effective, the continuity and consistency of field operations are disrupted" (Ghali 1993, 191). While UNIFIL is centrally commanded in principle, national command and control systems override UNIFIL command and control (Hillen 1998, 124). In terms of transferring knowledge during troops rotations, UNIFIL has not developed mechanisms that would transfer knowledge centrally (other than through the civil affairs cultural sensitivity trainings, as I explain later). Instead, institutional experience, when it is transferred at all, is passed through national battalion command structures (Hillen 1998, 123).

After 2006, the massive infusion of troops and equipment, mainly from France, Spain, and Italy, created new expectations among western powers that UNIFIL would be able to enforce the peace by providing military-based security guarantees. Many of the troops arrived after serving in NATO missions, where the force posture was geared for war fighting. This approach did not prove effective in South Lebanon.[20]

In 2007, six Spanish peacekeepers were killed, most likely by Hezbollah, which many interpreted as a message to back off from the robust force posture (and patrolling outside of UNIFIL's area of operation, north of the Litani River). In another example, in 2006, 1,600 French troops arrived with 13 Leclerc Main Battle Tanks. They insisted on patrolling in tanks, which led villagers to complain: "even the Israelis didn't wake our children up at night by patrolling in tanks!" (François 2015). As Timor Goksel exclaimed: "What are you going to do with 13 tanks? The Israelis have 13,000 tanks" (François 2015). One French commander explained to me: "The martial look is what people respect."[21] But the French eventually relented and now patrol mainly in light-armed vehicles and trucks. As one ethnographer explains: "The French and Spanish were treating the Lebanese like a foreign enemy;" the locals protested, and prevailed (Newby 2018, 131). She further explicates, "UNIFIL is unable to use force ... because were it to do so, it would necessarily alienate most of the local population ... Despite calls by Israel and the United States for UNIFIL to employ a more forceful posture and rid the area of ... Hezbollah weapons, in this environment, deterrence is not an option" (Newby 2018, 167).

Goksel further describes the ineffectiveness of attempts in 2006 toward a more compellent approach:

UNIFIL II is not an occupation force and they're not going to fight the Israelis or Hezbollah, so why all this machinery? When I go to the villages and I ask what the problem is when people complain about "this new

[20] Note that the French and American Multinational Force of 1983, Israel and Syria have each attempted to control Lebanon through compellent means and failed.
[21] Author interview with Colonel Benoit Aummonier, Southern Lebanon, 10 March 2015.

UNIFIL" they'd say, "they don't talk to us." That is what the people really want – they want you to walk around the village and say, "Hi, how are you? How's the family? How's life?" … because for 28 years they got used to a different kind of UNIFIL, a friendly UNIFIL who shared their lives in tough times under very difficult circumstances (Goksel 2007, 77).

"Walking around and asking about life" is what UNIFIL troops have reverted back to as their standard practice (Novosseloff 2015b, 772). On a daily basis, the troops' main activities are observation/surveillance, as they have always been, through "stationary observation posts, traffic control points, and patrols" (Hillen 1998, 129). Today, every month, "UNIFIL conducts on average ten thousand activities, including some eleven hundred in close coordination with the LAF. UNIFIL ensures every type of violation is attended to immediately to reassure the parties that the blue line is being monitored" (Newby 2018, 84).

UNIFIL troops observe and surveil, but they do not have the power of arrest – when there is a blue-line or other sort of violation, UNIFIL report it to the relevant sides and employ military diplomacy (as I describe later). When they are confronted with more serious challenges, "UNIFIL's strategy is always to stand back" (Newby 2018, 127). As one commander explained, "There are different degrees of the use of force, but there's an awful lot to be said for the guy who's in charge on the ground at the time showing a bit of restraint and common sense … having a bit of manners goes an awful long way" (Newby 2018, 140). In recent years, UNIFIL will often call the LAF to help diffuse tensions. This strategy serves to promote the principle that the LAF hold primary responsibility for security in the south, although Hezbollah may one day contest that notion.

In sum, UNIFIL troops may defend themselves and patrol/surveil, but further coercive action such as arrest, or military-based deterrence or compellence, are not possible. UNIFIL does not provide military-based security guarantees. UNIFIL troops calm disputes, but they cannot stop armies because they have neither the means nor the legitimacy. One of UNIFIL's important means of reducing conflict is through persuasion, which I explore next.

Persuasion: Military Diplomacy, Civilian Outreach, Symbolic Displays, and Training

Although UNIFIL does not compel, it has the capacity to employ persuasion effectively. Persuasion in UNIFIL comes in a variety of forms, including high-level military diplomacy. Over the 40-year course of its operations, UNIFIL's *military* diplomacy for de-escalating conflict spirals has undoubtedly proven more effective than its *political* efforts at concluding the conflict between Israel and Lebanon. I begin this section by clarifying how military and political diplomacy differ in UNIFIL, and then turn to exploring UNIFIL's points of persuasive power, including symbolic displays, outreach, and training. I also recap the conditions that enable UNIFIL to persuade effectively.

Unlike most peacekeeping operations, UNIFIL's top leader always comes from military, not civilian, ranks. The Head of Mission and Force Commander must "perform a diplomatic role, more often than not, dependent on the art of persuasion, not the use of force" (Allee 2009, 100). Although it is easy to critique this arrangement, since peace-keeping is intended to be more of a political rather than a military endeavor (Goulding 2002, 32; Weinberger 1995), for southern Lebanon, this institutional structure has shown to be both enduring and fairly effective.

Throughout its history, UNIFIL's military staff have nearly always managed to communicate with all sides in the ever-evolving conflicts. As one analyst explains, "While Israel never formally accepted UNI-FIL's presence, it nonetheless employed its mediation and negotiation capabilities, with its headquarters becoming a common meeting place for representatives of all of the parties to the conflict. UNIFIL was also the only reliable source of information from the region for the UNSC" (Nachmias 1996, 15). UNIFIL troops and civilians gather sensitive military and political information and pass it up the chain of com-mand, where the leadership works to avert violent crises.

After the 2006 war, UNIFIL formalized and made public the occur-rence of regular monthly "tripartite" meetings between representatives of the IDF and the LAF.[22] These meetings include the UNIFIL force commander, 14 senior UNIFIL staff, and 6 or 7 senior officials from the LAF and IDF each. The agenda is agreed several days ahead of time. Although the content of these meetings is not public and there is no formal account of liaisons between Hezbollah and the IDF, numer-ous people with whom I spoke in southern Lebanon suggested that military diplomacy, facilitated by UNIFIL, is the main mechanism

---

[22] https://unifil.unmissions.org/unifil-head-chairs-regular-tripartite-meeting-laf-and-idf-officials.

through which the parties communicate (See also S/2015/475, 25 June 2015, para. 18). According to the UN Secretary-General, these meetings are "the most significant stabilizing factor ... serving to build confidence between the parties and defuse tension in potential flashpoints, as well as providing a platform through which UNIFIL can facilitate practical arrangements on the ground between the LAF and IDF" (S/2013/381, 26 June, para. 7). The meetings allow both sides to "air their grievances [and] vent their feelings ... the liaison and communication channels appear to make a strong contribution to the prevention of war" (Newby 2018, 97).

While high-level military diplomacy appears effective at diffusing tensions between the IDF and the LAF, on a lower level, problems sometimes arise between regular UNIFIL troops and local civilians. Issues often stem from frequent troop rotations and the large number of European troops who are unaccustomed to the environment or standard practices in UNIFIL. As one local hotel owner lamented, "This frequent rotation hurts the relations a lot, because as soon as you make relations with someone, they disappear and you have to start from zero" (Newby 2018, 148). For example, local south Lebanese – 75 percent of whom are Shiite and many of whom support Hezbollah – fear that European troops favor Israel and might spy for Israel. Photo taking in the south is especially sensitive, and when performed by European troops, it is sometimes assumed to be spying. All UN bases have signs warning against taking photos, but new troops sometimes ignore them. Newly arrived Europeans are also more likely to behave arrogantly and assume what are perceived as aggressive or unfriendly postures. Speeding vehicles and patrolling in tanks or other heavy, armored means of transport are often perceived as offensive to locals (Newby 2018, 158).

Civil affairs officers smooth over these sources of friction through *outreach* and *training*. UNIFIL's approximately 600 civil affairs officers are comprised in nearly equal proportions of Lebanese nationals and international staff. Although contracts vary, UNIFIL has employed some civil affairs officers for 10 years or more. The civil affairs approach "is very much in tune with Lebanese village culture, which is very social and where dropping in to chat is regarded as very normal. During [these conversations] ... civil affairs officers inquire about local needs ... and explain [UNIFIL's programs] (Newby 2018, 119). In response to requests, civil affairs officers run trainings in organic agriculture, manufacturing agricultural products, [creating] agricultural cooperatives, training for medical staff, donating computers and sewing machines, and providing training in sewing" (Newby 2018, 143). The civilian affairs officers also hold frequent trainings for newly arrived UNIFIL troop battalions to help ease their entry into southern Lebanese society and culture. UNIFIL staff reiterate continuously to troop contingents that "they are guests in Lebanon" and must respect the local culture (Newby 2018, 151).

While civilian outreach efforts help to smooth sometimes-inconsistent relations between newly arrived troops and local Lebanese, many Lebanese recall important *symbolic displays* and sacrifices made by UNIFIL troops, which have endeared the mission to locals historically. For example, Indonesia, which is the world's largest Muslim-majority democracy – and one that is extremely diverse – has as the slogan on its main peacekeeping base and elsewhere: "Unity in Diversity." In another example of symbolic displays, Ghanaian troops – both Muslim and Christian – often pray with locals in mosques and churches.

Sometimes troops' symbolic displays of solidarity cross the line from immaterial to potentially life threatening. For example, some French troops appeared willing to make the ultimate sacrifice to dissuade Israeli forces prior to the Israeli invasion of 2000. Israeli troops had invaded a village and were preparing to bomb a home: "the French commander, without asking, ordered his guys to climb to the roof of the building and sit there. So 15 French ran to the roof of the building and sat there. People saw those things and it became legend" (Newby 2018, 63). Moreover, when fighting breaks out, UNIFIL troops have often suffered along with local civilians. Thus far, more peacekeepers have died in the service of UNIFIL (312 in total) than in any other UN operation, and people in southern Lebanon have a general sense of this sacrifice (United Nations 2018c). "Perhaps the most important contribution of UNIFIL is the moral support it has provided for the embattled civilian population in Lebanon" (Nachmias 1996, 15). As the previous UNIFIL force commander, Major-General Luciano Portolano, explained,

Operationally I define the relationship with the local population as my center of gravity. It means an element that, if it exists, might lead to success; if it doesn't exist it will lead, for sure, to complete disruption of the mission.

So the link between the UNIFIL members and the local population is the most important element I recommend for the future leadership to take into consideration.[23]

Thus military diplomacy (high and low), supplemented by civilian outreach, are important elements of UNIFIL's ability to persuade (S/2015/475, 25 June 2015, para. 22).

Although military diplomacy and civilian outreach may defuse conflict in a variety of localized ways, in terms of its more standard, politically oriented efforts at persuasion, UNIFIL has proven less effective. No political figures have managed to mediate a settlement either between the Israelis and the Palestinians, or, more recently, between the Israelis and Hezbollah.[24] It is therefore logical to deduce that a standard UN Special Representative head of this mission would not be able to achieve such a goal. Compounding the problems, the current structure of the UN's political efforts in the region render achieving the goal of peace even more remote, since the bureaucracy itself makes speaking with one voice nearly impossible. In the last decade, "UNIFIL has had to carry on its work in the company of no fewer than three high-level UN political representatives with a Lebanon portfolio, all of whom operate independently and under distinct but inter-related mandates ... the lack of integration has resulted in conflicting messages on some politically loaded issues" (Allee 2009, 93, 95).[25]

The most politically "loaded" issue is how to treat Hezbollah. UNIFIL's military troops must maintain functioning relations with Hezbollah in order to avert violent escalations; they thus liaise with

---

[23] https://unifil.unmissions.org/he-prepares-leave-unifil-head-says-relations-communities-critical-success.

[24] In addition, the UN tribunal to investigate the assassination of Prime Minister Rafic Hariri in 2005, allegedly by Hezbollah or by Syrian troops, remains mired in a political quagmire.

[25] The three political representatives are the UN Special Coordinator for the Middle East Peace Process, who has focused mainly on the Palestinian track and delineating the border between Israel and Lebanon. The UN Special Envoy for SC Resolution 1559 focuses on Syria, and is investigating the death of Lebanese President Rafik Hariri. The UN also has the Secretary-General's Personal Representative for Southern Lebanon, now called the UN Special Coordinator for Lebanon. All three have distinct but interrelated mandates, and they report through the Department of Political Affairs, not through the Department of Peacekeeping Operations.

Hezbollah counterparts. However, given the US, European, and Gulf Cooperation Council designation of Hezbollah as a terrorist organization, UNIFIL political and even non-governmental representatives are required to treat the group as hostile (Zahar 2012, 82).[26] The divisions within UNIFIL's political-diplomatic structures have created the conditions whereby the parties do not divide and rule, but they often "divide and outsmart" by playing different parts of the UN against each other (Allee 2009, 96). "Few who are familiar with the UN peace structures concerned with Lebanon would contest that the myriad missions and messengers extant have hindered unity of purpose and message" (Allee 2009, 96).[27]

In sum, UNIFIL's military diplomacy and civilian outreach have proven fairly effective. UNIFIL troops and civil affairs officers are able to speak with one voice (focusing on the message that they act impartially and actively seek consent of the local population). Civilian affairs officers serve to smooth over occasionally choppy relations between troops and civilians; the symbolic displays and sacrifices of UNIFIL troops also demonstrate an alignment of message and behavior. They thus generally employ persuasion effectively to *manage* conflict. In contrast, the higher-level political mediation structures – which seek to employ persuasion to *resolve* the conflicts – are divided and sometimes convey inconsistent messages, especially regarding Hezbollah. We have evidence of the persuasive means by which UNIFIL troops may effectively manage conflict, but its resolution remains elusive.

Elements of Inducement in UNIFIL

While I was conducting fieldwork in Lebanon in the spring of 2015, over the course of approximately 40 interviews and casual conversations with UNIFIL troops, civilian staff, and southern Lebanese citizens, I posed questions about UNIFIL's 2006 robust, "all necessary

---

[26] The UNIFIL Deputy Head of Mission and Director of Political and Civil Affairs, Imran Riza, asserted that despite the formal restrictions, "We have lots of ways to pass messages and understand concerns." Author Interview, Naqoura, Lebanon, 12 March 2015.
[27] Note also that approximately one quarter of UNIFIL's current troops – a total of 2,400, are from Bangladesh, Indonesia, and Malaysia – do not recognize Israel or maintain diplomatic relations with the state. While this may help on the Lebanese side of the Blue Line, it does not on the other.

action" mandate. I asked how troops carry out the mandate and how locals interpret UNIFIL actions. Nearly all interviewees responded that force has little if anything to do with the UN's operations in the south. They also nearly all conveyed, unprompted, that the UN's *financial contributions* to the south's economy were the main reason why people in southern Lebanon accept the UN's presence. It is this acceptance – conceived in peacekeeping doctrine as "consent" – that enables the UN to help manage conflicts in southern Lebanon.

Although my sample is not representative, the recurrent refrain of the UN's power of inducement is also supported by three recent ethnographic studies of UNIFIL – by Chiara Ruffa (2014), which focuses on UNIFIL military troops; Susann Kassem (2017), on the civilian side of UNIFIL and the ways in which the mission is perceived by south Lebanese; and by Vanessa Newby (2018), which explores both the military and civilian aspects of UNIFIL. All three studies are based on more than one year of participant observation, ethnographic, and in-country research in southern Lebanon. The studies demonstrate the myriad ways in which UNIFIL peacekeepers induce peace, namely by providing a variety of carrots – including the non-enforcement of weapons restrictions – and building institutions. These elements together comprise the peacekeeping economy of the south. I explore each mechanism of inducement – aid, restrictions, institutions, and the peacekeeping economy – in turn.

QIPs and Aid

When UNIFIL first deployed in 1978, most of south Lebanon did not have much in the way of basic infrastructure such as electricity, roads, or water and sewage systems (Newby 2018, 63). All of these systems were developed over the years – often through UNIFIL assistance programs – and then shattered in 2006. As a Lebanese civilian explained, "After the 2006 war UNIFIL contributed a lot. Our infrastructure was destroyed – our roads, water system, telecommunications, electric, everything. They helped us rebuild our water and electric system and cleared the roads" (quoted in Newby 2018, 144).

QIPs are a key component of post-2006 "civil-military cooperation" or (CIMIC) between UNIFIL and local south Lebanese, which moves into the domain of humanitarian and development aid. Ruffa explains, "CIMIC entails humanitarian and reconstruction activities aimed at

improving the living conditions of the Southern Lebanese and impli-
citly at promoting a good image of peacekeepers in their respective
area of operations" (2014, 208). UNIFIL peacekeepers provide
"humanitarian assistance to the local population, including medical,
dental and veterinary aid ... Specialized teams of de-miners have
destroyed [thousands of] explosive devices that included rockets, gren-
ades and cluster bombs. Troops are also involved with the reconstruction of infrastructures, especially roads and bridges" (Elron 2007, 34).
One UNIFIL member explained to me: "We help to build labs and
schools. We help with the energy supply, infrastructure, and health.
We always strive to help the most people. We come only when we are
invited."[28] In another example, the mission engages in such activities
as tree planting with the Ministry of Environment, "aimed at reducing
the mission's environmental footprint. UNIFIL also participated in the
'Greening the South' campaign, whereby thousands of trees were
planted across the area of operations" (S/2015/147, 28 February
2015, para. 18).

When I asked UNIFIL's deputy force commander how peacekeeping
works in southern Lebanon, he explained: "We support the local
population by providing medical supplies and regular clinic hours for
all types of medical treatment, in both the municipalities and on our
bases" (see Photo 3, p. 182).[29] He explained that UNIFIL's un-
mandated development projects total about $5 million per year, which
is significant in an impoverished, small farming region. However,
UNIFIL's work related to inducement often differs by nationality of
the troop-contributing country, and that country's wealth, and is thus
not uniform across the mission.

For example, historically, Ghana has served as one of the top troop
contributors to UNIFIL. The first-ever Force Commander for UNIFIL,
Lieutenant General Emmanuel Erskine, was Ghanaian. Ruffa asserts,
"the Ghanaian units contended that peacekeeping was the specialty of
their army" (2014, 213). One member of the Ghanaian battalion
affirmed: "We are the 57th Ghanaian contingent to deploy under
UNIFIL. We know what we are talking about when we talk about
southern Lebanon" (Ruffa 2014, 211). Ghanaian troops emphasize

---

[28] Author interview with Captain Ludivine Daman, Southern Lebanon,
    9 March 2015.
[29] Author interview with General Escerito Obbedio, Southern Lebanon,
    11 March 2015.

CIMIC activities, which, as Ruffa summarizes in her research, entails a certain set of behaviors:

> In the period of observation ... the Ghanaian army displayed lower force protection measures, did contact patrolling, and focused on CIMIC. For instance, the Ghanaian army patrolled mostly on foot and implemented large amounts of small civil-military relations projects based on limited resources. This is consistent with the overall low threat perception, [their] interpretation of the enemy, and the restrictive interpretation of the use of force. (Ruffa 2014, 216)[30]

In my own experience, one south Lebanese local explained to me that his favorite contingent was the one from Ghana, because they brought Bob Marley's "music of resistance" to southern Lebanon. He described that, in the 1980s, the Ghanaian troops would hang out in the local community center (which they helped to rebuild) and share their Bob Marley tapes with south Lebanese youth. The music spread quickly and can be heard even today throughout the south.[31]

In general, troops from developing countries employ inducement in different ways from that of the middle-income and wealthier: "The Nepalese have veterinarians, dentists, and doctors. The Indians have great veterinarians and teach yoga. The Koreans brought (expensive) solar-powered street lamps. They also teach Tae Kwon Do, and they have helped women form cooperatives to grow food and distribute it to the market."[32] According to Newby, the South Koreans are perceived to be the most generous, even offering cultural trips to South Korea (2018, 145).

Several observers and analysts have noted that French troops in particular have run into obstacles as they navigate the complex terrain of exercising different forms of power.[33] French troops often teach

---

[30] Rather than singling out Hezbollah or any parties as enemies, the Italian Force Commander, like his Ghanaian predecessor, would repeatedly state, "we have no enemies here."

[31] In this example, persuasion and inducement are at work simultaneously.

[32] Author interview with UNIFIL Spokesperson Andrea Teneti, Naquora, Lebanon, 12 March 2015.

[33] The roots of the problems probably stem from lingering resentment over the French colonization of Lebanon, as well as a rocky decolonization process. French troops are also wary, recalling the attack on their barracks when they served in the Multinational Force in Beirut in 1983, which killed 58 service members.

French in schools as part of their CIMIC programs, and they give generously to infrastructure projects. However, French troop acceptance is not uniform, given memories from French colonial times, a perception that France is partial to Israel, and the sometimes-arrogant or overly forceful approach of French peacekeepers (Ruffa 2014). Their assistance, therefore, is not always welcome. Kassem illustrates an episode she observed when the mayor of a village refused to allow French troops to teach the French language in a local school. As retribution, "the French CIMIC contingent decided to withdraw funding for a recently-approved electricity generator for the village" (Kassem 2017, 474). In other words, the French were linking carrots – and their removal – as a means of inducing the acceptance of French language education, but locals were not complying. I also heard stories of unintended consequences, such as villages playing battalions off one another, inadvertently creating tensions between villages, when wealthier battalions provide goods that troops from developing nations cannot. Newby and Ruffa found similar conflicts (Newby 2018, 147; Ruffa 2014).

Staff in UNIFIL headquarters have sought ways to equalize the ability of troops from nations of differing wealth to contribute to local projects (i.e., to induce) more equitably, through QIPs.[34] In recent years, UNIFIL has secured a $500,000 annual budget for QIPs. Several rules accompany such projects: (1) the expenditure must not exceed $25,000, (2) the project must be completed within three months, and (3) it must benefit the maximum number of people in a given village. A fourth standard practice is that the local mayor or municipal leader must be involved in the process from start to finish. These rules and guidelines emerged as a way to overcome inequalities in what troops of differing wealth can deliver to locals while trying to ensure that the projects are actually desired by locals.

In sum, UNIFIL troops provide a variety of inducements to local Lebanese. These projects ingratiate UNIFIL with people in the south, even if people do not always like the troops – some battalions employ soft power more expertly than others. UNIFIL peacekeepers also employ inducement in the realm of security-sector reforms.

---

[34] Author interview with UNIFIL Spokesperson Andrea Teneti, Naquora, Lebanon, 12 March 2015.

Trust Fund for DDR and Market (Weapons) Restrictions

UNIFIL works to induce military reforms through several mechanisms. A trust fund enables various programs for training and equipping the LAF. In principle, UNIFIL is also supposed to uphold a weapons ban in southern Lebanon, although restricting Hezbollah weapons procurement is beyond the capabilities of the United Nations alone.

In terms of inducing military reforms, in Lebanon, the "International Support Group for Lebanon" is the trust fund through which international finances are allocated for training and equipping the LAF. The Group is comprised of the P-5 Security Council members, Germany, Italy, the EU, and the Arab League. In recent years, the United States and the United Kingdom in particular have provided hundreds of millions of dollars in equipment to the LAF (The International Institute for Strategic Studies 2017, 40).

UNIFIL has been mandated to create a weapons-free zone in the south, but the only way to carry out this mandate is by building up, and working with, the LAF: "Many in the local population do not want UNIFIL to search for Hezbollah's weapons ... because they view Hezbollah as the only deterrent to another Israeli invasion" (Newby 2018, 8). Moreover, the mandate "does not include the interception of arms shipments from Syria unless requested by the Lebanese government, nor will [UNIFIL] directly disarm Hezbollah, but only support the LAF in doing so through assistance on the ground and by training personnel" (Elron 2007, 35).

UNIFIL's Maritime Task Force conducts joint operations with the LAF's incipient Navy (see Photo 4, p. 182). Together, UNIFIL and LAF Navy have inspected hundreds of vessels in order "to ensure that no unauthorized weapons or related material were transferred into Lebanon" (S/2015/475, para. 20). But again, UNIFIL will not restrict goods from the sea or land on its own.

As Karim Makdisi explains, "It must be remembered that during the immediate post-civil war period in Lebanon (1990–2004) Hezbollah was officially regarded as a legitimate and protected 'resistance' group and therefore, unlike other armed groups, entitled to carry arms as long as the state of war with Israel persisted" (Makdisi 2017, 149). For this reason, many south Lebanese are unwilling to assist UNIFIL in restricting Hezbollah's weapons into, and within, UNIFIL's area of operation in the south. But as UNIFIL assists in building the LAF and the LAF assumes greater responsibility for securing the south, the balance between the LAF and Hezbollah – of military capacity and legitimacy – is shifting. I explore LAF institution building next.

Institution Building

The third component of UNIFIL's original mandate is to assist "the Government of Lebanon in ensuring the return of its effective authority in the area" of southern Lebanon (S/RES/425, 19 March 1978). Even before the civil war began, the state was hardly present in south Lebanon from 1963, when the region last held elections, much less during the 15-year civil war or the 22-year Israeli occupation. After the Israeli withdrawal in 2000, citizens in the south had little if any experience with the principles or realities of a functioning municipal government that would collect taxes and provide services. For most of UNIFIL's existence, the third part of the mandate was simply not possible to help implement. Since 2006, however, UNIFIL has carved out some room in this domain. For the last decade or so, civil affairs officers have held technical workshops on how to establish a state municipality, how to prepare a budget, and how to issue requests to Beirut (Newby 2018, 118). Until recently, the political parties Hezbollah and its cousin Amal have been the main service providers alongside UNIFIL. "By bringing the state back down to the South, UNIFIL can be said to be working [to] reduce the space for other substate actors to provide material benefits" (Newby 2018, 123).

While UNIFIL works to help establish official municipal governing structures, arguably the most important element of its state-building efforts lie in its work with the LAF. For decades, UNIFIL has integrated LAF contingents into the UNIFIL force structure (Hillen 1998, 115). Even today, the "headquarters of every UNIFIL battalion has a LAF officer living in the compound to ensure that there is full communication between UNIFIL and the LAF at every level" (Newby 2018, 126).

After 2006, UNIFIL began training and equipping the LAF as a means to extend state authority to the south. In the 2008 Doha Agreement – arrived at under Qatari and Arab League patronage and approved by the UN Security Council – Hezbollah became reincorporated into the Lebanese government and acknowledged as coexisting with the LAF. The LAF, however, remained largely ineffective and symbolic until the mid-2010s.

The LAF does not have a set budget from the national government. Basic supplies including uniforms, and even meals are often funded by outside sources, most notably the United States and France (Byman 2018). UNIFIL's spokesperson described some of the mission's projects with security forces in general:

We are working to train a new Lebanese Navy. With the LAF, we provide equipment, matériel, and experience. Our goal is to allow the LAF to assume control of southern Lebanon. We are very committed to achieving this goal. The more credible they are, the more credible we are. They ask for training – especially people in the villages ask for police training. For example, the Italian Carabinieri are training local police in how to stop vehicles, search houses, and prevent criminality.[35]

A colonel in the French battalion provided further illustrations: "We teach young officers different military techniques. For example, how to command a patrol, the essentials of de-mining, physical fitness, and basic tactics of urban combat."[36]

UNIFIL carries out thousands of operational activities in the form of patrols, checkpoints, and manning observation points each month, approximately 10 percent of which are conducted in tandem with the LAF (S/2015/475, para. 19). Through its funding, training, and operational programs, "UNIFIL has helped to reintroduce the LAF into the region ... it has helped to build the credibility of the LAF (Newby 2018, 132–133).

Since the start of the Syrian civil war in 2011, the Lebanese army has functioned largely on its own in securing Lebanon north of the Litani, where UNIFIL is not deployed. The LAF has been challenged by operations to combat "rocket fire, suicide attacks and gun battles" from the war in neighboring Syria (Perry and Holmes 2014). Many Hezbollah troops are fighting in Syria, leaving the LAF to guard the homeland. Thus far, the LAF have risen to the occasion, with the assistance (funding and training) of UNIFIL. In sum, UNIFIL engages in inducement as a means of conflict management by assisting in bringing both municipal and security institutions of the Lebanese state

---

[35] Author interview with UNIFIL Spokesperson Andrea Teneti, Naquora, Lebanon, 12 March 2015.

[36] Author interview with Colonel Benoit Aummonier, Southern Lebanon, 10 March 2015.

to the south. But arguably its overall financial contributions are even more significant.

The Peacekeeping Economy

Over the course of more than four decades, local villagers in southern Lebanon have grown accustomed to UNIFIL and its role as an aid provider, service provider, and institution builder. From its early years, some UNIFIL analysts regarded its involvement in the local economy as problematic: "The force has been sucked into the economic and political fabric of the wider society in which it operates and of which it has become an integral part. UNIFIL increasingly has come to function as a pseudo-government for the south whose chances of being replaced by the appropriate authorities in the foreseeable future seem remote" (Heiberg 1991, 150–151). Over time, the PLO and Israel receded from their domination of the south, but rather than the "appropriate authorities" taking UNIFIL's place, Hezbollah has emerged.

With the rise of the global war on terror, for some, the tool of inducement has assumed a newly problematic angle. As Kassem explains, in the context of French and NATO-member attempts at inducement, "The linking of aid to the military and geostrategic security concerns of foreign powers needs to be understood as a form of external domination highly reminiscent of the period of classical European colonialism" (Kassem 2017, 468). As such, UNIFIL's "conflict resolution paradigms of funding, inaugurating, and documenting humanitarian projects can be understood as attempts to compete with Hezbollah's own humanitarian and social activities in the region" (Kassem 2017, 471). Indeed, the unspoken, implicit competition with Hezbollah underlies much of UNIFIL's work.

After the 2006 Israeli invasion and Hezbollah's successful land defense of southern Lebanon, the budget for UNIFIL increased from $94,252,900 in 2005–2006, to a high of $650,755,600 in 2008–2009; in 2017–2018, it stood at $470,759,800 (United Nations 2006, 2009, 2018d). Since the outbreak of the war in neighboring Syria, the UN's programs, funds, and agencies (mainly UNHCR, UNICEF, UNDP, and UNRWA) have also augmented their funding for Lebanon such that they "spent around USD 950 million on humanitarian aid and development activities in 2017... the financial needs for Lebanon are increasing ... the total UN Strategic Framework budget for 2018 is 1.7 billion USD"

(United Nations 2017a, 48). To put that sum in context, the total GDP of Lebanon in 2017 was approximately $51.8 billion (World Bank 2018). International aid accounts for about 3.3 percent of Lebanon's GDP (a percentage that has decreased since 2006–2007).

Today, UNIFIL troop numbers stand at about 10,500, with 900 civilian staff, approximately half of whom are Lebanese nationals (United Nations 2018c). Beyond direct employment, hundreds of other households in southern Lebanon are supported by expenditures and businesses associated with the large international presence.[37] In Lebanon, poverty rates are highest and education rates are lowest in the south (and extreme north) of the country; despite UNIFIL's presence, the south continues to have the highest rate of unemployment (Le Borgne and Jacobs 2016, 36, 38).

Lebanon is constantly in a fragile state of existence. Its ethnocratic government is frequently nonfunctional. After enduring more than a decade of occupation by Syrian forces it must now ward off spillover from the Syrian civil war raging on its northern and eastern borders; one-third of the six million people residing in Lebanon are Syrian and Palestinian refugees. To its southern border, Israel continues to be threatened by the presence of Hezbollah and remains prepared to re-invade Lebanon, potentially destroying the economy once again.

Although many economic analyses of peacekeeping focus on the unintended negative consequences of the presence of international forces for local markets, it is difficult to imagine how the economy of southern Lebanon would function without UNIFIL (and UNTSO). One member of UNIFIL explained to me that even though many south Lebanese are not enthusiastic about UNIFIL, "Lots of people are interested in the mission staying because it helps the local economy."[38] When people assent to peacekeeping, peacekeepers are better able to help keep the peace. In other words, despite problems in the peacekeeping economy that surrounds UNIFIL, inducement remains its most important means of power.

---

[37] Author interview with UNIFIL Spokesperson Andrea Teneti, Naquora, Lebanon, 12 March 2015.
[38] Author interview with Colonel Benoit Aummonier, Southern Lebanon, 10 March 2015.

Conclusion

There is a common perception in and around UN peacekeeping that in contrast to the large, multidimensional missions, the traditional missions are simple and easy. As I have demonstrated in this study of UNIFIL and UNTSO in Lebanon, this perception does not match the reality. UNIFIL deployed in 1978, in the context of a civil war where at least 36 warring factions were vying to control the territory. The Lebanese state was nearly nonexistent, and southern Lebanese civilians enjoyed very little in the way of electricity, sanitation services, or roads. Since then, Israel invaded five times and occupied the territory for 22 years.

Writing in the late 1980s, Bjorn Skogmo remarked that "UNIFIL is generally held to be the most complex and difficult UN peacekeeping operation ever, with the possible exception of the Congo operation in 1960–64" (1989, 1). Many other analysts have stated in various ways that UNIFIL's mandate is unachievable: "from the outset, the UN Secretariat was concerned that the UNSC had created an impossible mission for UNIFIL" (Makdisi 2014, 31). Hillen described UNIFIL's tasks as "seemingly impossible" (1998, 129). One scholar even wrote an article with the title, "The Impossible Mission: UNIFIL" (Nachmias 1996). Although some analysts contend that mandate implementation is unattainable, at the same time, most also argue that mission has helped to keep the peace – among militias during the Lebanese civil war, as well as between Lebanon and Israel since that time. Thakur explains that UNIFIL is "not a peacekeeping force, but a war-dampening force. Its mandated task is impossible to attain, yet its presence remains indispensable" (Thakur 1987, 67).

The UN's presence in Lebanon is paradoxical, and its missions are some of the UN's longest enduring; these circumstances render it important to delve into how the missions work. Through careful study, it is possible to understand the mechanisms of power the operations have sought to employ over time and which types of power have proven effective for achieving the UN's goals. UNTSO's persuasive means of power are derived from its mandate. UNTSO officers speak with one voice, have a deep understanding of south Lebanese culture, and match their message with their behavior. Their effective persuasion continues, even 70 years after the mission's establishment. UNIFIL, in contrast, is more complex.

UNIFIL began with a mandate to confirm the withdrawal of Israeli forces, restore peace and security, and assist the Government of Lebanon in extending state authority to the south. Israeli forces eventually withdrew; peace has generally held; and the state is extending to the south, albeit slowly. Given the assumed impossibility that these tasks could be performed by an external force, how has UNIFIL managed to achieve its objectives to the extent that it has? I contend that UNIFIL never possessed a compellent, coercive capacity, although the large influx of western troops to southern Lebanon in 2006 made it appear that it would supply security guarantees. UNIFIL has also not managed to transfer ownership of its activities to locals, although the employment of Lebanese in UNIFIL has certainly helped the mission to function.

Instead, UNIFIL troops persuade by walking around and talking to people. Its troops also effectively exercise persuasion through high-level military diplomacy. Its military ranks communicate and mediate with their counterparts in the IDF and Hezbollah, which serves to relieve tensions. Although the UN's political leaders are obligated to refrain from dealing directly with Hezbollah, apparently, the same does not hold for the military.

But beyond persuasion, UNIFIL exercises inducement. I have argued that inducement in peacekeeping tends to take on four basic forms: (1) the provision of services and goods such as humanitarian and development aid, (2) market restrictions such as on weapons of war, (3) institution building, and (4) the overall peacekeeping economy that develops around a large international presence. UNIFIL's official mandate does not indicate that peacekeepers in southern Lebanon would use the means of inducement (other than institution building) to influence behavior. Upon close observation, however, that is precisely what is occurring.

In this chapter, I have presented observations of UNIFIL's effective inducement. The mission not only provides services that communities need – such as health, veterinary, and dental clinics – it has become the south's largest formal sector employer. UNIFIL has not managed to restrict markets or Hezbollah's weapons, but it has helped to train the LAF and extend some municipal functions to the south, which foster local ownership. The Lebanese state, however, remains weak.

UNIFIL's inducement actions generally foster good will toward the mission. As Newby explains: "the relationship between UNIFIL and the local population appears to be largely positive, but is underwritten by instrumentality, often contingent, on the regular provision of material resources and a high level of responsiveness to local needs" (Newby 2018, 164). In the end, inducement paves the way for UNIFIL's members to be accepted by local communities. This acceptance renders it possible for UNIFIL to gather information on conflict episodes and dampen violence. At the same time, UNTSO manages conflict through purely persuasive means. In southern Lebanon, UNIFIL and UNTSO are tools of conflict management. Conflict resolution, however, remains elusive.

4 | Coercion in the Central African Republic

We are shifting the paradigm of peacekeeping to focus on law and order.

– Luis Carrilho, Police Commissioner MINUSCA[1]

Peacekeeping employs some aspects of coercive military power, but not all. Like standard militaries, peacekeepers may deter attack, defend themselves and others, and surveil. In the case of the Central African Republic, unlike most other operations, peacekeepers also hold the power of arrest. However, by design, peacekeepers do not possess a *compellent*, or offensive, force capacity. This crucial aspect of military power is what separates peacekeepers from other types of troops.

Three essential properties of peacekeeping preclude compellence as a means of power in peacekeeping: doctrine, composition, and the visual symbols that reflect these two dimensions. First, what distinguishes peacekeeping from other forms of military intervention are its doctrinal principles of impartiality, consent, and the nonuse of force (except in self-defense and, more recently, in defense of the mandate; see de Coning, Aoi, and Karlsrud 2017; Peter 2015). Standard military forces do not work according to these principles: they take sides; they do not seek the consent of all parties before they intervene; and they rely on compellent force as their primary form of coercive military power.

Second, in order to achieve consent and impartiality, peacekeeping missions are composed of troops from dozens of countries. This mak-up increases their legitimacy and overall effectiveness (Bove and Ruggeri 2016; Finnemore 2003), but decreases their ability to use compellence effectively. As I explained in Chapter 1, peacekeepers hail from dozens of different countries; their matériel is not always interoperable; they do not train together before deploying; they do not consistently speak common languages; and their command and control channels are such

---

[1] Author interview, Bangui, Central African Republic, May 2015.

that, unlike in national militaries, orders given from high are not legally binding below. For example, a commander from one country may request, but not order, a unit from another to do something. In other words, peacekeeping was not designed for compellence.

Third, symbolically, peacekeepers signal visually that their means and purpose differ from those of other troops. They wear blue helmets to convey a pacific intent. They patrol in white vehicles to symbolically situate themselves alongside humanitarian actors, who likewise exclusively use white vehicles (cars, trucks, planes, helicopters, etc.). Humanitarians drive in white vehicles in order to allow combatants to comply with the Geneva Convention on the treatment of sick and wounded in warfare. It is a violation of international humanitarian law to fire on a white vehicle with a humanitarian marking. Regular military forces do not use white or blue colors (except for medical staff), nor do they enjoy such protections.

Actual military forces may effectively and legitimately exercise compellence alongside peacekeepers, who may legitimately and effectively exercise *other* forms of coercive power – deterrence, defense, surveillance, and arrest. Such a division of labor proved effective, for a time, in the Central African Republic. There, in the wake of violent conflict in 2014, military and peacekeeping tasks were successfully divided between actual militaries (from France, the United States, and Uganda) on the one hand, and multinational UN peacekeeping troops (from dozens of countries) on the other. This model proved fairly effective from 2014 to 2016. During this short but important time period, the peace process was taking root; rebel groups stood down; citizens elected a new president; and the economy began to restart (S/2016/ 305, paras. 2, 3, 40).[2] As a result, fewer civilians were being killed, and tens of thousands returned to their homes.

The French troops withdrew in 2016, followed six months later by the Americans and Ugandans (each for different reasons, as I explain later), removing the international levers of compellence. The indigenous Central African military, police, and gendarme had not yet been trained or reconstituted. UN peacekeepers were mandated by the UN

---

[2] "The economic outlook foresees a 5.2 percent economic growth rate for 2016. The country recorded a 4.5 percent growth rate in 2015, compared with 1 percent in 2014 … Financial needs are expected to decline from 4.8 percent of GDP in 2016 to 3.2 percent in 2019 if the trend towards peace consolidation continues" (S/2016/284, para. 41).

Security Council to take on the compellent tasks of actual military forces – tasks for which peacekeeping is not designed. While the UN's and the Central African state's coercive power receded, reports of sexual abuse, and an inadequate UN response undermined the persuasive power of the UN and other external actors. The consequences, as of this writing, have been new waves of violence and rebounding rates of displacement. Many observers warn of an all-out war between the government (with the UN on its side), led by the current president, Dr. Faustin-Archange Touadéra, and the Front Populaire pour la Renaissance de la Centrafrique (FPRC), whose top leaders are Michel Djotodia and Noureddine Adam, the instigators of Central Africa's most recent coup d'état. No entity holds a monopoly over the use of force, legitimate or otherwise.

In this chapter, I first explain how I conceive of the relationship between legitimacy and coercion. I then categorize different forms of military power, and I delineate which aspects peacekeeping and standard troops share. Finally, I illustrate the different types by way of an in-depth case study of recent interventions in the Central African Republic. Events there offer something of a natural (and terrifying) experiment in the effective application of externally-enforced compellence, and the violent results when such a capacity is removed before a legitimate domestic counterpart arises in its place. They show how unintended actions – such as sexual abuse – may undermine a UN mission's persuasive power, legitimacy, and effectiveness. The events of late 2016–2018 also demonstrate the inadequacy of the main alternative hypothesis in this study, by revealing the extent to which UN peacekeepers do not supply compellent, military-based security guarantees. Although involvement of local actors is generally not conceptualized in the literature as a hypothesis, we see in this case that turning over control too quickly to local actors can work to undermine a fledgling peace.

Definition of Coercion and Legitimacy

I define coercion as the act of using, or threatening to use, force in order to gain compliance. An act of coercion occurs when a physically strong entity (e.g., person, government, or intergovernmental organization) changes the behavior of another party by means or threat of violence or deprivation of liberty. Recall Dahl's classic definition of power: "A has power over B to the extent that he can get B to do something that B would not otherwise do" (Dahl 1957, 202–203). Coercion means B has no choice but to comply. The successful application of coercion is contingent on actor A possessing the *physical capacity* to impose its will on actor B; it is also contingent on A's resolve (often conceived as the willingness to bear the costs of employing harm; see Art and Greenhill 2018, 10). For the purposes of this study, I limit my scope to military- and police-based coercion. The effective use of this type of power is contingent on the material capability and resolve to employ violence.

Some scholars conceptualize coercion as a phenomenon that lies in opposition to legitimacy (Hurd 2007, Whalan 2013). Legitimacy is the belief that the wishes of an actor should be followed.[3] Hurd states, "As a source of following rules in a society, legitimacy stands in contrast to other equally grand concepts from sociology: coercion and self-interest. Legitimacy, coercion, and self-interest constitute ideal-types for modes of social control, and each generates compliance with society's rules by a different mechanism" (2007, 35).

However, Max Weber – the father of modern sociology – conceptualized legitimacy and coercion differently. For Weber, there are legitimate and illegitimate manifestations of coercive force. Weber is probably most famous for his classic definition of the state: "a state is the social entity that holds the monopoly over the *legitimate* use of force within a given territory" (Weber 1978; italics added). In other words, states (and other entities) may exercise legitimate – or illegitimate – compellent military force.

In civil wars, the distinction between legitimate and illegitimate uses of force is of crucial importance. Some actors are deemed by their constituents and outside actors to wield force legitimately, while others are not. Thus, both theoretically and empirically, the categories of legitimacy and coercion do not lie in opposition. Rather, in Weberian fashion, I consider legitimacy to be a quality of coercion. We can only assess when an exercise of power is legitimate by the actions of B. If B complies, and B and other external actors deem A's actions to be worthy of following, we can determine that A has exercised legitimate power.

---

[3] With respect to peacekeeping, Jeni Whalan defines legitimacy as "the belief by local actors that a peace operation and its goals are fair, right, and appropriate, within a particular normative context" (Whalan 2013, 6).

In relation to the relative coercive power of A and B, there is debate in the literature about asymmetry, especially if B is much weaker. Many scholars deem coercive capacity to be the essential basis of power, and more is better (Lieber 2012; Mearsheimer 2001; Waltz 1979). There is debate, however, about what happens when B is significantly weaker militarily, and what effects asymmetry may have on outcomes. Others disagree. As Rob de Wijk has argued, "military superiority scarcely matters [and may] ... prevent the coercer from reaching his objectives" (2005, 10; see also Byman and Waxman 2002). Some have even argued that "the greater the disparity in power between compeller and the target, the less likely the former is to get its way vis-à-vis the latter" (Art and Greenhill 2018, 31).[4] Thus peacekeepers' inability to use compellence may actually be part of the reason why peacekeeping has a better rate of success than standard military interventions. I will return to this idea in this book's concluding chapter.

Circling back to how legitimacy and coercion relate, legitimacy in peacekeeping may derive from its doctrinal principles (Paddon 2011; Peter 2015); its multilateral composition (Bove and Ruggeri 2016; Harland 2004); or by protecting civilians and providing services to people in need of assistance (Newby 2018). Thus, legitimacy is both a causal variable and an outcome. I conceptualize the UN's attempts at employing three types of power – coercion, inducement, and persuasion – as legitimate or illegitimate depending on whether both UN employees and domestic actors follow through on stated peacekeeping goals (in this way, I conceive of legitimacy as more of a dependent variable).

In order for force to be viewed as legitimate, however, most scholars agree that it must be authorized multilaterally (Claude 1996; Coleman 2007; Elliot 2010; Finnemore 2003; Hurd 2007; Johnstone 2016; Thompson 2009; Voeten 2005; Zaum 2007). For peacekeeping to be seen as legitimate, peacekeepers must embody the ideals of multilateralism by hailing from multiple – even dozens of – UN member states. But this basis of peacekeeping legitimacy undermines the efficacy of its coercive capacity. When peacekeepers attempt to exercise deadly force

---

[4] Note that in civil wars, Kalyvas and Ballcells (2010) see the emergence of weakness on both the side of the state and rebels. The question is whether general weakness might lead to better outcomes or simply the continuation of grinding, low-level conflict.

outside of self-defense (and sometimes in defense of others), they also lose moral legitimacy, both because they are supposed to be representatives of peace and not war, and because they are not effective warriors by design. However, they may and do effectively exercise *other* forms of coercion: defense, deterrence, surveillance, and arrest.

Types of Coercion

In the following paragraphs, I delineate the specific types of coercive power. There is a vast and nearly endless array of *purposes* for which states and others use coercion. However, the specific categories or *means* may be reduced to a handful of types. Building on Thomas Schelling's seminal distinction between compellence and deterrence, Robert Art's classic typology of military power, and Michel Foucault's path-breaking work on surveillance, I outline five basic subtypes or mechanisms of coercive power: (1) compellence, (2) deterrence, (3) defense, (4) surveillance, and (5) arrest. The final form – the power of arrest – is my addition. I argue that it should be considered as a type alongside the others, because the deprivation of liberty is a coercive means by which uniformed forces exercise power.[5] I explain each type in the following sections. Although military forces may employ all types, I contend that peacekeeping encompasses only the last four. If peacekeepers employ compellence, they are no longer peacekeepers.

Compellence

Thomas Schelling delineated the compellent use of force in his seminal studies of nuclear weapons (1963 and 1966) as "initiating an action ... that can cease, or become harmless, only if the opponent responds. The overt act, the first step, is up to the side that makes the compellent threat" (Schelling 1966, 72). Robert Art further specifies compellence as "the deployment of military power so as to be able either to stop an adversary from doing something that he has already undertaken or to get him to do something that he has not yet undertaken" (Art 1980, 7); in other words, both A and B are acting, and B changes its behavior.

---

[5] Note also that I have removed "swagger" from Robert Art's classic typology. All uniformed forces – peacekeeping and otherwise – do engage in swagger, but it is not a form of coercion. It is a symbolic display, meant to intimidate others and make the swaggerer feel more confident, and, thus, it fits better with persuasion.

Some theorists understand compellence to include both threats to use force and the actual use of force. Schelling, for example, viewed compellence often in terms of threats, followed by the kinetic use of force (1963 and 1966). In contrast, Art, along with most international relations theorists, emphasizes the active, kinetic understanding of compellence in that he discusses mainly preemptive and preventive uses of force in this category (Art 1980; Greenhill and Krause 2018).

Compellence is the most crucial subtype of coercive power that militaries have used to fight and win wars. Compellence is predicated on possessing the military capacity to wage and win an offensive attack. Offensive weapons and positions must be mobile, which allows attacking forces to move and advance past a line of demarcation (Quester 2003, 1–3). Offensive capabilities refer "to technology and techniques that reward counterforce initiatives, destroying more weapons on the other side than are lost in the attack and incapacitating more soldiers than are lost (Quester 2003, 6). Taking the initiative on the battlefield is often what commanders prefer (Cruz, Phillips, and Cusimano 2017; Kier 1997). However, as in the case of World War I, "If both sides are primed to reap advantages by pushing into each other's territory, war may be extremely likely whenever a political crisis erupts. If the defense holds the advantage, by contrast, each side in a crisis will probably wait a little longer, in hopes that the other will foolishly take the offensive" (Quester 2003, 7; see also Lynn-Jones 1995).

The United Nations was devised to limit the use of offensive compellence by states. After the devastation of World Wars I and II, which together claimed the lives of more than 100 million people, the victors of World War II joined together in 1945 to form a new international body. The opening lines of the Charter of the UN explain the justification for creating the organization:

We, the peoples of the United Nations, determined to save succeeding generations from the scourge of war, which twice in our lifetime has brought untold sorrow to mankind, and to reaffirm faith in fundamental human rights … unite our strength to maintain international peace and security, and ensure, by the acceptance of principles … that armed force shall not be used, save in the common interest.

Given the founding principles of the United Nations and UN peace-keeping doctrine, compellence was never supposed to be a central feature of UN peacekeeping. Peacekeeping forces are designed to be able to keep the peace but not fight wars. As one of the leading figures in the practice of UN peacekeeping explains,

> Unity of command, normally seen as an essential element of effective military operations, is largely lacking in the UN context. Yet it is the singular weakness of the UN that is also its greatest strength in international administration. Constrained by the compromises of its huge membership, and need to accommodate a broad spectrum of views and constituencies, it is the least illegitimate of all possible outside actors. It may not represent the will of the people administered, but it derives some legitimacy from the breadth of international support. (Harland 2004, 17)[6]

While peacekeeping missions are *purposefully constituted* to be ineffective at using compellent force, as of 1999, every multidimensional peacekeeping mission was either authorized from the start or eventually assumed a "peace enforcement" mandate (Howard and Dayal 2018). Under peace enforcement mandates, UN peacekeepers may use compellent force to protect themselves and civilians. The mandate in DR Congo goes even further, with language about using compellence to defend the mandate, and "neutralize" armed actors.[7] There is only one instance of the UN successfully employing compellent force to defeat an armed group on the battlefield (the M-23 in DR Congo, in the spring of 2013). Other than this example, there are a handful of instances when peacekeepers have successfully employed some force, but not to the extent that they defeated an armed group outright.

The problems associated with the use of compellent force are numerous. In civil wars and multilateral intervention, it can be difficult for external and internal parties to agree on who holds the monopoly over the legitimate use of force. Beyond questions of legitimacy, compellence is often difficult to use as an effective means of power because it involves not only the physical harm to the target, but also, very importantly, psychological damage: "compellent actions directly engage the prestige and the passions of the put upon [party] ...

---

[6] Note that Vicenzo Bove and Andrea Ruggeri (2016) find that mission diversity in peacekeeping missions decreases the level of violence against civilians, demonstrating that problems of chain of command do not make civilians more vulnerable to violence.

[7] The mandate in Malí moves toward involving the UN in counterterrorism.

compellence is intrinsically hard to obtain ... because it demands more humiliation from the compelled" (Art 1980, 10). Similarly, Hurd explains that compellence tends "to generate resentment and resistance, even as [it] produces compliance, because [it] operates against the normative impulses of the subordinate individual or group" (Hurd 2007, 36). Christian Davenport, Erica Chenoweth, and Maria Stephan have demonstrated that the myriad ways in which compellent tactics have been used – both by governments and by opposition parties – are often less effective than nonviolent means (Chenoweth and Stephan 2011; Davenport 2017). In sum, although compellence may spark temporary compliance in the short run, it can also inspire sustained resistance unless it is viewed by the compelled as legitimate.

Observable implications of the use of compellence (both successful and unsuccessful) are fairly easy to detect. On the rare occasions when the UN actually uses force, it is public knowledge and thus directly observable, and the justification and goals are generally clear. It is also public knowledge whether the results successfully change the behavior of the peacekept. As I demonstrate in the case of the Central African Republic, French forces successfully employed compellence from 2014 to 2016. After the French Sangaris mission passed on its compellent mandate to UN peacekeepers, Central African civilians and the peacekeepers themselves have been increasingly under attack; UN peacekeepers have not managed to respond effectively. In general, compellence is harder to achieve but easier to demonstrate empirically than other forms of coercion such as deterrence.

Deterrence

According to Thomas Schelling, "deterrence and compellence differ in a number of respects, most of them corresponding to something like the difference between statics and dynamics" (1966, 71). Deterrence concerns the use of military "threats by one party to convince another party to refrain from initiating some course of action. A threat serves as a deterrent to the extent that it convinces its target not to carry out the intended action because of the costs and losses the target would incur" (Huth 1999, 2). Deterrence is employed to prevent hostile actions against oneself and/or to dissuade attack against another party (Brodie 1959; Schelling 1966, 73). Deterrence has been the subject of heated debates in international relations for several decades. Debates generally revolve around how deterrence differs for nuclear and conventional weapons and how to measure deterrence; most scholars employ rationalist assumptions.[8]

Much of deterrence theory concerns the concepts of credibility and resolve. For Paul Huth, "a threat is considered credible if the defending state possesses both the military capabilities to inflict substantial costs on an attacking state in an armed conflict, and if the attacking state believes that the defending state is resolved to use its available military forces" (Huth 1999, 5). In other words, like compellence, deterrence requires both the ability and the will to inflict punishment (see Kertzer 2016; Press 2004; Press 2005). The defender must also be able to sustain the threat through multiple rounds of fighting if attacked (Mearsheimer 1983). Military deterrence requires a credible threat of retaliation against not only military, but also often civilian targets (as in "mutually assured destruction" in nuclear deterrence).

Deterrence is difficult to measure because it relies on the counterfactual that an actor did not act because of a specific threat and not for some other reason. Deterrence *failures* are easier to pinpoint. If we witness the ignition of a crisis, the use of military compellence, or the avoidance of crisis by making unacceptable concessions, then deterrence has failed.

Peacekeeping appears to work by deterring attack given that peacekeepers and the peacekept are not often attacked. However, peacekeepers do not necessarily wield the capacity to inflict substantial costs on belligerents nor forge a second-strike counterattack. Peacekeepers also do not uniformly share the resolve to use force.[9]

Kofi Annan, who served as the head of the UN's Department of Peacekeeping Operations from 1993 to 1996 before serving as two-term Secretary-General of the UN from 1997 to 2006, succinctly explained the problems of compellence and deterrence when attempted by UN peacekeepers: "We can use force today, and maybe we will be successful, but what about tomorrow, when they come with reinforcements?" (François 2015). Any individual UN peacekeeping battalion

---

[8] In other words, they assume that actors base their actions on cost-benefit analyses. Exceptions to the purely rational view are Jervis (1982), Lebow and Stein (1989), and Sagan (1993).
[9] As I explore in the conclusion, most troop contributing countries have not signed the 2015 "Kigali Principles," which emphasize the idea that peacekeepers should use compellence.

may possess the capacity and resolve to strike once, but taken as a whole mission, peacekeepers do not possess the capacity or resolve necessary for multiple strikes.

I thus contend that the deterrent effect of peacekeepers stems not from their ability to provide military-backed security guarantees, but, rather, the sources of deterrence in peacekeeping are more financial and psychological. Belligerents do not fear physical punishment from peacekeepers, but they may fear sanctions or exclusion from economic and political processes, or shame, if they do not comply with peacekeepers' requests. I include a discussion of deterrence here, under the concept of coercion, as it is most associated with a military deterrent, even though in peacekeeping, according to my typology, the mechanism falls into the categories of both inducement and persuasion.

Observable implications of deterrence are notoriously difficult to demonstrate because we must demonstrate a negative, whereas failures of deterrence are easier. The widespread existence of "post-conflict violence" attests to the failure of deterrence in peacekeeping (Autesserre 2010). The absence of violence in the presence of peacekeepers suggests a deterrent effect, but it is necessary to process-trace through each case to try to uncover the reasons why parties chose not to attack. In Namibia, deterrence rested on persuasion (see Chapter 2 of this book). In Lebanon, the sources of deterrence generally stem from financial inducement (Chapter 3). In the case of the Central African Republic, French Sangaris forces, as well as the presence of American and Ugandan troops in the southeast, functioned as an effective military deterrent to local groups taking up arms. Although the American and Ugandan forces were not deployed with this function in mind (they were on the hunt for notorious warlord Joseph Kony), after they departed, rebel activity increased dramatically in a part of the country that had previously not experienced such trouble – a clear indicator of a military-based deterrence failure (following initial success).

Defense

Like deterrence, defense is intended to protect both oneself and possibly a third party from attack. As Art explains, "defense dissuades by presenting an unvanquishable military force. Deterrence persuades by presenting the certainty of retaliatory devastation" (Art 1980, 7).

Deterrence requires some sort of a second-strike capacity or other punishment if attacked. Defense requires only the ability to ward off an attack. Adequate defensive capabilities are also helpful for minimizing the damage of attack, and especially for maintaining the status quo. As the Prussian military historian, Karl von Clausewitz explains: "A may feel too weak to attack B, from which it does not follow that B is strong enough for an attack on A ... Therefore, it may so happen that both parties, at one and the same time, not only feel themselves too weak to attack, but also are in reality... [which can] tame the elementary impetuosity of War" (Clausewitz 1968, book 3, chapter 16).

UN peacekeepers, from the advent of this unique tool, have always had the mandate to defend themselves if attacked. Since 1999, that mandate has extended to protecting (defending) civilians in conflict zones, and sometimes in defense of the mandate (Howard and Dayal 2018). The requirements of defense are much lower than compellence or deterrence, and thus defense is a standard component of military power that is both possible for peacekeepers and often deemed legitimate – internationally and domestically – in post-conflict societies.

For example, in South Sudan, UN peacekeepers have not only warded off attacks on themselves but also created "protection of civilian" camps in or adjacent to their own, where tens of thousands of civilians rely on UN peacekeepers for safety. The camps have increased the UN's legitimacy in the eyes of many civilians in South Sudan, among its own staff and among NGOs. However, in the summer of 2016, after numerous attacks on protection of civilian camps (signaling a failure of deterrence), American staff in the UN Mission in South Sudan (UNMISS) operation initiated a drive to allow UNMISS peacekeepers to acquire an offensive military capacity.[10] The justification was to give UNMISS peacekeepers a more credible military deterrent capacity, which would only be possible by bolstering peacekeepers' ability to wage offensive maneuvers. The offensive/deterrent mandate was approved by the UNSC on August 12, 2016, with 11 votes in favor and 4 votes in abstention (Russia, China, Egypt, and Venezuela). The essential problem with mandating

---

[10] Author's email exchange with a senior State Department official who chose to remain anonymous, August 2016.

peacekeepers to wage compellent force, rather than using force only in self-defense, is that they become a party to the conflict. By definition, therefore, they are no longer peacekeepers.

Observable implications of legitimate and successful defense are when peacekeepers and civilians are not attacked during a peacekeeping operation (similar to deterrence). However, if deterrence fails but the attack ends quickly and is not repeated, this also signals successful defense. Successfully holding the line and repelling an offensive attack are prime indications of an effective defense.

Surveillance

A fourth means of military-based coercion is surveillance. All troops – standard, peacekeeping, or police – employ surveillance as an essential form of power. Indeed, patrol is the modal activity of all uniformed personnel, and information gathering is a prerequisite for all military action. Although surveillance contributes to the capacity to engage in compellence, deterrence, and defense, I conceive of it as a stand-alone category of coercion. As Michel Foucault argued some forty years ago, surveillance alone has the effect of changing behavior: "it is a type of power, a modality for its exercise, comprising a whole set of instruments, techniques, procedures, levels of application, targets; it is a 'physics' or an 'anatomy' of power, a technology" (Foucault 1977, 215).[11] Surveillance has often been associated with repression of civil society, dissidents, and other condemnable purposes (Bozzini 2011; Giddens 1987; Lyon 2007; Starr et al. 2008).[12] However, other studies characterize surveillance not simply as an element of brutal government control, but also "care," depending on the intent of both the surveiller and the surveilled (Coyne and Hall 2018; Karlsrud and Rosen 2013; Lyon 2001; Lyon, Ball, and Haggerty 2012).

Surveillance is nearly synonymous with the original concept of peacekeeping as observation. From its very inception, parties to conflicts have consented to impartial peacekeepers' monitoring compliance with peace agreements, especially ceasefire lines. The original idea and

---

[11] Note that Michel Foucault's (1977) *Surveiller et punir* was (mis) translated into English as *Discipline and Punish*. Here I use the term "surveil" rather than "discipline" because it is closer in meaning to the original.

[12] Surveillance can inspire resistance, even in peacekeeping (Browne 2015; Gilliom 2001; Zanotti 2006).

purpose of the traditional "observation missions" was to surveil as a means to establish and ensure order. By providing unbiased, trusted third-party information, all parties to a conflict may know whether the others are complying with agreements. A joint ceasefire committee, with representation from all sides, may function as a forum for investigating alleged infringements, in a "kind of facilitated self-governance mechanism."[13] Information from surveillance alone has the power to influence behavior even if the punishment processes for violations of ceasefires may be vague.[14]

This elementary means of power in peacekeeping has become more complex, and sometimes contentious, with the expansion of peace-keeping mandates and advances in technology. Whereas with earlier mandates, observation could be conducted by very lightly armed peacekeepers (i.e., in the original mandate for the UN Truce Supervision Organization in the Middle East), observation and surveillance have transformed into tools of coercion and potential punishment – as opposed to tools of consensual and cooperative order building – as peacekeepers have been increasingly asked to use force. Technological advances in the use of unarmed drones (Karlsrud and Rosen 2013) and geospatial surveillance (Convergne and Snyder 2015) have made it possible for peacekeepers to gather vast quantities of information. The UN is presently in the process of determining how to manage this information, how to classify it, and how to act on it. Despite these debates, most analysts agree that greater capabilities have meant, and will probably continue to mean, better peacekeeping (Dorn and Semken 2015; Karlsrud and Rosen 2013). New technologies are being used as a way to "appear omnipresent," both for peacekeepers and for regular military forces, as exemplified in the Central African case (Bozzini 2011).

Observable implications of successful surveillance are challenging to establish, because the ramifications of disobeying peacekeepers remain vague. Surveillance is similar to deterrence in that the purpose is to prevent an activity (such as harming civilians) from happening. It is therefore necessary to demonstrate the possibility that the peacekept would have taken an action were it not for the surveillance capability.

---

[13] In the words of peacekeeping expert Cedric De Coning. Written communication with the author, August 2018.

[14] The phenomenon is similar to what happens with unarmed electoral observers (see Kelley 2012).

If civilians are being harmed, the first purpose of surveillance has failed. However, surveillance can still serve as an important tool for understanding how external and internal forces might stop and prevent harm. Information from surveillance may be used to aid all of the other types of coercion – for compellence (by military forces), deterrence, defense, and, the final category, arrest.

Arrest

Arrest is a category of coercion in its own right. Whereas compellence is based on the threat of losing one's life/physical existence, arrest is based on the threat of deprivation of liberty. Arrest is an action designed to forcibly change behavior and may be practiced by domestic or international police or gendarme, and sometimes military. Arrest can function as a brief, short-term act of coercion, "as an end in itself, as a way of terminating a problem," without further engagement in judicial processes (Feeley 1979, 46). In other words, arrest or detention coupled with quick release may be a simple and stand-alone means of trying to change the behavior of criminals or armed actors. However, arrest is often the first and essential component of larger processes of state or UN control that involve building and prosecuting legal cases (contingent on a fully developed judicial system), and depriving those found guilty of freedom longer term through imprisonment (contingent on a functioning prison system). I do not explore the full extent of judicial and prison systems here, but I do address the institution of the police, the power of arrest, and how they relate to peacekeeping.

Currently, all UN peacekeepers in multidimensional missions in civil wars are mandated by the UN Security Council to use deadly force to protect civilians – however, very few peacekeepers are empowered to *arrest* belligerents (Howard and Dayal 2018; Oswald 2011; Trenkov-Wermuth 2010, 74). There are potentially three categories of targets for arrest in peacekeeping: those who are suspected of committing a criminal offense, those who pose a security threat, and those who fall into both categories (Oswald 2011, 138).[15] Arrest and detention are

---

[15] In some of today's civil wars, organized crime and its intersections with terrorist organizations present difficult barriers to peace (Dziedzic 2016; Boutellis and Fink 2016a). According to scholars of terrorism, the most effective means of addressing such obstacles are through police-like activities (Byman 2007; Crenshaw 2000).

linked, but they are not the same. For detention, the extent to which the detainee is deprived of liberty is of crucial importance. In consent-based peacekeeping, UN peacekeepers may stop an individual to ask questions but not deprive them of their right to walk away (Oswald 2011, 133). Beyond this step, peacekeepers may detain armed actors in the act of breaching the peace, as long as peacekeepers hand over detainees to the state as soon as possible. Arrest, however, is a trickier tool.

In general, peacekeepers are reluctant to exercise the power of even detention, and certainly arrest. According to one study, "the common reaction of UN officials to inquiries regarding detention procedures was to deny involvement" (Hirschmann 2017, 188). In 2009, the UN Department of Peacekeeping Operations issued a new edition of the Criminal Justice Standards, "which deals with the rights of detained and imprisoned persons as well as the conditions of detention and imprisonment" (Hirschmann 2017, 189). These new standards were created at the same time as the "Specialized Training Material for Police on Human Rights Standards in Arrest and Detention" (United Nations 2009a, 2009b). Even with these new regulations, however, detention and arrest remain uncertain forms of coercive power in peacekeeping, and there is no known database of individuals under UN detention or arrest (Hirschmann 2017, 198). The reluctance to deprive people of their liberty is bound to the absence of judicial and penitentiary institutions in the UN system that might substitute for those on the domestic level, which is in and of itself a result of adherence to principles of state sovereignty.

Concerns about international peacekeepers infringing on host government sovereignty date back to the earliest peacekeeping missions (Oswald 2011, 124). In an analysis of UNEF in 1956, the UN Secretary-General observed that "[the] authority granted to the United Nations group cannot be exercised within a given territory ... in competition with representatives of the host Government. ... A right to detention which normally would be exercised only by local authorities is extended to UNEF units. However, this is so only within a limited area where the local authorities abstain from exercising similar rights, whether alone or in collaboration with the United Nations" (Cordier and Foote 1975, 284).

Thus, although peacekeepers assumed some tasks of policing early on, the first UN constabulary police deployed with the UN Operation in the Congo (ONUC) in 1964–1965. It was later, beginning with the mission in Namibia starting in 1989, that the contemporary concepts, principles, and practices of UN civilian policing were born (Dwan 2002, 3). Today, UN civilian police are the second most numerous of all peacekeepers, after military forces. UN civilian police, now called UNPOL, constitute about 10 percent of UN peacekeepers, numbering about 11,000 officers from more than 80 countries (UN Chiefs of Police Summit 2018).[16]

In 1995, the Department of Peacekeeping Operations formalized UN policing principles as the "SMART" doctrine: "Supporting human rights; Monitoring the performance of the local enforcement authority; Advising the local police on best practice; Reporting on situations and incidents; and Training local enforcement in best practice for policing and human rights" (Dwan 2002, 3). In other words, UN civilian police were limited to monitoring, reporting, advising, and training – employing the means of persuasion and inducement. Although they were armed, they did not possess the coercive power of arrest.

This largely ideational approach gave way to the "executive policing" mandates in Cambodia in 1992, and again in Kosovo and Timor Leste in 1999, where the UN Security Council charged the Department of Peacekeeping Operations with substituting UN police for deeply dysfunctional or nonexistent domestic police forces. The executive policing mandates authorized UN police to uphold the law by endowing them with the powers of arrest, detention, bearing arms, and carrying out all aspects of law enforcement while simultaneously training a new police force to whom they would eventually transfer policing functions (Howard 2008, chapter 4; Howard 2014). However, most notably in Kosovo, UN peacekeepers were criticized by the Organization for Security Cooperation in Europe and the Council of Europe, "who shamed the UN in Kosovo for not complying with core human rights principles and suggested institutional provisions for a better protection of detainees' right to due process" (Hirschmann 2017, 188). Given the difficulties of having the UN build its own justice system within peacekeeping missions, with all proper rights protections, UN peacekeepers have not again held an "executive policing" mandate. In the Central African Republic, however, the policing

---

[16] Due to budget cuts, the number of police has been nearly halved in recent years.

mandate approaches this authority because it includes the power of arrest, as I describe next.[17]

In many countries transitioning from civil war, the military and police were closely allied, if not jointly constituted, and both possessed the power of arrest. In peacekeeping, the UN has sought to separate military and police personnel, responsibilities, and actions, but such separation can prove difficult. The differences between police and military action blur in many European and formerly colonized countries, where military units may be tasked with civilian policing. The best known of these are the French gendarme, literally, "people of arms."[18] Police may engage in all types of coercion – compellence, deterrence, defense, surveillance and arrest. The most notable and important difference in function between military and police is that police target criminal activity, and, unlike most UN military officers, they may hold the power of arrest and the authority to gather evidence to build criminal cases. Generally, gendarme and military focus on public order, including countering armed actors, whereas police target criminal activity.

As UN police and military assume the responsibilities of public security in war-torn countries, some observers lament the "militarization" of the police, especially in the executive mandates (Hansen 2002, 70). The UN Mission in the Central African Republic presents a novel attempt at the opposite: "the policization of the military."[19] For the first year of this mission, the main military battalions responsible for upholding peace and public order in Bangui were under police, not military command. I explore this innovation here. For this and other cases, causal process observations of the power of arrest and legitimate policing in action would include the mandate and physical capacity to arrest and adequately detain individuals of interest; reductions in violence and crime; and international police upholding their own codes of conduct, international human rights, and domestic law and order.

As I summarize in Table 4.1, military, police, and peacekeepers share some aspects of coercive power, but not all. All three types of

---

[17] Thus, peacekeepers now have the mandate to shoot but not arrest because, in the end, shooting is much less complicated than arresting.

[18] There are also the *Carabinieri* in Italy, the *Guarda Nacional Republicana* in Portugal, the *Guardia Civil* in Spain, the *Royal Marechaussee* in the Netherlands.

[19] Author interview with Luis Carhillo, Force Commander, MINUSCA, Bangui, 17 May 2015.

Table 4.1 *Coercion: Mechanisms, Observable Implications, and Actors*

Mechanism/ Tool of Coercion	Description	Observable Implications (Effect on B)	Actors
Compellence	Active, kinetic, preemptive or preventive force	Changes behavior	Military, Police
Deterrence	Mainly static, with capacity for second-strike if attacked	Does not change behavior	Military Peacekeepers, Police
Defense	Ward off attack on self or others	May or may not change behavior	Military Peacekeepers, Police
Surveillance	Observe, patrol, gather intelligence	May or may not change behavior	Military Peacekeepers, Police
Arrest	Deprive of liberty	Changes behavior	Peacekeepers, Police, Gendarmerie

uniformed forces deter, defend, and surveil. Police, and sometimes peacekeepers – not often military – hold the power of arrest. Military and police employ compellent coercion regularly. Effective coercion is predicated on three conditions: having the capacity or means to perform the given task, the mandate/legal authority, and the resolve. Peacekeepers in civil wars have the mandate to use compellence but not the means, the legitimacy, or resolve to effectively do so. The differences between the different forms and effectiveness of armed coercion are best illustrated in the recent interventions in the Central African Republic.

The Central African Republic

The violence in the Central African Republic is often characterized as a continuous condition of life. Sometimes this characterization dates back to the privatization of abusive French colonial rule. More recently, especially in news articles, this "continuous violence" narrative pinpoints the Muslim-majority Séléka takeover of Bangui in

March 2013 as the start of the recent "sectarian" conflict, when undoubtedly violence spiked. But if one examines trends in death and displacement, there are significant recent shifts that require explanation. Civilian deaths decreased dramatically in 2014 but then rose again in late 2016 (see Figure 4.3, p. 158). Why?

In the paragraphs that follow, I provide some of the background for understanding the current conflict and the international responses to it. I then lay out the general picture of changes in death and displacement rates in recent years. Subsequently, I trace the efforts to exert power by the UN's multidimensional peacekeeping mission, MINUSCA; the French Sangaris mission; and others. The mandate and actions of MINUSCA and Sangaris allowed for the killing to stop and for the displaced to return for a couple of years. But the peace did not last. I explain the precipitating causes of increasing death and displacement in 2017. I outline the ways in which the UN and France attempted, and succeeded, in exercising power, and the sexual abuse and civilian deaths that undermined their persuasive capacity.

I argue that the fluctuations in death and displacement are the result of the recent shifts in international interventions. I am not alone in advancing the notion that Central African politics are in large part as regional and international as they are domestic. In other words, the Central African Republic, from its very origin, has not really been sovereign. The most recent death and displacement shifts mirror the exercise of compellent/offensive force on the part of the French military forces, combined with non-compellent coercion and other forms of power exercised by the UN peacekeepers. Although the French troops made some serious mistakes early in their intervention, after they corrected course, they stabilized the country through the use and threat of offensive, compellent and deterrent military force. This "hammer" function – a monopoly over the use of force – allowed for the deployment of an innovative and initially highly effective UN multidimensional peacekeeping mission. MINUSCA utilized all forms of power in peacekeeping – most notably inducement and non-compellent coercion. However, with the departure of French troops in October 2016 (and American special forces in May 2017), events in Central Africa have taken a steep downward turn . The central coercive mechanisms of the state – the police, gendarmes, and the Forces armeés centrafricaines (FACA) had not been reconstituted by the fall of 2017. As a result, upon the French and American withdrawal, MINUSCA peacekeeping troops assumed the foreign (and local, by default) forces' responsibilities – but not their capacity. In the absence of any monopoly over the use of force – legitimate or otherwise – neighborhood groups sought to provide for their own, local-level safety and inter-communal tensions have escalated. In April 2018, MINUSCA engaged in an attempt at an urban warfare battle, and failed. Russian troops (not affiliated with the UN peacekeepers) deployed in May 2018 to protect the presidency of Central Africa and other key state offices. As of this writing, the situation remains unstable.

Background

The Central African Republic has yet to enjoy a single decade of stable, non-abusive political rule. However, neither had it experienced widespread killing between its citizens until 2013. The country suffers from multiple generations of traumatic experiences. After decades of slave-raiding and trading, which created a "pervasive atmosphere of distrust," France annexed and named the territory Ubangi-Shari in the 1880s (Prioul 1981, 81). But rather than putting Ubangi-Shari under French state control, France partitioned out concessions to rapaciously exploitative commercial firms in an atypical colonial arrangement (Lombard 2016; Prioul 1981; Smith 2015). The concessionary companies worked Central Africans to their deaths while introducing new diseases, such that between the years of 1880 and 1940, it is estimated that half of the local population perished (Saulnier 1998, 81–96; Smith 2015, 19). Beginning in the 1920s, Central Africans initiated violent protests against cruel and unfair treatment, which eventually led to direct Central African representation in the French parliament by the widely respected leader, Barthélemy Boganda. Boganda perished in a suspicious plane crash in 1959, the year after independence. The joys of independence were not long-lived. In 1966, army commander Jean-Bédel Bokassa seized power and later proclaimed himself president for life and "Emperor" of the "Central African Empire"; his rule endured nearly 14 years – the longest-serving head of state thus far. Although some media analyses described his rule in "pornographic" terms, many Central Africans viewed him as "a tough man, one who knew how to speak forcefully and justly, even if he was cruel" (Bigo 1988, 9, author's translation). Bokassa used violence, extravagant pageantry, and patrimonial networks to consolidate something of a Central African state and nation, alongside his own personal wealth (Bigo 1988).[20] Bokassa was eventually ousted in a coup in 1979, followed by five or six more coups, several non-inclusive elections, five military interventions by France, and many rounds of peace talks.

Throughout its history, the Central African state has not held much sway beyond the capital, Bangui. This important city is located in the middle of the southern edge of the Central African Republic, across the Ubangi River from the Democratic Republic of the Congo, in the very heart of Africa. This large, lush, landlocked, and resource-rich country is slightly smaller than the US state of Texas (or slightly bigger than metropolitan France). More than one quarter of the country's 4.5 million people reside in Bangui, where electricity is scarce, potable tap water is nonexistent, and the vast majority of roads are unpaved (and unnamed). School children have not enjoyed an uninterrupted school year in 20 years.[21] Of 187 countries classified on the Human Development Index, Central Africa ranks as the lowest for its short life expectancy, low GDP (the lowest PPP in the world), low levels of literacy, high unemployment, and high infant and maternal mortality rates.[22]

There are somewhere between 7 and 50 ethnic groups in Central Africa (Central Intelligence Agency 2014). Most people speak French as well as the national language, Sango. Although estimates of precise religious proportions vary, and many Christian and Muslim families are intermarried, about 50 percent of the people are Protestant or Catholic (in roughly equal measures, although probably more Protestant), about 35 percent adhere to indigenous, animist beliefs (although this percentage is probably higher), and 15–20 percent profess some variant of Islam (Carayannis and Lombard 2015, 322; Central

---

[20] Those familiar with history of the Democratic Republic of the Congo, just south of the Central African Republic, will recognize the sequence of an "exploitative, terror-based [colonial] regime" followed by a violent, extravagant national leader (Smith 2015, 22).

[21] Interview with Rebecca Hunter, State Department, Washington DC, 14 April 2015. In 2012, dozens of schools were repeatedly attacked and looted, mainly by factions of ex-Séléka (S/2016/133, paras. 34, 35, 56).

[22] Note that in 2012, the Central African Republic was ranked 180 of 187 on the Human Development Index. Now it is the lowest (UN Development Programme 2017).

Intelligence Agency 2014). Muslim Central Africans are diverse, but most are Sunni. Many came several generations ago from Chad, Cameroon, Lebanon, or Nigeria through slave raiding and various forms of trade and have often concentrated on commercial activities in Bangui (Kilembe 2015). Given the extreme poverty of Central Africa, Muslims are often considered relatively wealthy. At the same time, many Central African Muslims are nomadic and have traditionally moved across borders and throughout the country during the seasonal "transhumance" period, when livestock and people transit from northern territories bordering Chad and Sudan, through to the southern parts of the country to sell beef in Bangui, and to neighbors in Cameroon, Congo-Brazaville, and Congo-Kinshasa.

Historically, tensions have arisen from time to time between landed farmers and nomads seeking pastures for cattle grazing, especially during the dry season from December to May, but traditional agropastoralist mediation practices prevented conflicts from escalating past the local level, and these disputes did not take on overtly religious tones (Agger 2014; Brown and Zahar 2015; International Crisis Group 2014, 14). Anthropologists have made a convincing case that in the absence of state authority, Central African society developed practical responses involving not only mediation, but also popular punishment and vengeance (BBC Afrique, 2014; Lombard and Batianga-Kinzi 2015). These practices, however, render the establishment of a legal-rational Weberian state difficult.

Throughout its history, the Central African Republic has also endured "a vicious cycle of conflict [that is] grounded in and perpetuates inequality" (Brown and Zahar 2015, 17). The agropastoralist conflicts in the countryside have manifested themselves in a variety of ways, but often separately from conflicts in and around the capital Bangui, where the political and economic elite regularly appropriate resources from the state to the disadvantage of average citizens. In much of the countryside, battles can be characterized more as raids. In the absence of a state or more peaceful means of employment, young people may take up arms to raid another village, especially one inhabited by people who belong to another identity group. The people in the village evacuate and subsequently regroup to seek revenge, maybe on the initial attacker and then beyond, and thus the cycle of violence expands.[23]

---

[23] Polarized identity is thus a product, rather than a cause, of the violence.

In the last decade or so, the Lord's Resistance Army from Uganda has added to difficulties, most notably in the southeastern parts of the country, exacerbated also by refugees from South Sudan, Darfur, and the Democratic Republic of the Congo. A continuous and augmenting theme in Central African discourse involves who is genuinely Central African, and who is an outsider, with particular focus on people from Chad (Chauvin 2018).[24]

The nature of the Central African state is one of debate. The UN frames the problem as the absence of a traditional Weberian state. Anthropologist Louisa Lombard argues that Weberian notions of territoriality and the distinction between public and private have not applied and do not apply to governance in the Central African Republic (Carayannis and Lombard 2015; Lombard 2016). The borders of Central Africa are porous, and its neighbors – both political leaders and citizens – frequently determine the nature of political processes in the country.[25] Most external interveners, however, maintain the frame of a state as one that governs a specific territory, provides services, and remains separate from private companies. Thus, for example, the second-ranked task in MINUSCA's mandate is "extension of state authority and preservation of territorial integrity" (S/RES/2149, 10 April 2014, para. 30, b). Lombard argues, however, that the Central African state "has always been privatized," and that "the extreme porousness and non-territorial nature of the CAR state have fed a desire for a more stable and closed system," which might never be attainable (Lombard 2016, 24). She contends that a less porous state would require "something entirely new, something nearly impossible to imagine" (Lombard 2016, 24). Perhaps the Central African state is not "fragile"; but, rather, it is of a different form.

Although I agree that reimagining what might count as "the state" may be necessary for Central Africa, I contend that Lombard and others miss the centrality of *violence* and its control as a defining characteristic of any legitimate state or foreign intervener. For Weber, in his definition of the state, the notion of holding a monopoly over legitimate violence precedes the part about territory (and the economy). I would contend

---

[24] Note that some parts of northern Central Africa were formerly considered parts of Chad.

[25] For example, Idriss Déby of Chad resolved the crisis of who would govern after Michel Djotodia stepped down in January 2014, choosing Bangui Mayor, Catherine Samba-Panza (who was born in what is now Chad).

that, although the state and economy in Central Africa are difficult to separate, and its borders are porous, violence and who controls it are essential for understanding governance – whether internationally imposed or domestically built. In other words, although some aspects of the Central African state defy Weberian ideal types, the importance of controlling violence remains in line with notions of what it means to be a functioning Weberian state. And since the state has not monopolized violence, other actors have sought to do so, with varying effects.

International actors have sought to quell violence in Central Africa for the last twenty-some years (although sometimes they spur it, usually inadvertently). Beginning with the Mission Interafricaine de Surveillance des Accords de Bangui in 1997, Central Africa has hosted nearly a dozen different interventions (Olin 2015). Neighboring Chad is a frequent player in all interventions (Chauvin 2018). Official *regional* interventions include those by the Economic and Monetary Community of Central African States, the Community of Sahel-Saharan States, and the African Union. The European Union, the United States, Uganda, France, and the United Nations have conducted *international* interventions. The largest and most expensive have been waged by the last several entities on this list (S/2016/565, 22 June 2016, para. 2), which are thus the focus of my analysis. All of the interventions suffer from "the failure to profit from periods of stability, and the search for cheap solutions leading to quick exits" (Olin 2015, 195).

2012 December, Séléka rebels begin capturing towns.
2013 March, Séléka rebels storm through the countryside and seize Bangui. Bozizé ousted in coup and Djotodia installed. Massive killing of people associated with Bozizé; looting of state institutions; the national military (FACA) disintegrates.
2013 December, UNSC authorizes France (Sangaris) and the African Union to send forces to stabilize. Generalized violence; ethnic cleansing of Muslims; then decrease in violence.
2014 January, Djotodia resigns, Samba-Panza becomes interim leader.
2014 September, MINUSCA arrives, AU forces re-hatted to UN, Sangaris remains.
2015 February, Battle for Bria.
2015 May, Bangui Forum peace talks, displaced return home, economy grows.
2015 August, Reports of sexual abuse surface, SRSG fired, UN battalions sent home.
2015 November, Pope visits.
2015 December, New constitution approved by referendum.
2016 February, Dr. Touadéra wins presidency in runoff.
2016 October, Sangaris departs; uptick in violence and displacement.
2017 April, U.S. forces announce September departure; displacement soars again.
2017 July, Several major western aid agencies depart amid increase in violence.
2018 April, Sukula battle in PK5, Bangui; armed groups control 80 percent of country.
2018 May, Russian troops arrive.

Figure 4.1 Central African Republic Timeline

Effectiveness

Overview of Death and Displacement in the Central African Republic since 2000

Although Central Africa has been poor and ill governed for a long time, its people have not been dying or displaced from war until very recently (Marchal 2015, 167). The problems of inequality, unfair treatment, economic scarcity, political exclusion, religious differences, and the dismantling of whatever state existed all came together and exploded in three major waves of cross-country violence in December 2012–March 2013, re-igniting in December 2013–early 2014, dissipating for nearly two years, and returning again in late 2016 (see Figure 4.1, p. 153). The violence has generally emerged as a result of conflicts between two groups of loosely aligned militias: the Séléka and the Anti-balaka. The Séléka, which means both "alliance" and "wedding ring," was a mainly (but not exclusively) Muslim group headed by Michel Djotodia and has always been more hierarchically coordinated (Wohlers 2015).[26] The Anti-balaka, which means both "anti-machete" and "anti-bullets from Automatic Kalashnikov rifles" (in French: *balles A.K.*) are an even looser, non-hierarchical group of neighborhood defense forces, mainly Christian and animist, dating back to the 1990s. Anti-balaka forces, initially aligned with the former president/ dictator, François Bozizé, banded together temporarily in the wake of Séléka advances in late 2012.[27]

In December 2012, protesting Bozizé's corrupt and exclusive rule and failure to follow through on promises made during peace talks several years earlier, the Séléka marched through the north and center of the country, and eventually past a regional peacekeeping force (MICOPAX), to seize and loot Bangui. "The country faced a total breakdown of law and order, and already fragile state institutions completely collapsed" (S/2016/565, 22 June 2016, para. 2). Bozizé fled in March 2013, the national military – the Forces armeés centrafricaines (FACA) – collapsed, and Djotodia declared himself president.

---

[26] However, various ex-Séléka groups are now fighting each other (S/2018/125, para. 17).

[27] The Anti-Balaka recruited and used thousands of child soldiers, in much greater numbers than the Séléka (S/2016/133, 12 February 2016, para, 20). In the attacks of 5 December 2013, "hundreds of children were killed and maimed, often brutally" (S/2016/133, 12 February 2016, para, 26).

While at first many Central Africans of all religious persuasions welcomed the change in power, the celebration was short-lived, as Séléka militias – lacking a hierarchical chain of command or uniting purpose – ran rampant through Bangui and the countryside, plundering villages, committing atrocities, and killing hundreds of people – mainly non-Muslims who were seen to be supporters of the former president Bozizé. By May of 2013, after Séléka militias looted several state armories and small arms washed across many neighborhoods of Bangui, the UN's special representative in Central Africa informed the UN Security Council that the country had "descended into a state of anarchy" (UN Information Department 2013). US Ambassador to the UN Samantha Power named it "the worst crisis most people have never heard of" (Power 2013). The UN Office for the Coordination of Humanitarian Affairs proclaimed that "both sides are committing unimaginable atrocities." The Séléka and Anti-balaka were not necessarily directly fighting each other. Instead, each would target mainly defenseless civilians in "a devastating cycle of reprisal attacks" (McCormick 2015).

Under international pressure, Djotodia disbanded the Séléka in September 2013 (Smith 2015). On December 9, 2013, French "Sangaris" forces arrived and began disarming any remaining Séléka, which ushered in an unintended counter-wave of violence and displacement that disproportionately affected Muslim civilians (Brown and Zahar 2015, 11; Marchal 2014; Olin 2015, 213; S/2016/133, 12 February 2016, para. 10).[28] As a National Geographic photographer who witnessed this period described it, for six weeks, from January to March 2014, "the country went psychotic" (Gwin 2015). Mainly Christian militias carried out an "ethnic cleansing" of the Muslim population, short of genocide but nevertheless criminal under international humanitarian law (Cinq-Mars 2015; S/2014/928, 22 December 2014). According to the official record, approximately 6,000 people

---

[28] "On 5 December 2013, Anti-Balaka attacked ex-Séléka positions in Bangui and in Bossangoa (Ouham prefecture), which triggered widespread violence between Christian and Muslim communities across the country. Close to 2,000 civilians were reportedly killed in Bangui in just a few days. It is estimated that these attacks generated the highest number of internally displaced persons and refugees over the past decade, including 435,000 displaced persons and 450,000 refugees, the majority of whom were Muslims, who fled to neighboring countries between 2013 and 2014" (S/2016/133, 12 February 2016, para. 10).

perished, though the UN Commission of Inquiry's final report "considers that such estimates fail to capture the full magnitude of the killings that occurred" (S/2014/928, 22 December 2014). Meanwhile, during the height of the fighting, an interagency group headed by the UN Population Fund documented more than 60,000 cases of sexual and gender-based violence, "of which about 30,000 involved victims of sexual violence, including rape. That is about 100 people a day" (Aichi 2015).

After acknowledging the unintended effects, the French forces corrected course and began to protect vulnerable Muslim populations. Eventually the French forces quelled the violence, including the widespread gender-based violence, paving the way for a July agreement on the cessation of hostilities signed by most parties in Congo-Brazzaville. In September 2014, the UN deployed a large, multidimensional, integrated peacekeeping mission (MINUSCA). The UN helped to organize the Bangui Forum peace process in May 2015, subsequent elections that resulted in a new constitution in December 2015, and the popular choice of President Faustin-Archange Touadéra in early 2016.[29] Touadéra was the former Rector of the University of Bangui and former Bozizé-chosen Prime Minister, known for holding two doctoral degrees in math – one from the University of Yaoundé in Cameroon and the other from Lille University of Science and Technology in France.[30]

Clouding the trends toward peace were widespread reports of sexual abuse committed by both French troops and UN peacekeepers. The French departed in the fall of 2016, and American and Ugandan special forces six months later. Since the departure of the troops from France, the United States, and Uganda, new rebel groups are forming and tightening bonds, especially in the northeast and southeast; some call for the partition of the country.

Figures 4.2–4.4 depict some of the human results of these shifts in politics and international interventions. Figure 4.2 shows the Uppsala

---

[29] Note that the constitution, approved by voter referendum in December 2016, includes such state organs as the Ministry of Social Affairs and National Reconciliation, an economic and social council, a national mediation council, a high council for communication and a high committee on good governance.

[30] Although warnings of potential genocide against Muslims in Central Africa are serious, and discrimination abounds, President Touadéra has not used anti-Muslim narratives as a way to gain in popularity which are a precondition for genocide. See Straus 2015.

Conflict Data Program's (UCDP) yearly rates of deaths due to violence, beginning in 2000.[31] Although there had been sporadic rounds of killing in the 2000s, nothing compares to the cataclysmic years of 2013 and 2014. The overall yearly death rate then decreases significantly in 2015 and 2016 (UCDP data are not yet available for subsequent years).

Figure 4.2 presents the Armed Conflict Location & Event Data Project (ACLED) data for the same time period, but their data are more current and can be broken down monthly.[32] The ACLED data make it clear that violent deaths subsided significantly from late 2014 to late 2016, picking up again after the withdrawal of French and American troops. In turn, Figure 4.3 presents the toll of events on displacement – both within and outside of the Central African Republic. Again, we see people fleeing the violence of 2013 and 2014. But then, notably, we see internally displaced people returning

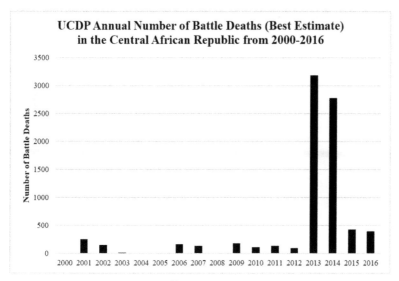

Figure 4.2 Death Rates by Year[33]

[31] UCDP is housed in the Department of Peace and Conflict Research at Uppsala University in Sweden.
[32] ACLED employs different coders and uses some different data-gathering methods from UCDP. ACLED is funded by the US Department of State and the European Research Council.
[33] These data were originally published in Pettersson and Eck 2018.

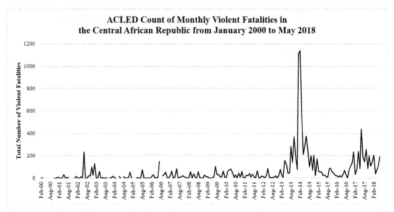

Figure 4.3 Death Rates by Month

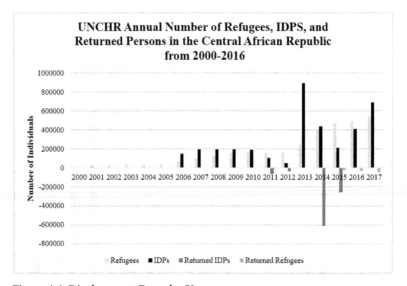

Figure 4.4 Displacement Rates by Year

to their homes from 2014 to 2016; this trend reverses thereafter. The most recent data are not included in this chart, but as of April 2018, the number of IDPs increased dramatically from 2017, even worse than 2013:

The upsurge of violence during the first three quarters of 2017 led to an increase in the number of internally displaced persons, bringing the total to over 688,000 people – a 70 percent increase in one year. The number of refugees increased by 26 percent, surpassing 545,000 refugees in neighboring countries. By the end of 2017, as a consequence of the conflict in the Central African Republic, a total of 1.24 million people, the highest number yet recorded, had been forcibly displaced, either as refugees or as displaced persons (S/2018/125, 15 February 2018, para. 29).

The following two sections explain how French, American, and UN forces exercised power, as well as internal reactions to these efforts, which resulted in these shifts in death and displacement.

Sangaris and Other Military Forces: Compellence, Deterrence, Surveillance

Sangaris is the name of a small central African butterfly that has a short lifespan. The French Special Forces in the Central African Republic from 2014 to 2016 were anything but gentle like a butterfly, but the French government certainly wanted them to remain in Central Africa for as short a time as possible. The French mission suffered from three self-inflicted wounds: (1) the time pressure to leave as quickly as possible, (2) disarming the Séléka without securing the safety of Muslim civilians, and (3) reports of sexual abuse against children (as I explain in the section on persuasion). These are the three negative elements of Sangaris that are most recounted in the news media, as well as in NGO and UN reports. However, Sangaris played an extremely important role in stopping the violence and making it possible for IDPs to return home. It was effective most notably because it functioned as a centralized, hierarchical, and compellent source of overarching coercive power, in a country where there was no other.

The French forces exercised compellence as their main form of coercive power (see Photo 5, p. 183). The effective exercise of compellence had an additional military-based deterrent effect. Sangaris forces also engaged in surveillance, or at least promoted the perception of constant surveillance, as a way to change the behavior of belligerents. As one analyst explains, Sangaris sought "to create a sense of ubiquity" (Hémez 2016, 79).

The French government conceived Sangaris as a "bridging operation," and not one of stabilization, although its primary effectiveness was in its stabilization function (Hémez and Leboeuf 2016, 80). The UN Security Council mandated Sangaris "to take all necessary measures to support MISCA," the small, multilateral African Union mission that deployed simultaneously with the French forces, before a UN peacekeeping mission could be developed (S/RES/2127, 49; Welz 2016).[34] Although Sangaris "did not resolve the CAR's crisis, it helped avoid genocide, it jump-started the disarmament process while fostering a nascent administrative structure, and it restored the supply of essential goods ... Above all, [it] managed to be a 'bridging operation' to ... MINUSCA, the desired end state" (Hémez 2016, 73).[35]

Sangaris only had 2,000 troops at its full operational strength in January 2014, but the mission managed to gain control over the violence through its mobility – both by ground and air. As one information officer explained at the time, "Sangaris surveils from on high. They help to find criminals and Anti-balaka, and ex-Séléka."[36] Their goal was never to control the whole country, but to give the impression that they were under control. On the ground, they secured key roads where supply lines had been disrupted, as well as villages and cities where civilians were under threat by Anti-balaka, ex-Séléka, and various unaffiliated bandits (such as the *coupeurs de routes*).

The operation unfolded in three phases: (1) Sangaris secured Bangui, where most civilians were under threat; (2) it secured the west of the country, most notably the supply road from Bouar to Bangui, over which goods from Cameroon and elsewhere travel; and (3) it pushed north and eastward, toward Kaga Bandoro and Bria (but not much further), in order to protect civilians (Hémez 2016). The strategy of modern counterinsurgency is that international forces help governments to "clear, hold, and build" (United States Army 2006). In this framework, French forces successfully "cleared" and "held," but unlike UN peacekeepers, they were not designed, nor could they "build." Sangaris functioned effectively as a compellent, coercive force, but they did not base their power on the other forms – persuasion or inducement. As one UN official explained: "Sangaris has a simple

---

[34] Large, multidimensional peacekeeping missions take at least nine months to prepare and deploy (UN General Assembly 2000; United Nations 2008).

[35] The UN Security Council mandated MISCA with 4,500 African Union soldiers – many from Chad – who were "re-hatted" into MINUSCA nine months later. The new troops were not as trained, mobile, or equipped as the single-nationality French forces. The presence of Chadian "peacekeepers" was not well received by many Central Africans, who accused them of being partial to the ex-Séléka.

[36] Author interview with Alexandra Simpson, Information Officer, Bangui, 6 May 2015.

mandate. They go in hard and then step back and watch."[37] Another extolled Sangaris' deterrent effects: "The only thing preventing the Séléka from taking over again is Sangaris."[38] Numerous UN officials in and around Bangui in 2015 expressed frequently to me, and in different ways, the extent to which Sangaris was effective in its use of compellence and deterrence. These means of power were entirely different from those of the UN peacekeepers. But they were similar to the ones being used effectively by US and Ugandan forces, active in the southeast of Central Africa.

In the eastern areas of the country, where Sangaris forces were not deployed, US special forces were, alongside Ugandan infantry. The Americans and Ugandans were on the hunt for the Lord's Resistance Army (LRA); they did not have a stabilization or peacekeeping mandate. Rather, in 2012, President Obama authorized "a small number of combat-equipped US forces to deploy to Central Africa to provide assistance to regional forces that are working toward the removal of Joseph Kony from the battlefield" (Wilson and Whitlock 2011). The American forces trained and assisted some 800 Ugandans (exact numbers are not public, see Cakaj 2015, 276), who had been chasing Kony for years after his rapacious plundering of villages in northern Uganda left tens of thousands of people – especially children – dead or traumatized, and hundreds of thousands displaced (Wilson and Whitlock 2011). Overall, the United States has spent approximately $800 million in this effort – an enormous sum in an impoverished area.[39] Much of the funds went to "providing housing, food and medical care for the US Special Forces and a series of classified items believed to be part of intelligence, surveillance, and reconnaissance systems" (Cakaj 2015, 284). Although the Americans and Ugandans did not capture or kill Kony, they were reported to be having several positive effects: improving the behavior of sometimes-abusive Ugandan forces; cutting down on LRA violence; and, unintentionally, preventing armed Central African groups from harming civilians

---

[37] Author interview with Adrian Foster, Major General, Deputy Military Adviser, Bangui, 4 May 2015.
[38] Author interview with Political Affairs Officer with MINUSCA who preferred anonymity, Bangui, May 2015. See also Smith 2015, 45.
[39] Author interview with anonymous official in the US Department of Defense with knowledge of the mission, Washington, DC, 3 May 2018.

(Cakaj 2015, 285).[40] Many observers have linked the uptick in violence in the southeast to the departure of the Americans and Ugandans (Kleinfeld 2018; S/2017/865, 18 October 2017, paras. 13–23). In other words, similar to the French Special Forces, the American Special Forces, alongside Ugandan military, used surveillance as a means of power – just like peacekeepers. But unlike peacekeepers, they were also effective at compellence and military-based deterrence – types of power for which peacekeeping was not designed.

Mechanisms of Power in MINUSCA

Given the success of Sangaris and the other forces in stabilizing Central Africa and the existence of a peace accord signed in neighboring Congo-Brazzaville in July 2014, MINUSCA was supposed to be an easy mission. Although the conflict in 2013–2014 could be characterized as "a total breakdown of law and order" (BBC 2013), Central Africa was not in a generalized or organized state of *war*. The country is vast – the size of continental France and the Benelux countries combined – but with only 4.5 million people it is not ungovernable. Central Africa has abundant natural resources (diamonds, gold, uranium, etc.), fertile earth, an equatorial climate, and plenty of water. Nourishment should not be a problem. Muslims and Christians have been living and working together, and intermarrying, for generations (Kilembe 2015). As a top UN political advisor explained, in contrast to other civil wars, "the sides are not hardened against each other. People are fighting because they are unemployed and this gives them something to do."[41] At the start of MINUSCA, according to most external and internal analyses, the troubles in Central Africa stemmed from three interrelated sources: an absence of development, an absence of the state, and lawlessness.[42] The mission, therefore, concentrated on tackling these problems.

---

[40] Author interview with Najat Rochdi, Deputy Special Representative of the UN Secretary-General in the Central African Republic, Washington, DC, 7 November 2017.

[41] Fifatin Grace Kpohazounde, Political Advisor, New York, Interview in François 2015.

[42] The International Crisis Group has famously coined it the "phantom" state (2007).

Mandate

The UN Security Council's mandate for MINUSCA is long and compli-cated – it is the longest peacekeeping mandate ever. To simplify, some members of the mission described MINUSCA's mandate in 2015 as having three central pillars: (1) the protection of civilians, (2) the support of a transitional political process, and (3) the restoration of state authority. The full mandate, however, includes many more tasks, which I list below. The mission's leadership sought to implement both the letter and the spirit of the mandate by instituting two central innovations for a peacekeeping mission, one based on inducement and the other on coercion: first, a deeply integrated structure with the UN Development Programme (UNDP), and second, a unique policing concept, whereby military battalions would serve under police com-mand. This configuration has allowed MINUSCA troops to engage in "urgent temporary measures," which include the power of arrest. As the Under-Secretary-General for Peacekeeping at the time described it, "this is a new experiment in peacekeeping, focusing on policing, but with a classic infantry [Sangaris] as back-up."[43]

Authorized under Chapter VII of the UN charter, MINUSCA was to take the reins from two other international interventions: The African Union's peace enforcement mission (MISCA) and the UN's peacebuild-ing mission (BINUCA). Troops and staff – and buildings and equip-ment – from both operations would be reassigned to MINUSCA by September 15, 2014. The full list of tasks included the following: protecting civilians, especially women and children, under threat of physical violence (within its capabilities and areas of deployment) and identifying and recording threats and attacks against civilians; support-ing the transition process (from the transitional government under Catherine Samba-Panza to a constitutional referendum and elections), the extension of state authority, and the preservation of territorial integrity through technical assistance, mediation, and national dia-logue, and helping IDPs and refugees to return; facilitating humanitarian aid delivery; protecting the UN itself and ensuring free-dom of movement for staff; promoting human rights including

[43] Author interview with Hervé Ladsous, UN Under-Secretary-General for Peacekeeping, Goma, Democratic Republic of the Congo, 25 April 2015. Author's translation.

monitoring and investigating abuses; supporting national and international justice processes by arresting war criminals for the ICC, building a new national justice system, and reinstating the police and criminal justice system; and disarming, demobilizing, reintegrating, and repatriating (DDRR) former combatants and armed elements, implementing community violence reduction and justice programs, coordinating international DDRR assistance, and seizing, collecting, and storing arms in support of the international arms embargo imposed on the Central African Republic since 2013 (S/RES/2127, 5 December 2013).

In addition, the UN Security Council gave the mission a variety of other tasks, such as helping to find the Lord's Resistance Army, protecting and reintegrating child soldiers, incorporating gender advisors in DDRR processes, assisting all regional political reconciliation efforts, helping the EU in its military training missions, and instituting a zero-tolerance policy for sexual abuse and exploitation committed by international personnel. The authorizing mandate also asks France to use "all necessary means" to help MINUSCA carry out its mission and requests that DPKO work on a "concept of operations" for sequencing the benchmarks and tasks in the mandate while envisioning an exit strategy. Paragraph 40 (of 51 total) indicates that the UN Security Council decided "that MINUSCA may, within the limits of its capacitates and in areas of deployment, at the formal request of the Transitional Authorities and in areas where national security forces are not present or operational, adopt *urgent temporary measures* on an exceptional basis and without creating a precedent and without prejudice to the agreed principle of peacekeeping operations, to maintain basic law and order and fight impunity" (my italics). The resolution also requests frequent reports back to UN headquarters, including full Secretary-General Reports to the UN Security Council, every four months. As one UN staff member remarked, "The mandate is twenty pages long. It's very difficult to figure out what the priorities are, and to think about achieving anything concrete when we are mired in daily crises and constantly having to write reports."[44] But early on, the leadership chose to focus, as much as possible, on the development and policing functions as the most viable paths that external actors could take in assisting the Central African Republic in its hoped-for transition to peace.

[44] Author interview with senior UN Official, Bangui, Central African Republic, May 2015.

In 2016, after the elections, which marked the end of the "transitional" period, followed by the withdrawal of the Sangaris forces, the Security Council recalibrated the peacekeepers' mandate. Protection of civilians, safeguarding delivery of humanitarian assistance, and return and resettlement of IDPs and refugees remained priority tasks. But the Council also wanted MINUSCA to advance towards its proposed end state by focusing on supporting "the sustainable reduction of the presence of armed groups through a comprehensive approach" (S/2016/565 22 June, 2016, para. 32). Unfortunately, although the UN's approach has, indeed, been comprehensive and innovative, the precise opposite has occurred with regard to the armed groups – there are more such groups than ever before; currently, they are killing not only civilians, but also each other (S/2018/124, 15 February 2018, para. 12).

Elements of Coercion in MINUSCA

MINUSCA has sought to employ all forms of coercion – compellence, deterrence, defense, surveillance, and arrest – but thus far, it has exercised only the last three effectively. With Sangaris exercising compellence and military-based deterrence in the background, MINUSCA had the mandate, the capacity, and the leadership necessary to use the deprivation of liberty as a tool to reduce the proliferation and effectiveness of the various armed groups. MINUSCA troops were also able to defend civilians for a time, and they developed something of a surveillance capacity – both by land and air. But MINUSCA has not effectively wielded the hammer of compellence in the manner of, for example, Sangaris. I provide evidence of the different aspects of MINUSCA's coercive capacity, and illustrate its varying effectiveness in two battles that members of the mission often cite by way of comparison: in the town of Bria, near the center of the country, on 10 February 2015, and then three years later, in the PK5 neighborhood in Bangui on 8 April 2018, known as the "Sukula" operation. In the following sections, I examine each type of coercion as it has been employed in MINUSCA, starting with arrest.

Arrest

The mandate that MINUSCA take "urgent temporary measures" to engage in law enforcement opened a window for the mission's leadership to experiment with a new form of peacekeeping: having police in charge of military battalions. In the capital city of Bangui, as of mid-2015, MINUSCA had six formed police units (of about 250 officers each) and several other "military battalions under the tactical control of the police. This is how we are establishing order in the most difficult neighborhoods like Boy Rabe and PK5 ... we are putting police interventions ahead of stabilization" (see Photo 8, p. 184)[45] Under this unusual configuration, military, even those not under police command, have the authority to arrest, and military and police forces are often colocated. The mission established MINUSCA police outposts, often also colocating in Central African police stations, in towns across the country. Starting in Bangui, and working through other towns north and west. As one staff member described the configuration: "Our police co-locate with local police and gendarme in order to suppress large-scale banditry."[46]

From its inception in September 2014 until mid-2015, MINUSCA arrested "more than 365 criminal suspects and facilitated their transfer from various regions to Bangui under its urgent temporary measures mandate" (S/2015/576, 29 July 2015, para. 53). The arrests of prominent Anti-balaka leaders sometimes triggered reprisal attacks against international workers (including against UN staff and any others driving white vehicles), but the disputes were generally diffused through legal proceedings and mediations (S/2015/227, 1 April 2015, paras 5, 7).

After the transition to the Touadéra government, the central innovation in policing – having military battalions under police command – reverted back to the usual chain of command in UN peacekeeping missions, where the two are separate. In other words, unless directly ordered, military troops are not inclined to engage in arrest.[47] At the time of transition to the Touadéra government, the Central African Police were still severely understaffed and underfunded. "Of the 3,700 registered police and gendarmerie officers, only 800 are deployed

---

[45] Author interview. Luis Carrilho, Police Commissioner, 2 May 2015. Note that Boy Rabe is considered to be a rough Anti-Balaka (Christian) neighborhood, and PK5 is historically more Muslim. PK5 has become a Muslim enclave, associated with ex-Séléka.

[46] Author interview with Alexandra Simpson, Information Officer, Bangui, 6 May 2015.

[47] Several MINUSCA mission staff suggested to me that the military were not happy about being under police command.

outside Bangui. The police-citizen ratio of 1:1,250 is extremely low. There is a high rate of ageing officers with no institutionalized pension system and salary arrears are common. There has been no recruitment since 2010 and no retirements since 2005. A draft five-year development and capacity-building plan has been developed with the support of MINUSCA" (S/2016/565, 22 June 2016, para. 22). UN policing efforts shifted to focus not only on training, but also on arresting members of the ex-Séléka. At the request of President Touadéra, MINUSCA assisted the government in arresting a variety of prominent ex-Séléka leaders (S/2016/824, 29 September 2016, paras. 44, 45). After the transition, the UN Secretary-General reports to the UN Security Council do not mention specifically the arrest of Anti-balaka forces or leaders – only ex-Séléka – signaling a shift away from adhering to the peacekeeping principles of impartiality and consent, and toward favoring the government.

Surveillance

Surveillance is a tool of both intelligence gathering and the coercive conditioning of behavior. Peacekeepers surveil in many ways, most often through patrol (see Photo 6, p. 183). The UN Security Council mandated MINUSCA to protect civilians "including through active patrolling" (S/RES/2149 10 April 2014, para. a, point i). MINUSCA also devised "community-based early-warning analysis and rapid-response tools" and conducts joint patrols with national police, gendarmes, and military. In addition, the mission has hired dozens of community liaison assistants to better understand events at the village level (S/2015/227, 1 April 2015, para. 37).

In a country where many roads are impassable or difficult to traverse, even in the dry season, MINUSCA planes and helicopters move people and goods around the country and give the impression of continuous UN presence. MINUSCA's police and military are organized by static stations and bases, as well as mobile units, all of which conduct daily patrols. Patrol is a way to demonstrate the presence of peacekeepers and attempt to prevent illegal behavior by creating a widespread impression on the part of potentially nefarious actors that they are being watched.

Aside from physical patrol and community liaisons, MINUSCA also employs new technologies, including an unmanned aerial surveillance drone. It has attempted to "create a common operating picture by integrating various sensors, including cameras, unmanned aircraft systems, and aerostat, static and mobile sensors, into a single framework" (S/2016/565, 22 June 2016, para. 58). Members of MINUSCA use the information gathered from these technologies to guide "the location of checkpoints, buffer zones and areas of active patrolling" (S/2017/94, 1 February 2017, para. 25). In the last year, the new technology has enabled MINUSCA forces to "conduct long-range patrols along migratory corridors and maintain a presence in key hotspots" (S/2017/94, 1 February 2017, para. 26).

Surveillance alone conditions behavior, but it is more likely to mitigate negative behavior if there are known consequences for committing crimes or acts of violence. With the knowledge provided by surveillance and intelligence gathering, if someone infringes on the rules and if there are other forms of coercive capacity, then it is possible to conceive of consequences. As the MINUSCA Police Force commander explained, during patrols and roadblocks, peacekeepers not only watch, but also "stop anyone with arms or committing crimes."[48] Stopping and depriving liberty are possible through coercive and community policing alone. But surveillance and arrest alone are probably not sufficient to dissuade thousands of members of armed groups who are intent on using violence against each other and civilians. That is where compellence and deterrence are absolutely critical.

Compellence and Deterrence

In 2015, when, in the course of surveilling and patrolling, MINUSCA personnel found evidence of armed actors targeting civilians, they would inform French Sangaris troops of the activity (see Photos 5 and 6, p. 183). UN representatives would first attempt to mediate, and if that proved ineffective, Sangaris would use compellent force in order to gain compliance. For example, in the town of Bria, on 10 February 2015, two armed groups were targeting civilians that the other group claimed to be protecting. MINUSCA peacekeepers (civilians and military) "talked with them for weeks, but they would not stop."[49] Based on these events and knowledge obtained through patrol and

[48] Author interviews with Luis Carrilho, Bangui, Central African Republic, May 2015.
[49] Author interview with Aurelien Agbenonci, Deputy Special Representative of the Secretary-General, 8 May 2015.

other surveillance activities, Sangaris forcibly disarmed the combatants (or chased them out of the city) while UN troops arrested others. Subsequently, MINUSCA set up protection points around hot spots and began to rebuild looted public administration buildings.[50] This type of joint effort was effective at dampening violence against civilians for nearly two years. However, Bria succumbed to violence as soon as Sangaris departed in October 2016.[51] Since that time, MINUSCA troops have assumed the Sangaris tasks, but their ability to use compellence or military-based deterrence has proven wanting. The "Sukula" operation in early April 2018 – MINUSCA's first venture into "urban warfare" – illustrates this point.

The predominantly Muslim neighborhood of PK5 has been an area of contention for some time. One resident explains, "formerly a hotspot for commerce, social bricolage, music, dance and parties, [PK5] has been at the center of several conflicts in recent years" (Kilembe 2015, 95). PK5 was nearly completely destroyed in Anti-balaka reprisal attacks against anyone associated with the ex-Séléka in late 2013–early 2014. Although it remains an economic hub, PK5 has become a Muslim "enclave" in Christian-majority Bangui; many of its residents feel trapped and vulnerable to a variety of threats.

In early 2018, residents complained to MINUSCA of illegal taxing and other abuses by (fellow Muslim) armed groups. Residents requested that MINUSCA arrest or disarm the armed actors. But somewhere, a breakdown of communication occurred. On 8 April MINUSCA police and military, together with members of the Forces armeés centrafricaines, entered PK5 with the intent to arrest and disarm. They were met, however, by hundreds of young civilians who attacked the UN peacekeepers, removed their barricades, and burned a police commissariat that was still under construction (Ourdan 2018). A four-hour gun battle ensued. More than 30 Central African civilians were killed and more than 100 wounded; 1 Rwandan peacekeeper was killed, and 8 others were injured.

In a symbolic gesture to protest UN killings, residents of PK5 took approximately 17 of the bodies to the main MINUSCA peacekeeping

---

[50] Author interviews with Babacar Gaye, Special Representative of the Secretary-General, 6 May 2015; and Frank Dalton, Chief of the Justice and Corrections Division, Bangui, 7 May 2015.
[51] Author interview with Grace Kpohazounde, Political Affairs Officer, New York, 25 June 2018.

base and laid them out in a row on the ground before the front gates. (The Red Cross later removed the bodies for proper burial.) The Under-Secretary-General for UN peacekeeping, Jean-Pierre Lacroix, was in Bangui at the time and responded, "We are very angry, but not against these young people, who were manipulated. We're very angry with those manipulating them, who arm them and use them for their selfish reasons" (Kokopakpa 2018).

Soon thereafter, President Touadéra requested that MINUSCA transition from a peacekeeping to a genuine peace enforcement mission (Kelly 2018). The main rebel leader in PK5 responded, "if the UN blue helmets want a war, they only have to tell residents to leave the area and we will defeat them" (Muggah 2018). The rebel response reveals the extent to which UN peacekeepers do not supply military-based security guarantees for peace enforcement. Many fear that UN peacekeepers will be sucked into a counter-insurgency, fighting on behalf of the government.

Since the shootout, self-defense forces (Anti-balaka) and ex-Séléka have waged reprisal attacks; ex-Séléka militias in the northeast have regrouped and "threatened to march on the capital, saying the military operation there had singled-out Muslims" (Kelly 2018). The June 2018 Secretary General's report to the Security Council describes the turn of events:

The situation in the CAR has steadily deteriorated in recent months, including in Bangui and other localities. Self-proclaimed self-defense groups, loosely connected to some members of the Anti-balaka movement, have continued to operate in south-eastern CAR, targeting Muslims. Ex-Séléka, largely consisting of Muslim factions, continue to establish illegal parallel administration and taxation structures in areas under their control, preying on the population ... There has been a resurgence of sectarian rhetoric and intercommunal strife, which has undermined popular support for the state and its institutions, and the credibility of MINUSCA. (What's in Blue 2018)

In sum, starting in 2014, MINUSCA engaged effectively in some aspects of coercion. The leadership created a new and effective peacekeeping model, predicated on the coercive power of arrest.

The peacekeepers also effectively surveilled and defended. Meanwhile, Sangaris, and American and Ugandan forces, exercised compellence and deterrence in their respective areas of operation. After the compellent forces departed, and MINUSCA assumed the mantle of compellence, the UN's capacity to bring peace is in question.

Nevertheless, MINUSCA has tried and continues to try to employ other forms of power: inducement and persuasion.

Inducement in MINUSCA

The United Nations and its peacekeepers employ inducement in both direct and indirect forms. They seek to induce changes in behavior by supplying items directly, such as humanitarian assistance and quick impact projects (see Photo 7, p. 184). They also directly take things away, such as the availability of arms in the country. In addition, they seek to change behavior indirectly by building institutions. At the beginning of the MINUSCA mission, the Central African Republic ranked the second-lowest country on the Human Development Index; now it ranks the lowest (UN Development Programme 2017; see also Glawion, de Vries, and Mehler 2018). Central Africans have the lowest GDP in the world, in purchasing power parity (World Bank 2018). The UN's Office for the Coordination of Humanitarian Affairs deems that half of the population is in dire humanitarian need. Given that Central Africans are in great need, inducement might be a winning strategy for changing behavior to decrease violence.

The MINUSCA mission began by employing various innovative, and largely effective, inducement strategies. Many of its staff had prior experience in Central Africa, as well as elsewhere, and were determined to integrate not only the various UN branches but especially Central Africans into the process of rebuilding the country. As one otherwise somewhat cynical UN official remarked, "The idea of integrated missions is finally working here. The UN is not a unified organization, but it's changing. We are much more integrated here than in Haiti, DR Congo, Mali, or South Sudan. The technicalities of integrated missions are overwhelming, but not impossible."[52]

Often in multidimensional peacekeeping missions, the military-oriented peacekeeping wing conflicts with the development wing. With MINUSCA, however, they were structured from the start to work together. The Deputy Special Representative of the Secretary-General (DSRSG) in MINUSCA is also the head of the UN Development Programme offices. As the DSRSG explained, "I consider the UN like a human body. If a body doesn't use all of its parts, it doesn't work

---

[52] Author interview with UN official, Bangui, 1 May 2015.

well. The UN needs to use all of its capacities, especially in justice and development."[53]

Indeed, MINUSCA initiated a wide variety of programs to help in the transition to peace, most notably in rebuilding (or building) the justice sector institutions, and steering people toward work and employment outside of armed groups. The Peacebuilding Fund provided much of the financing, in addition to occasional, direct infusions of capital from France and the United States.

For example, in 2014, the UN estimated that 7,000 fighters would need to be disarmed and reintegrated into society. The mission thus created dozens of "labour-intensive income generating projects for youths at risk in communities affected by armed groups ... to rehabilitate local infrastructure" (S/2015/227, 1 April 2015, para. 32). By early 2016, more than 12,000 young people had directly benefited from these initiatives (S/2016/305, 1 April 2016, para. 15).

The mission was mandated to restore and extend state authority, not only in Bangui but also to the rest of the country. Members of the mission, working directly with Central Africans, labored to rehabilitate dozens of hospitals, prefectures, police stations, courts, and prisons. As MINUSCA's Chief of Field Offices explained: "Local priorities determine our priorities. Our quick impact projects focus on social projects like rebuilding markets to be used by all communities. These projects help re-establish social cohesion."[54]

One of the most important innovations is the Special Criminal Court, composed of 13 national and 12 internationally recruited magistrates (the prosecution office is headed by an international prosecutor) with a mandate to prosecute crimes committed during the violence. Beyond this important institution, one of the key development strategies was to "re-establish the justice system. We have international judges and UNPOL supporting criminal investigations. We have new provisions to protect both the courts and witnesses."[55] These types of projects influence behavior, both directly, by employing people, and indirectly, by building institutions to establish order.

---

[53] Author interview with Aurelien Agbenonci, Deputy Special Representative of the Secretary-General, 8 May 2015.

[54] Author interview with Baboucarr Jagne, Chief of Field Offices, Bangui, 5 May 2015.

[55] Author interview with Adrian Foster, Major General, Deputy Military Adviser, Bangui, 6 May 2015.

MINUSCA's substantial innovations and efficacy in working to induce changes in behavior bore fruit for a couple of years, but recently, the tables are turning. A final source of direct inducement came in the form of arms sanctions and restrictions on trade in natural resources. In 2013, the UN Security Council agreed to a full arms embargo on the Central African Republic, even for the national armed forces, rendering it difficult for all armed groups to acquire weapons and use them against each other or civilians. For natural resources, diamonds were Central Africa's biggest export prior to the conflict, and Central Africa ranked "as the world's 10th-biggest diamond producer by value in 2012" (Koursany 2017). When violent conflict broke out, under the Kimberley Process provisions, Central Africa was prohibited from exporting diamonds. In 2016, some areas were "green-lighted" for diamond mining and exporting.

Central Africa is home to not only important diamond reserves but also gold, oil, timber, and uranium. The uranium for France's first nuclear weapon came from the Central African Republic. The absence of a functioning state coupled with the existence of natural resources are significant drivers of violent conflict. Given MINUSCA's slide downward after the departure of French and American troops in late 2017, Russia requested and was granted permission by the UN Security Council to sell arms to the Central African Government (McGregor 2018). "Russia is now believed to have signed a range of bilateral deals with the government; Russians provide security for President Faustin-Archange Touadéra … a number of militia groups say they have been approached by Russian figures to mediate in conflicts … 'The West has missed the boat,' a western diplomat at the United Nations said. 'The Russians are now everywhere in the CAR state apparatus'" (Hauchard 2018). Thierry Vircoulon, a longtime expert on Central Africa explained: "the state is on its knees, which is for sale … The West is no longer a buyer" (Hauchard 2018). Russia is stepping into the picture, primarily exercising inducement but also coercion (reportedly upwards of 1,000 Russian private military troops have deployed), as well as persuasion, in the form of mediation (McGregor 2018).

In sum, MINUSCA employed a wide and innovative variety of tools to induce changes in behavior away from violence. These efforts were effective for a time, until the absence of an overarching compellent force undermined the projects. In the wake of this unraveling, Russia has stepped in with its own strategies, including all three forms of power: coercion, inducement, and, finally, persuasion.

Persuasion, Civilian Deaths, and Sexual Abuse

I have posited that effective persuasion by an international organization is predicated on three conditions: having a coherent and unified message, behaving according to that message, and understanding how the target audience might receive the message. Even if these conditions are met, international organizations will not necessarily exercise persuasion effectively, because behavior change based on externally directed arguments, leading to ideational change, is intrinsically difficult to realize. Such shifts are all the more difficult to help bring about in a country like the Central African Republic, where rumor abounds, the traditions of popular punishment and vengeance run deep, and the economic situation is so dire that the means of communication are severely limited (i.e., most of the country does not have electricity, and word travels in idiosyncratic ways).

Despite these obstacles, MINUSCA peacekeepers exercised persuasion to the best of their capacities. Before 2016, they had a unified message of peace, justice, and reconciliation. They explained to anyone who would listen that their mandate was to protect civilians. They devised hundreds of trainings and other mechanisms to get their messages across. However, some members of the mission misused their power by sexually abusing the very people they were sent to protect. Moreover, since the departure of French troops, MINUSCA has ventured into urban warfare, most notably in the Sukula battle. The operation thus has an inherent contradiction in its messaging and symbolism. Are UN peacekeepers there to persuade or compel? To help or to inflict punishment? Do they seek to be loved, or feared? Are they there as an impartial presence (to help all), or as counterinsurgents (helping mainly the government)? What are Central Africans supposed to think when they see blue helmets driving in white UN vehicles? The answers to these questions are not obvious. In other words, the basic persuasive message is muddled and thus undermined.

For a time, however, Central African civil society leaders, as well as members of the UN, had made significant progress in convincing Central Africans, and the outside world, that peace is a worthwhile cause. Three important religious leaders – Imam Omar Kobine

Layama, president of the Central African Islamic Community; Dieu-donné Nzapalainga, Archbishop of Bangui; and Nicolas Guéré-koyame-Gbangou, president of the Evangelical Alliance of the Central African Republic – frequently tour together (see, for example, Sullivan and Stigant 2014). In 2014, they were featured in *Time* magazine's 100 most influential people (Wallis 2014). The three have ventured tirelessly throughout Central Africa, encouraging their fol-lowers and others to talk rather than fight; internationally the three have worked to drum up support for peace. Similarly, Pope Francis made Central Africa his first trip to a conflict-ridden country. He visited the main Mosque in the PK5 neighborhood when it was still surrounded by Christian militias. He removed his shoes, bowed to Mecca, and delivered a message of peace and reconciliation: "Together, we must say no to hatred, to revenge and to violence, particularly that violence which is perpetrated in the name of a religion or of God himself. God is peace. *Salaam*" (Nzwili 2015). Throughout PK5, young people wore T-shirts with the Pope's image and shouted, "it's over!" referring to the violence.

The Pope's visit came several months after the momentous Bangui Forum, during which representatives of 9 of 10 armed groups at the time, the three top Central African religious leaders, and 600 other influential people in Central African politics and society came together to work out a path forward. They adopted the "Republican Pact for Peace, National Reconciliation and Reconstruction in the Central African Republic" as well as a plan for "Disarmament, Demobilisa-tion, Rehabilitation and Repatriation" (DDRR) (S/2015/344). Profes-sor Abdoulaye Bathily, Special Representative of the United Nations Secretary-General for Central Africa, convened the forum.

In addition to Bathily's work, since its deployment in 2014, MINUSCA staff have conducted hundreds of trainings on topics such as mediation and conflict-resolution practices, human-rights monitor-ing, investigation and reporting, security and respect for prisoners' rights, how to conduct elections, legal trainings, and a variety of other conflict-reducing techniques (S/2015/227, 1 April 2015, para. 42; S/206/305, 1 April 2016; S/2016/824, 29 September 2016, paras. 48–50). MINUSCA conducted a large-scale "awareness-raising cam-paign on human rights, focusing on peace and social cohesion between communities, due process, and the role and importance of the judiciary, with more than 2,500 participants from civil society, including

university students, community leaders and community members"
(S/2015/576, 29 July 2015, para. 37). In 2016, the trainings began to
shift toward the police and gendarmerie "with the aim of strengthening
judicial police skills, investigation techniques, community policing and
responses to gender-based violence" (S/2016/824, 29 September 2016,
para. 43). As part of its efforts to include everyone in the country,
MINUSCA devised a radio station, Radio Guira, and expanded its reach
outside of Bangui to include Bambari, Bria, and Kaga Bandoro (S/2015/
227, 1 April 2015, para. 58). As a top military advisor explained to me:
"Peacekeeping is about teaching a population to change its behavior."[56]

As an observer of peacekeepers, I have witnessed them in Central
Africa protecting civilians by maintaining their positions in contentious
areas, watching (surveilling), and, when tensions arise, *mediating*.
A MINUSCA spokesperson explained: "We are trying to create a
new ambience in the country, trying to instill hope and confidence in
the future."[57] In sum, MINUSCA was making a concerted, creative,
and multi-faceted effort at exercising effective persuasion (see Photo 8,
p. 184).

However, sexual abuse – and deaths at the hand of the UN – as well
as the UN's response to these harms, worked to undercut the message
of peace, justice, and reconciliation. Although UN peacekeepers have
sexually abused civilians, the initial story of "UN sexual abuse" had
nothing to do with UN peacekeepers. Rather, it was Sangaris forces,
operating under an entirely separate chain of command from the UN,
before UN peacekeepers ever deployed to the country, who were
accused of "repeated acts of sexual violence reportedly committed
between December 2013 and May 2014 ... in and around the M'Poko
camp for internally displaced persons" (S/2016/133, 12 February
2016, para. 49). During the summer of 2015, reports of French Sangaris soldiers exchanging sex with children for food and water – in
other words, the systematic and repeated sexual abuse of minors in
need – came to light. However, the story reported in most major
Anglophone publications, including the *New York Times*, blamed the
United Nations for the abuse, repeating in nearly one dozen stories
the phrase "French peacekeepers" (see, for example, Sengupta 2015a,

---

[56] Author interview with Adrian Foster, Major General, Deputy Military Adviser,
Bangui, 4 May 2015.
[57] Author interview with Hamamadoun Tourre, Bangui, 9 May 2015.

2015b, 2015c). "French peacekeeper," however, was not a reality at that time: there were French special forces under a French chain of command, and, only several months later, United Nations peacekeepers under their own, separate command. The story of "French peacekeeper abuse" took on sensational proportions, including reports that defy the imagination, such as one widely retold story about troops tying up girls to a tree and forcing them to have sexual intercourse with a dog (Code Blue 2016).

The stories of abuse caught fire and were repeated in dozens of publications. UN peacekeepers were accused of both rape and killing civilians. In the summer of 2015, Amnesty International reported that during a shootout over an arrest in PK5, some UN peacekeepers killed several civilians, while another UN peacekeeper raped a 12-year-old girl (Amnesty International 2015). The MINUSCA spokesman at the time, Hamadoun Touré, fed the fire by reportedly telling a journalist from *Foreign Policy* magazine during a phone interview that in his "personal opinion, the allegation of rape is not credible. When peacekeepers arrived … they were attacked immediately with heavy, heavy weapons … I'm sorry, but I don't think someone would think of raping someone at this time. I think they will think of how to escape. He will think, 'I'm a human being before I'm a man.' When you're under fire, I think you think of saving your life. Really, really, really in this situation you don't think of a girl" (Wolfe 2013). This response infuriated many readers, mainly outside of the Central African Republic.

The reputation of the entire United Nations was at stake (Gowan 2015a). Under pressure, especially from the United States' UN Ambassador, Samantha Power, in August 2015, UN Secretary-General Ban Ki-moon fired his Special Representative and head of MINUSCA, Babacar Gaye (among others). Never before in the history of UN peacekeeping had a Special Representative been fired. The Secretary-General appointed the former Deputy Director of US Homeland Security, Dr. Jane Holl-Lute, to serve as Special Coordinator on improving the United Nations response to sexual exploitation and abuse (SG/A/1634, 8 February 2016). But allegations of rape by UN peacekeepers did not end, and by then, instances of abuse perpetrated by individuals who were indeed UN peacekeepers (as opposed to French special forces) became apparent.

The United Nations now keeps track of, and makes public, all accusations of sexual abuse and exploitation in all missions, as well as the status in the investigative process (pending, unsubstantiated, substantiated), the nationality of the accused, and which body is overseeing the investigation – the country that sent the peacekeeper, the UN's Office of Internal Oversight, or both. According the UN's records, since MINUSCA deployed in 2014, the mission has received 98 allegations of sexual exploitation and abuse (SEA), more than half of which (52) came in 2016 (UN Conduct in Field Missions 2018; S/206/305, 1 April 2016, para. 60). Since then, even as reporting mechanisms have improved, the number of allegations has decreased. MINUSCA has devised a variety of programs to report abuse, compensate victims, train peacekeepers in sexual misconduct awareness, and has implemented strict non-fraternization policies (S/2018/125, 15 February 2018, para. 68–69). The number of allegations for 2018 as of midway through the year is five (there are some 14,000 UN personnel in the Central African Republic). Individual troops from 13 different countries have been accused of SEA. Because UN member states have not permitted the UN to devise its own forms of internal accountability mechanisms, the greatest punishment the UN can inflict on abusers is to send them home; in some cases, in the Central African Republic and elsewhere, entire battalions have been sent home. The legacy of sexual abuse and exploitation weigh heavily on the citizens of the Central Africa Republic, and on MINUSCA. It is an understatement to say that the mission's persuasive power is deeply diminished by its prior history in this domain and each time an act of sexual abuse or exploitation is committed.

Conclusion

The United Nations Stabilization Mission in the Central African Republic began with great hope and promise. In a land beset by underdevelopment and very low-level violence until recently, UN staff aspired to great transformation. The mission innovated in important ways. By putting military battalions under police command, it employed the power of arrest as a way to reduce violence, the circulation of small arms, and crime, especially in Bangui. By integrating development and peacekeeping, it used the power of inducement to jump-start the economy, and build institutions of justice. The mission also had a unified and persuasive message of peace – one that was supported by influential thought-leaders both in and outside of the Central African Republic. But each of these levers of power could not hold without some form of compellence against the rise and splintering of armed groups. Sangaris possessed and used its compellent power effectively, until it departed. Similarly, American and Ugandan forces in the eastern part of the country had a military-based deterrent effect. Since their departures, armed groups have gained control of approximately 80 percent of the country.[58]

As of mid-2018, the national military, the FACA, is reported to be the most trusted institution of the Central African state.[59] The European Union is in charge of FACA training, and it hopes to establish a 9,800-strong force by 2021 (SC/13220, 22 February, 2018). Because of UNSC weapons sanctions, the FACA remain largely unarmed, although Russia has secured a UNSC exemption to provide weapons to the FACA. The Central African government controls only the area around the capital city of Bangui; it is desperately trying to take steps to secure itself with Russian and UN assistance. The main opposition force, the *Front Populaire pour la Renaissance de la Centrafrique* is growing in strength and has control over nearly half of the country; other groups control another 30 percent or so. A new "Africa Initiative," led by African Union powers, has held consultations with FPRC leaders to restart a dialogue. Russia and Sudan are also mediating. Meanwhile, child soldier recruitment is on the rise (Losh 2018). Civilians are dying and fleeing their homes. Some warn of an impending all-out war between the government and the FPRC.[60]

Turning over the reins of governing to local actors in early elections has not had the hoped-for results. The recent turn of events demonstrates that UN peacekeepers are incapable of supplying compellent-based security guarantees. The UN was, for a time, effective at leveraging its bases of power, through the coercive power of arrest, community-oriented inducement programs, and persuasion. Together with the compellent force of Sangaris and others from 2014 to 2016, external actors were helping Central Africa to tip the balance toward peace. But since the compellent forces departed, the scales have tipped in the other direction. The future remains uncertain.

Coercion is the least-preferred type of power employed by the United Nations. Indeed, the body was designed precisely to decrease the

[58] "Thematic Brainstorming for MINUSCA's Strategic Review." United Nations, Department of Peacekeeping Operations, 20 June 2018.
[59] Ibid.
[60] Informal social media communication with colleague in Bangui, 27 June 2018.

reliance on coercion in international politics. That said, UN peacekeepers do employ some types of coercion effectively. They may deter (though their deterrent effect is often not military based). Peacekeepers also defend (by warding off attack) and surveil, as ways of exerting power to decrease acts of violence. In the case of the Central African Republic, peacekeepers have also successfully employed the power of arrest. What peacekeepers in the Central African Republic and elsewhere do not possess is a compellent or offensive military capacity. Other entities – especially single-state militaries – are designed to compel. Militaries may also deter, defend, and surveil, but their primary means of coercion lies in the capacity and resolve to use offensive force. The UN peacekeepers, by design, do not physically possess this capacity, nor is there a consensus – nor, by extension, the resolve – to have the United Nations develop and exercise this form of coercion.

Photo 1 Persuasion in Namibia: Training and Symbolic Display
Special Representative Martti Ahtisaari (second right), and Deputy Special Representative for UNTAG, Joesph T. Legwaila, visit the ballot-counting center at the Windhoek Showgrounds. UNTAG election experts help train, while Ahtisaari and Legwaila symbolize interracial cooperation.
Windhoek, Namibia
UN Photo # 262883 Milton Grant, 1989

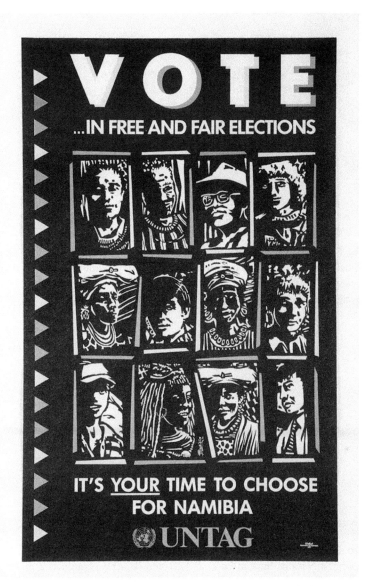

Photo 2 Persuasion in Namibia: Public Information and Symbolic Display
Linocuts of Namibian faces/ethnic groups. *Vote … in free and fair elections: it's your time to choose for NAMIBIA* poster.
Canadian War Museum 19890335–026, 1989

Photo 3 Inducement in Lebanon: Aid
Medical staff from the Italian battalion of UNIFIL provide wellness checkups in free weekly clinic.
Copyright Mathieu Pansard and Pierre-Olivier François, 2015

Photo 4 Inducement in Lebanon: Institution Building
The United Nations Interim Force in Lebanon (UNIFIL) conducts a maritime exercise off the coast of southern Lebanon with the incipient Lebanese Navy. Naqoura, Lebanon
UN Photo # 167846 Jorge Aramburu, 2008

Photo 5 Coercion in the Central African Republic: Compellence
French "Sangaris" Special Forces on tank patrol in downtown Bangui, Central
African Republic.
Photo taken by the author, 2015

Photo 6 Coercion in the Central African Republic: Surveillance and Arrest
The Congo-Brazzaville battalion on patrol with a rusted anti-aircraft gun bolted
to the back of a white UN pick-up truck. Near Mbaiki, Central African Republic.
Photo taken by the author, 2015

Photo 7 Inducement in the Central African Republic: Aid and Institution Building
UNDP-MINUSCA help to build a youth community center in the Boy-Rabe
neighborhood of Bangui.
Copyright Pierre-Olivier François, 2015

Photo 8 Persuasion in the Central African Republic: Outreach and Mediation
MINUSCA Police Commissioner Luis Carrhilo talks with residents of the PK5
neighborhood.
Copyright Mathieu Pansard and Pierre-Olivier François, 2015

5 | *Toward a More Effective Use of Power in Peacekeeping*

The most surprising fact about UN peacekeeping is that it is generally effective. Peacekeepers are not sent to the easy places – they deploy where no other states or organizations are willing or able to help and where prospects for peace are low (Doyle and Sambanis 2006; Fortna 2008; Gilligan and Stedman 2003; Kathman and Wood 2014; Melander 2009). And yet, of the most complex, concluded missions, two-thirds have succeeded at implementing their mandates (Dobbins et al. 2005; Howard 2008; Chapter 1 of this book). The evidence is overwhelming that peacekeepers reduce civilian and military casualties, contain the spread of conflict both within and across borders, end civil wars, and prevent their recurrence (Beardsley and Gleditsch 2015; Bove and Ruggeri 2016; Carnegie and Mikulaschek 2018; Doyle and Sambanis 2006; Fjelde, Hultman, and Nilsson 2019; Fortna 2008; Hultman, Kathman, and Shannon 2013, 2014; Kathman 2011; Melander 2009; Ruggeri, Dorussen, and Gizelis 2012, 2017). No other form of international intervention has enjoyed such a record.

At the same time, however, peacekeeping is not without its problems. International peacekeepers and peacebuilders suffer from misunderstanding and even disrespect toward the societies and cultures in which they work, inadequately seeking local input, failing to act impartially, establishing routines and structures that undermine purported goals, failing to learn, forcing political and economic liberalization too quickly, trying to implement lengthy and ill-fitting mandates, sexually exploiting and abusing people, and otherwise misusing their power (Autesserre 2010, 2014; Barnett and Finnemore 2004; von Billerbeck 2017; Campbell 2017; Caplan 2005; de Coning 2011; Donais 2009; Howard 2008; Karlsrud 2018; de Vries 2015). These problems contribute to, but are not the sole cause of, the essential troubles in today's largest UN peacekeeping efforts, sometimes referred to as the "big five" in the Central African Republic, the Democratic Republic of the Congo, Darfur (in Sudan), Malí, and South Sudan. Peacekeepers in the big five have not been able to consistently work toward fulfilling their mandates and depart.[1] Too many civilians and peacekeepers are dying. How might peacekeeping become more effective?

"Identifying where leverage lies" is a first step toward improving peacekeeping (Landgren 2018). In this book, I have delineated and demonstrated the three basic ways in which peacekeepers exercise power. Power is the ability of one actor to change the behavior of another. By better understanding the essential forms of how peacekeepers change behavior, it might be possible to improve peacekeeping. As I have shown, peacekeepers persuade, induce, and coerce. I have explored a positive case of each form of power in Namibia, Lebanon, and the Central African Republic (the last also serves as a negative case of all three). I highlight observable implications of the causal mechanisms in each case. Nowhere – not in these cases nor anywhere else – have peacekeepers provided military-based security guarantees as the main cause of their effectiveness in keeping the peace. Actual militaries may legitimately and effectively employ compellence, but not peacekeepers. Peacekeepers effectively and legitimately use other types of power.

I structure this concluding chapter in four parts. First, I recap the basic steps in my argument and evidence. Second, I review the scholarly literature on nonviolence and counterinsurgency and what makes the two strategies effective, and I relate the main findings to what I see emerging in peacekeeping. Third, I lay out the instances where peacekeeping (nonviolent) and military (violent) forces functioned in tandem with positive results. Finally, I survey recent ideas about peacekeeping reform and explain why moves toward making UN peacekeeping more "robust" will most likely decrease effectiveness.

Summary of Argument and Evidence

In this book, I delineate three ideal types of power in peacekeeping and match each with a positive case (and one negative case for all three). The three primary forms of power are persuasion, which is nonmaterial (mediating, shaming, displaying symbols, training), alongside the two material forms – inducement (giving aid, restricting markets, and building institutions) and coercion (forcing compliance in a variety of

[1] The African Union–led mission in Somalia is also proving slow to progress.

ways, not only through compellence). Each chapter explores a peace-keeping mission that effectively employed a different form of power.

Persuasion

Persuasion is the power of nonmaterial factors to change behavior. It is a social process of interaction that occurs in the absence of overt material inducements or coercion. I contend that UN peacekeepers may employ persuasion in five basic forms. Most of the time, when confronted with obstacles, peacekeepers *mediate* to prevent disputes from escalating. In all peacekeeping missions, troops and civilians, from the top of command structures to the very bottom, engage in this essential mechanism of persuasion. Peacekeepers may also employ the key psychological motivator of *shame* when positive-sum mediation techniques fail. Additionally, peacekeepers engage in numerous *symbolic displays* that are intended to convey their message of peace (e.g., by patrolling in white vehicles and wearing blue hats). *Outreach and information dissemination* is a fourth mechanism of persuasion, whereby peacekeepers engage directly with people in local communities to understand their needs and convey the intentions of peacekeepers; strategic information is also increasingly centralized and disseminated at higher levels via the UN's Department of Peacekeeping Operations. Finally, peacekeepers increasingly rely on *education and training* programs that aim to persuade the peacekept to behave differently. Ultimately, persuasion is difficult to achieve and is only effective when peacekeepers agree on their central political message, understand very well the targets of their messaging, and behave in ways consistent with their message.

I provide an example of the effective use of persuasion in the United Nations Transition Group, which deployed to Namibia in the April of 1989. This was the first of the UN's post–Cold War, complex missions. At that time, in what was then called South West Africa, there was no peace to keep and no formal peace accord because South Africa and its supporters in Namibia would not share a table with the South West African People's Organization. Namibia was emerging from decades of multiple abusive colonial rulers, including 40 years of apartheid, regional war, and civil war. With abundant natural resources, Namibia is prone to be resource cursed. All arrows point toward deep and continuous violence. The leaders of UNTAG set out to aid Namibia's transition to peace and democracy with few resources, few peacekeeping troops, and a lot of civilians with good ideas. Because the mission did not have other means and because its leader (eventual Nobel Peace Prize winner H. E. Martti Ahtisaari), had been working with Namibians toward Namibian independence for more than a decade before the mission began, he and his staff were able to invent creative ways to persuade people on all sides to go along with the transition to peace and democracy. The mission employed all five of the mechanisms of persuasion I have delineated – mediation, shame, symbolic displays, outreach, and education and training. Their messages were clear (although sometimes they had to re-calibrate when they were not), the peacekeepers understood their target audience well because they included Namibians in their efforts, and they aligned message and behavior. Namibia today is not without problems, but it remains at peace, with a stable government and a growing economy; its literacy rates have moved from less than 40 percent to greater than 80 percent in one generation. Using the power of persuasion, UNTAG proved successful, and its effects endure.

Inducement

I delineate inducement as the second form of power in peacekeeping. It is a broad category, encompassing at least four basic, material mechanisms to change behavior. These include, first, the carrots of QIPs, humanitarian and development *aid,* and trust funds. Second, *market restrictions* in the form of weapons bans, mineral trade restrictions, and economic sanctions. Third, building municipal, electoral, legal, military, and other *institutions*. Fourth and finally, the overarching *peacekeeping economy* that develops around large, long-standing international missions, with both positive and negative, largely unintended effects. All peacekeeping missions employ elements of inducement in order to keep the peace. Effective, intentional inducement is predicated on the external party having the means to induce, coordinating inducements with a persuasive/political strategy, and understanding the potential effects (both intended and unintended) of the inducement strategy. An example of the UN's effective use of the power of inducement can be found in Lebanon.

The UN's "Interim Force" in Lebanon has been anything but interim. It deployed to southern Lebanon more than 40 years ago, in

1978, in the midst of a brutal civil war that featured 36 warring factions vying to control an underdeveloped territory with little if any state infrastructure; the factions were also fighting (against or alongside) neighboring Israeli forces. Into this morass, the UN Security Council decided, at the behest of the United States, to deploy several thousand lightly armed UN peacekeepers and almost no civilian staff. UNIFIL's mandate was to oversee the withdrawal of Israeli forces, restore peace and security to the region, and assist the Government of Lebanon in extending state structures to the south. In 2006, after the most recent of several Israeli invasions, the mandate and mission were augmented by several thousand European (NATO) troops.

Over time, neither UNIFIL – nor anyone else – has managed to persuade Lebanon and Israel (or Hezbollah) to make peace. Neither does UNIFIL possess a compellent capacity – the Israeli Defense Forces and Hezbollah are capable of defeating UNIFIL's multinational troops at any moment. And yet, UNIFIL has been implementing its mandate. After 22 years, the Israeli forces withdrew, southern Lebanon remains at peace despite the civil war raging next door in Syria, and state structures are slowly developing in UNIFIL's areas of operation. UNIFIL has become effective at implementing its mandate not by providing security guarantees but by *inducing* parties to cooperate.[2] UNIFIL troops and civilians provide humanitarian and development aid in a wide variety of forms, including QIPs and other projects. While they cannot restrict Hezbollah's weapons or disarm the group, they render it difficult for anyone to display their arms, in part through coercion, in the form of surveillance, and in part through persuasion, through mediating and shaming. UNIFIL troops have helped to build or create state institutions in the south – most notably the Lebanese Armed Forces. Finally, the UN has become the largest employer in southern Lebanon. Although most studies of the "peacekeeping economy" explore the negative externalities of the presence of massive numbers of internationals, in the case of Lebanon, many observers contend that the UN's economic presence is beneficial and has provided meaningful opportunities for local economic development. Through a variety of

---

[2] In Chapter 3, I also explore the unarmed UN observers in Lebanon – UNTSO. These highly ranked troops only exercise the power of persuasion, and have been doing so fairly effectively for 70 years.

mechanisms – some of which are not specified in its mandate – UNIFIL effectively exercises the power of inducement.

Coercion

The third and final type of power in peacekeeping is coercion. Coercion is about restricting choice. Military-based coercion lies in using or threatening to use force in order to gain compliance, and has five basic forms. First, as delineated by Thomas Shelling and elaborated by Robert Art, militaries exercise *compellence* through the kinetic, active, preemptive, or preventive use of force. What distinguishes peacekeepers from other military forces is that, by their very nature, peacekeepers do not have the capability to compel (even if they may have the legal authority to do so). Second, when a military force possesses a second-strike capacity, it may also deter attack. *Deterrence* is about preventing attack through fear of retribution. Peacekeepers generally exercise deterrence not through military might but, rather, through inducement and persuasion. Potential attackers may decide not to attack because they fear potential economic or political consequences, but not the destructive wrath of UN peacekeepers. Third, peacekeepers and military troops alike exercise *defense*. Troops of all sorts may defend themselves and vulnerable populations. The military means necessary for warding off an attack and defending a position or civilians are lower than for exercising compellence or military-based deterrence; peacekeepers have always had this capacity. Fourth, all troops – military and peacekeepers – exercise the coercive power of *surveillance*. Observation or surveillance by patrolling and gathering information/ intelligence is one of the key forms of coercion in both peacekeeping and military action. Finally, sometimes UN peacekeepers are endowed by the UN Security Council with the power of *arrest*, as in the Central African Republic.

    Central Africa plunged into violent conflict in late 2012, when the Muslim-majority Séléka rebels swept over the country and took the capital, Bangui, in a violent and bloody coup. Approximately one year later, dozens of mainly Christian neighborhood-watch groups formed, began fighting, and retook the capital in even bloodier retribution. French stabilization forces entered the fray in late 2013 and effectively stabilized this vast and resource-rich country (larger than the size of metropolitan France, but with only 4.5 million people). In 2014, peacekeepers in the United Nations Multidimensional Integrated Stabilization Mission in the Central African Republic set about effectively deploying their means of power: *persuading* people to stop fighting through mediation, outreach, and training efforts, *inducing* by providing aid and building institutions, and *exercising coercion* by using the power of arrest, surveillance, and defense, but not attempting compellence. When rebels attacked civilians, French special forces would attack back. (American special forces, alongside members of the Ugandan military, were deployed in the southeast, on the hunt for the notorious warlord Joseph Kony. They did not have a mandate to stabilize Central Africa, but their presence served as an effective deterrent in preventing armed groups from attacking.) From 2014 to 2016, this division of labor worked well. Peacekeepers were keeping the peace by using the power of persuasion, inducement, and coercion (short of compellence), while actual military forces were effectively exercising compellence and deterrence – i.e., providing security guarantees. For two years, the death rates plunged, refugees and displaced people were returning home, the economy was growing, and Central Africans elected a popular former professor of math as their president.

But then it came to light that some French troops had abused their power by exchanging aid for sex with children on a regular basis in a camp for displaced persons. The French mission, which was supposed to end anyway, departed in a cloud of shame in late 2016. While the UN was incorrectly blamed for the French sexual abuse, it also came to light that individuals from several UN battalions were engaging in sexual abuse and exploitation of the very people they were sent to protect. Then in early 2017, President Trump called the American special forces (and Ugandans) home for budgetary reasons. Following the departure of the French and US forces, since the Central African government had not yet reestablished its own armed forces, UN peacekeepers were mandated to assume the task of compellence. Peacekeepers, however, were not designed – in principle or in practice – to exercise compellence. Their efforts have been faltering. An attempt at forcibly disarming a militia in the Muslim-majority PK5 neighborhood of Bangui in April 2018 went horribly wrong, resulting in the deaths of nearly three dozen civilians (and one peacekeeper). Demonstrators then laid many of the corpses at the front gates of the UN's main peacekeeping base in a symbolic gesture highlighting the extent to which MINUSCA was losing its powers of coercion and persuasion.

In the summer of 2018, armed groups mobilized and came to control more than 80 percent of the territory. Russia has stepped in to attempt to help stabilize. This case demonstrates how violent and nonviolent international actors may effectively stabilize a volatile situation and then lose control when UN peacekeepers assume the task of compellence.

Peacekeeping, Nonviolence, and Counterinsurgency

Peacekeeping is a form of intervention that is grounded in three doctrinal principles. The first is *impartiality* on the part of the peacekeepers. Peacekeepers do not take sides, and they hail from dozens of different countries (usually non-P-5) in order to credibly maintain impartiality. They are not neutral (they will call out violations of peace accords and the laws of war), but, like a judge in a court of law, they are supposed to behave impartially. Second is the *consent* of the peacekept. Peacekeeping cannot function without active consent and local input. The third and final principle is the *nonuse of force*, except in self-defense (and, more recently, in defense of the mandate). These principles were derived from insights of the nonviolent decolonization movements of the 1930s, 1940s, and 1950s, where eschewing the use of force proved effective in bringing about social change. The principles still appear at the front of the UN's peacekeeping website today (United Nations 2018a).

Impartiality, consent, and the nonuse of force are what separate peacekeeping from other forms of military intervention. The principles run in diametric opposition to the doctrine and practice of modern counterinsurgency, which is by definition partial (counterinsurgents take the side of the government); counterinsurgents do not seek the consent of the insurgents; and, most importantly, counterinsurgency relies on compellence as its central means of power. I lay out here some of the main scholarly findings about the sources of effectiveness in nonviolence and counterinsurgency and relate them to peacekeeping.

Nonviolent resistance is "a technique of socio-political action for applying power in a conflict without the use of violence" (Sharp 1999, 567). Nonviolence was developed primarily by Mohandas Gandhi in the 1920s as a method to confront unjust regimes. His challenges to British rule eventually resulted in Indian independence and inspired many similar movements, most notably the American civil rights movement. Based on an extensive dataset comparing violent and nonviolent movements, Erica Chenoweth and Maria Stephan have found that since the early days of nonviolence in practice, "nonviolent resistance has been strategically superior to violent resistance" (2011 17). Although violence may grant rebels an invitation to participate in negotiations and gain concessions (Thomas 2014), much of the literature on the efficacy of violence (including in terrorism) builds on or echoes Chenoweth and Stephan's basic findings about the utility of nonviolence (Abrahms 2006; Chenoweth and Schock 2015; Cunningham 2013; Cunningham et al. 2017; Dudouet 2013; Fortna 2015; Karakaya 2018). Chenoweth and Stephan contend that the mechanism behind the effectiveness of a nonviolent strategy is that it enables more people to participate in and support the movement (2013, chapter 2). This insight – that it is easier for a population to support a nonviolent actor – is important for understanding mechanisms of support and persuasion in peacekeeping, and why peacekeeping was created in the first place (Bunche 1950; Urquhart 1987, 1998).

Although nonviolence has certainly proven an important tool for bringing about peaceful change, no modern society – even free and democratic – has managed to remain peaceful without some sort of coercive state apparatus that holds final authority over control and order (Hobbes 1651/2017; Huntington 1957; Kalyvas 2006; Weber 1978). Based on this insight, coercion is the main lever of power applied by counterinsurgents. Counterinsurgency takes the opposite approach of nonviolence in that it seeks to reestablish state order and control through compellence. Counterinsurgency – whether waged by a domestic government or external forces – seeks to control violence by monopolizing it. There are two basic paradigms in counterinsurgency doctrine and research: the "enemy-centric" and the "population-centric" (Pampinella 2015). The debate about the effectiveness of these two models has proven inconclusive, and both sides have merit.

Proponents of the "enemy-centric" paradigm argue for the efficacy of employing overwhelming force in order to defeat an enemy, even if it may entail brutality against civilians (Arreguín-Toft 2001; Boot 2003; Gentile 2013; Hazelton 2017; Porch 2013). In contrast, the population-centric approach, also sometimes referred to as the "hearts and minds" or "good governance" theory, focuses more on political dimensions of counterinsurgency and the hypothesized need to protect and win over civilians (Byman 2006; Galula 1963, 1964; Jardine and Palamar 2013;

Nagl 2005; Paul et al. 2016; Paul, Clarke, and Grill 2010; Petraeus 2010; Ricks 2009; United States Army et al. 2006). Both schools acknowledge the centrality of compellence as the essential form of power in counterinsurgency, and both address the problematic question of efficacy in counterinsurgency – historically, most efforts have failed, and the rate of failure has been increasing over the last 100 or so years, as war has become more mechanized (Lyall and Wilson 2009).

Although it is not explicit, many scholars in the population-centric school imply that counterinsurgency will become more effective the more it comes to resemble complex UN peacekeeping. In Afghanistan and Iraq, counterinsurgents have increasingly assumed some of the elements that enabled peacekeepers to enjoy greater legitimacy, such as diversifying the number of troop contributors (i.e., making the mission more multilateral) and seeking to treat domestic groups impartially. The "hearts and minds" theory of counterinsurgency also draws on an assumption of legitimacy through inducement, or service delivery (Berman, Shapiro, and Felter 2011). Karsten Friis has pointed out that modern peacekeeping and counterinsurgency share six essential similarities of the purported need to (1) encourage civilian local solutions, (2) protect civilians, (3) `integrate and unify a wide variety of international actors, (4) seek host nation ownership, (5) use intelligence to support operations, and (6) use force judiciously (Friis 2010, 50). In other words, counterinsurgents are adopting some key elements of complex UN peacekeeping. At the same time, peacekeeping missions have increasingly been mandated by the UN Security Council under Chapter VII of the UN Charter to use force (Howard and Dayal 2018). The upshot is that the current "big five" complex UN peacekeeping mandates are increasingly resembling counterinsurgency efforts in Afghanistan and Iraq. Given the records of all of these missions, conflating peacekeeping and counterinsurgency does not appear to be a winning strategy. Dividing violent and nonviolent international actors, however, has proven effective.

Peacekeeping and Ad Hoc Military Intervention

Since the early 2000s, on occasion, the UN Security Council has authorized small, ad hoc military interventions in order to secure the peace, often working in tandem with large UN peacekeeping missions (see Table 5.1). These interventions, dubbed "peace enforcement"

Table 5.1 *Completed Multidimensional UN Peacekeeping Operations with Ad Hoc Military Assistance*

Number	Country and Mission	Year PKO Ended	Military Intervention in Tandem with UN PKO
SUCCESSFUL			
1	Namibia UNTAG	1990	
2	Cambodia (mixed success) UNTAC	1993	
3	Mozambique UNMOZ	1994	
4	El Salvador	1995	
5	Guatemala	1997	NATO
6	E. Slavonia/Croatia	1998	
7	Timor Leste	2002	INTERFET (Australia)
8	Sierra Leone	2005	British Special Forces, ECOMOG
9	Burundi (mixed success)	2006	African Union
10	Cote d'Ivoire	2017	French Infantry, Air Force
11	Liberia	2018	American Marines, ECOMOG
UNSUCCESSFUL			
1	Somalia	1993	United States
2	Angola	1993	
3	Rwanda	1994	France
4	Bosnia (Srebrenica)	1995	NATO
5	Haiti	2017	

missions, have generally been conducted by single states or small coalitions of the willing. They are not massive efforts at counterinsurgency. And because they use compellence, they look and function differently from UN peacekeepers.[3]

Examples of successful, completed missions include the operations of the British Special Forces to defeat the Revolutionary United Front

[3] As we see in Photo 5 (p. 183), standard military troops prefer camouflage colors – they do not wear blue helmets or travel in white vehicles – in a symbolic display that situates them as coercive actors and not UN peacekeepers.

in Sierra Leone, the United States Marines stationed off the coast of Monrovia to help stabilize Liberia, the French Special Operations in the Central African Republic and Côte d'Ivoire, and the Australian-led coalition in Timor Leste. The regional organizations have also often played the role of peace enforcer, such as NATO in Bosnia-Herzegovina and Kosovo, the Economic Community of West African States Monitoring Group (ECOMOG) in Liberia and Sierra Leone, and the African Union in Burundi. Generally speaking, single states, small coalitions, and regional organizations have proven fairly successful at peace enforcement. In the five most recent of the UN's successfully completed multidimensional missions – Eastern Slavonia, Timor Leste, Sierra Leone, Burundi, and Côte d'Ivoire – UN peacekeepers deployed after, or in tandem with, regular military forces. This partnership worked well in these cases. The unsuccessful cases in the early-to-mid-1990s of US forces in Somalia, French in Rwanda, and NATO in Bosnia all share the common denominator of not effectively coordinating with UN peacekeeping efforts (Howard 2008, chapter 2). Although we see this division of labor employed successfully in a number of places, this trend has not been highlighted in the recent peacekeeping reform proposals. Instead, most proposals blur the distinctions between military and peacekeeping action.

UN Peacekeeping Reforms

The original doctrines of peacekeeping and counterinsurgency differ in fundamental ways, and complex peacekeeping missions have proven effective when backed by even a small number of actual military forces. However, trends in the practice of both peacekeeping and counter-insurgency fail to acknowledge the fundamental strengths and weaknesses of each form of intervention, opting instead to blend the two. UN peacekeeping proposals of the last 20 or so years have conflated, rather than clarified, the issue. These proposals include the Rwanda, Srebrenica, and Brahimi Reports; the High-Level Independent Panel on Peace Operations (HIPPO) Report; the Kigali Principles and the Cruz Report; and, the most recent, the Action for Peacekeeping (A4P) initiative. The reports are far-reaching and too lengthy to summarize in a comprehensive way here. They offer numerous excellent suggestions and avenues of reform, such as enabling preventive action, incorporating local perspectives, and bettering peacekeeping training. Rather than attempting a comprehensive summary, I highlight the key refrain of increasing "robustness" in contemporary peacekeeping as a continuous theme.

After the devastating peacekeeping failures leading to genocide in Rwanda in 1994, and the genocidal massacres in Srebrenica and several other towns in Bosnia in 1995, UN Secretary-General Kofi Annan called for a deep rethink of peacekeeping. In 1999, he commissioned soul-search critiques of the tragedies in Rwanda and Bosnia, as well as the Brahimi Report – the first major review of UN peacekeeping in history. All of these reports took UN peacekeeping failures as their main objects of study. Among numerous recommendations, they suggested that "traditional" peacekeeping doctrine and practices were no match for current civil wars, and that multidimensional peacekeeping should become more "robust," despite the numerous (unexamined) examples of successful missions that did not employ compellence (A/55/305, 21 August 2000, paras. 48–50). The Brahimi report emphasized that "mandates should specify an operation's authority to use force ... with better equipped [peacekeepers], able to be a credible deterrent" (A/55/305, 21 August 2000, x). Since that time, all complex peacekeeping missions have been *mandated* by the UN Security Council to use force, even though they are still *not structured or equipped* to serve as a compellent or deterrent military force (Howard and Dayal 2018).

The next major evaluation of UN peacekeeping, the 2015 HIPPO report, acknowledges that "clarity is needed on the use of force" in peacekeeping (A/70/95 17 June 2015, 12). The authors recognize "the well-known capability limits of United Nations forces and the potential that those limits may be ruthlessly exposed" (A/70/95, 17 June 2015, para. 118). But the report does not clarify who the authors think *ought* to use force. On the one hand, maybe it is regular militaries (para. 118), but on the other, the authors assert that "Different threats must be met with the appropriate use of military force, ranging from containment via deterrence and coercion to direct confrontation ... attackers [must] perceive and know United Nations troops have the determination and capabilities to respond forcefully in case of attack" (para. 128). In other words, because military-based deterrence is contingent on an effective compellent capacity, perhaps peacekeepers should move beyond defense, and toward an offensive, compellent posture.

The Kigali Principles of 2015 and the Cruz Report of 2017 take the notion of peacekeepers using compellence a step further. The Kigali Principles were promoted by Paul Kagame, the former military leader–turned–political ruler of Rwanda, and former US Ambassador to the United Nations, Samantha Power, with the goal of better protecting civilians (High-Level Conference on the Protection of Civilians 2015). Of the 18 principles, key changes lie in 3, 8, and 13, whereby peacekeepers pledge "to be prepared to use force to protect civilians"; "not to hesitate to take action to protect civilians"; and "to take disciplinary action against our own personnel if and when they fail to act to protect civilians." In other words, if peacekeepers do not use proactive force to protect civilians, they could be relieved of duty. In everyday peacekeeping, the principles encourage tactical uses of force that directly contradict the original three principles of peacekeeping.

Furthering the trend, the Cruz Report, spearheaded by retired Lt. Gen. Carlos Alberto dos Santos Cruz, pushes peacekeeping more explicitly toward counterinsurgency, with the goal of better protecting UN peacekeeping troops (who died in higher numbers in 2017 than in previous years). The report recommends "changing the mindset ... beliefs and values" of experienced troop contributors who are "gripped by a Chapter VI syndrome of traditional" peacekeeping to "new [troop contributors who] are normally receptive to a change in mindset" (dos Santos Cruz, Phillips, and Cusimano 2017, 10–11).[4] Among many recommendations, dos Santos Cruz and his coauthors assert that "'proportional' force is a sound concept. However, in higher-risk environments ... the United Nations must employ overwhelming force ... [peacekeepers] must take the initiative to use force to eliminate threats" (dos Santos Cruz, Phillips, and Cusimano 2017, 10, 12). In other words, perhaps UN peacekeepers should assume rules of engagement even more proactive than today's counterinsurgents.

Unsurprisingly, the Kigali Principles and Cruz Report have met some resistance (Howard 2018; Karlsrud 2018; Williams 2018).[5] In the

---

[4] The UN Charter's Chapter VI concerns the "Pacific Settlements of Disputes," and lists a variety of diplomatic strategies to secure peace. Chapter VII, "Action with Respect to Threats to the Peace, Breaches of the Peace, and Acts of Aggression" outlines coercive measures, including the use of force (by UN member states, not the UN itself). The UN Charter does not explicitly mention peacekeeping because it had not yet been invented in 1945. Before 1999, multidimensional peacekeeping missions were authorized under Chapter VI or Chapter VII. Now they are all authorized under Chapter VII (Howard and Dayal 2018).

[5] Thus far, of 124 current Troop Contributing Countries to UN peacekeeping, about 47 have signed the Kigali Principles pledge. www.globalr2p.org/media/files/kp-signatories-31-july-2018.pdf.

spring of 2018, Secretary-General António Guterres announced a new Agenda for Peacekeeping (A4P) and called for member states to refocus on politics and mediation in peacekeeping. At the same time, however, he wants to ensure that the UN has "well-trained, well-equipped peacekeepers that are mobile and agile, and can be proactive in dealing with challenges and threats. Too often in the past, our troops have been reduced to waiting in a defensive posture, giving hostile forces time and space to plan attacks" (Guterres 2018). Although Guterres stops short of endorsing the Kigali Principles or the Cruz report recommendations, he echoes some of their ideas.

Despite pressure to move toward increasing peacekeepers' compellent power, UN peacekeepers still hail from dozens of different countries (which increases their legitimacy but not their compellent capacity). They do not train together in advance, their equipment is not uniform or interoperable, and they do not speak each other's languages. They do not function by a typical, unified command and control structure (when challenged, often answering first to their home governments rather than the UN's force commander). Although they may have a mandate to compel, UN peacekeepers have neither the capacity nor the resolve to do so.

Reform in peacekeeping is notoriously difficult (Gowan 2015b; Guéhenno 2002; Paris 2010). In the current era, civil wars are becoming more difficult to end as the great powers increasingly disagree, rebel groups proliferate, and violent jihad motivates people to fight (Howard and Stark 2017–2018). In this context, as in the Cold War era, most peacekeepers continue not to resort to using "force when civilians are under attack … missions perceive themselves as having insufficient resources to respond to force with force; and contingent members themselves are concerned about possible penalties if their use of force is judged inappropriate" (A/68/787, 7 March 2014, 1–2). Authorizing peacekeepers with a compellent mandate has not endowed them with the capacity or legitimacy to use force effectively. Nevertheless, the "big five" missions are currently deployed in active war zones, where there is little "peace to keep." The missions protect as many civilians as they can, but their protection is not, and cannot be, comprehensive.[6] UN peacekeepers cannot substitute for a functioning

---

[6] Even fully functioning states cannot protect all their citizens all the time, as the United States knows well from recent school shootings.

state – they cannot, by definition, hold a monopoly over the legitimate use of force or provide military-based security guarantees.

As I have shown in this book, however, peacekeeping has proven effective even in exceedingly difficult situations. United Nations peacekeepers have enjoyed remarkable success by relying primarily on nonviolent means – persuasion, inducement, and coercion short of compellence – as their main forms of power. At times, in tandem with peacekeepers, actual military forces have effectively delivered a compellent lever of power. Recognizing this division of labor and from where peacekeepers derive their power may provide a first step toward better peacekeeping.

Bibliography

Abrahms, Max. 2006. Why Terrorism Does Not Work. *International Security* 31 (2): 42–78.

Acemoğlu, Daron, and James A. Robinson. 2012. *Why Nations Fail: The Origins of Power, Prosperity, and Poverty*. New York: Crown Publishing Group.

Adler, Emanuel. 1997. Seizing the Middle Ground: Constructivism in World Politics. *European Journal of International Relations* 3 (3): 319–363.

Agathangelou, Anna M., and L. H. M. Ling. 2003. Desire Industries: Sex Trafficking, UN Peacekeeping, and the Neo-Liberal World Order. *Brown Journal of World Affairs* 10 (1): 133–148.

Agger, Kaspar. 2014. *Behind the Headlines: Drivers of Violence in the Central African Republic*. Washington, DC: Enough Project. Available at https://enoughproject.org/reports/behind-headlines-drivers-violence-central-african-republic.

Ahtisaari, Martti 1994. Planning and Operation. In *The Namibian Peace Process: Implications and Lessons for the Future*, edited by Heribert Weiland and Matthew Braham. Freiburg: Arnold Bergstraesser Institut.

Aichi, Dalia Al. 2015. Human Rights Day: Abuses Rife in Central African Republic. Human Rights Watch, 10 December.

Allee, Susan S. 2009. UN Blue: An Examination of the Interdependence between UN Peacekeeping and Peacemaking. *International Journal of Peace Studies* 14 (1): 83–107.

Amnesty International. 2015. CAR: UN Troops Implicated in Rape of Girl and Indiscriminate Killings Must Be Investigated. 11 August.

Amukugo, Elizabeth Magano. 1993. *Education and Politics in Namibia: Past Trends and Future Prospects*. Windhoek: Gamsberg Macmillan.

Aoi, Chiyuki, Cedric de Coning, and John Karlsrud, eds. 2016. *UN Peacekeeping Doctrine towards the Post-Brahimi Era? Adapting to Stabilization, Protection and New Threats*. Abingdon: Routledge.

Ariffin, Yohan, Jean-Marc Coicaud, and Vesselin Popovski. 2016. *Emotions in International Politics: Beyond Mainstream International Relations*. New York: Cambridge University Press.

Aristotle. 2015. *Rhetoric*. Aeterna Press.

Arreguín-Toft, Ivan. 2001. How the Weak Win Wars: A Theory of Asymmetric Conflict. *International Security* 26 (1): 93–128.

Arnault, Jean. 2015. A Background to the Report of the High-Level Panel on Peace Operations. *Global Peace Operations Review*. Available at https://peaceoperationsreview.org/thematic-essays/a-background-to-the-report-of-the-high-level-panel-on-peace-operations/.

Art, Robert J. 1980. To What Ends Military Power? *International Security* 4 (4): 3–35.

Art, Robert J, and Kelly Greenhill. 2018. Coercion: An Analytical Overview. In *Coercion: The Power to Hurt in International Politics*, edited by Kelly M. Greenhill and Peter Krause, 3–32. New York: Oxford University Press.

Art, Robert, and Patrick Cronin. 2003. *The United States and Coercive Diplomacy*. Washington, DC: The United States Institute of Peace Press.

Ausderan, Jacob. 2014. How Naming and Shaming Affects Human Rights Perceptions in the Shamed Country. *Journal of Peace Research* 51 (1): 81–95.

Autesserre, Séverine. 2010. *The Trouble with the Congo: Local Violence and the Failure of International Peacebuilding*. New York: Cambridge University Press.

2011. The Trouble with the Congo: A Précis. *African Security Review* 20 (2): 56–65.

2014. *Peaceland: Conflict Resolution and the Everyday Politics of International Intervention*. New York: Cambridge University Press.

Baker, Bruce. 2010. Poverty and Policy in Liberia's Post-Conflict Policing. *Police Practice and Research* 11 (3): 184–196.

Balcells, Laia. 2017. *Rivalry and Revenge: The Politics of Violence during Civil War*. Cambridge: Cambridge University Press.

Baldwin, David A. 2016. *Power and International Relations: A Conceptual Approach*. Princeton, NJ: Princeton University Press.

Barma, Naazneen. 2017. *The Peacebuilding Puzzle: Political Order in Post-Conflict States*. Cambridge: Cambridge University Press.

Barnett, Michael. 1995. Partners in Peace? The UN, Regional Organizations, and Peace-Keeping. *Review of International Studies* 21 (4): 411–433.

1998. *Dialogues in Arab Politics: Negotiations in Regional Order*. New York: Columbia University Press.

2011. *Empire of Humanity*. Ithaca, NY: Cornell University Press.

ed. 2016. *Paternalism beyond Borders*. Cambridge: Cambridge University Press.

Barnett, Michael, and Martha Finnemore. 2004. *Rules for the World: International Organizations in Global Politics*. Ithaca, NY: Cornell University Press.

2005. The Power of Liberal International Organizations. In *Power and Global Governance*, edited by Michael Barnett and Raymond Duvall, 161–184. Cambridge: Cambridge University Press.

Barnett, Michael, and Raymond Duvall. 2005. Power in International Politics. *International Organization* 59 (1): 39–75.

Barnett, Michael, Songying Fang, and Christoph Zürcher. 2014. Compromised Peacekeeping. *International Studies Quarterly* 58 (3): 608–620.

Barrera, Alberto. 2015. The Congo Trap: MONUSCO Islands of Stability in the Sea of Instability. *Stability: International Journal of Security & Development* 4 (1): 1–16.

Barry, Colin M., K. Chad Clay, and Michael E. Flynn. 2012. Avoiding the Spotlight: Human Rights Shaming and Foreign Direct Investment. *International Studies Quarterly* 57 (3): 532–544.

Barry, Joseph A. 2012. Bolstering United Nations Intelligence: Cultural and Structural Solutions. *American Intelligence Journal* 30 (1): 7–16.

Bauer, Gretchen. 1998. *Labor and Democracy in Namibia, 1971–1996*. Athens, OH: Ohio University Press.

Bauer, Gretchen, and Scott D. Taylor. 2011. *Politics in Southern Africa: Transition and Transformation*. Boulder, CO: Lynne Rienner.

BBC. 1995. No Place to Hide. Documentary Film by Sir Brian Urquhart.

2013. Central African Republic in Chaos, Says UN Chief Ban Ki-moon. 10 August.

BBC Afrique. 2014. Attaque Meurtrière en Centrafrique, 23 October.

Beardsley, Kyle. 2011. Peacekeeping and the Contagion of Armed Conflict. *Journal of Politics* 73 (4): 1051–1064.

2014. The UN at the Peacemaking–Peacebuilding Nexus. *Conflict Management and Peace Science* 30 (4): 369–386.

Beardsley, Kyle, and Kristian Skrede Gleditsch. 2015. Peacekeeping as Conflict Containment. *International Studies Review* 17 (1): 67–89.

Beber, Bernd. 2012. International Mediation, Selection Effects, and the Question of Bias. *Conflict Management and Peace Science* 29: 397–424.

Beber, Bernd, Michael J. Gilligan, Jenny Guardado, and Sabrina Karim. 2016. Peacekeeping, Compliance with International Norms, and Transactional Sex in Monrovia, Liberia. *International Organization* 71 (1): 1–30.

Bellamy, Alex, and Paul Williams. 2005. Who's Keeping the Peace? Regionalization and Contemporary Peace Operations. *International Security* 29 (4): 157–195.

Benedict, Ruth. 1946. *The Chrysanthemum and the Sword: Patterns of Japanese Culture*. New York: Houghton Mifflin Company.

Benner, Thorsten, Stephan Mergenthaler, and Philipp Rotmann. 2011. *The New World of UN Peace Operations: Learning to Build Peace?* Oxford: Oxford University Press.

Bennett, Andrew. 2013. The Mother of All Isms: Causal Mechanisms and Structured Pluralism in International Relations Theory. *European Journal of International Relations* 19 (3): 459–481.

Bercovitch, Jacob, and Karl DeRouen. 2004. Mediation in Internationalized Ethnic Conflicts: Assessing the Determinants of a Successful Process. *Armed Forces and Society* 30 (2): 147–170.

Berdal, Mats, and Hannah Davies. 2013. The United Nations and International Statebuilding after the Cold War. In *Political Economy of Statebuilding*, edited by Berdal, Mats, and Dominik Zaum, pp. 111–139, Abingdon and New York: Routledge.

Berdal, Mats, and David H. Ucko. 2014. The United Nations and the Use of Force: Between Promise and Peril. *Journal of Strategic Studies* 37 (5): 665–673.

2015. The Use of Force in UN Peacekeeping Operations. *RUSI Journal* 160 (1): 6–12.

Berdal, Mats R., and Dominik Zaum, eds. 2013. *Political Economy of Statebuilding: Power after Peace*. Abingdon and New York: Routledge.

Berman, Nicolas, Mathieu Couttenier, Dominic Rohner, and Mathias Thoenig. 2017. This Mine Is Mine! How Minerals Fuel Conflicts in Africa. *American Economic Review* 107 (6): 1564–1610.

Berman, Eli, Jacob N. Shapiro, and Joseph H. Felter. 2011. Can Hearts and Minds Be Bought? The Economics of Counterinsurgency in Iraq. *Journal of Political Economy* 119 (4): 766–819.

Bhargava, Vikas. 2011. Blood Electronics: Congo's Conflict Minerals and the Legislation That Could Cleanse the Trade. *Southern California Law Review* 84: 981–1034.

Bhaskar, Roy. 1979. *The Possibility of Naturalism: A Philosophical Critique of the Contemporary Human Sciences*. Abingdon and New York: Routledge.

Bhatia, Michael. 2005. Postconflict Profit: The Political Economy of Intervention. *Global Governance* 11 (2): 205–224.

Bigo, Didier. 1988. *Pouvoir et obeisance en Centrafrique*. Paris: Karthala.

von Billerbeck, Sarah. 2017. *Whose Peace? Local Ownership and United Nations Peacekeeping*. Oxford: Oxford University Press.

Bishnoi, Rati. 2006. Deployable Joint Public Affairs to Help Commanders' Media Outreach. *Inside the Pentagon* 22 (6): 18–20.

Boockmann, Bernhard, and Axel Dreher. 2011. Do Human Rights Offenders Oppose Human Rights Sesolutions in the United Nations? *Public Choice* 146 (3–4), 443–467.

Boot, Max. 2003. The Lessons of a Quagmire. *The New York Times*, 16 November. Opinion. Available at: www.nytimes.com/2003/11/16/opinion/the-lessons-of-a-quagmire.html.

2014. *The Savage Wars of Peace: Small Wars and the Rise Of American Power*. New York: Basic Books.

Boulden, Jane. 2015. Mandates Matter: An Exploration of Impartiality in United Nations Operations. *Global Governance* 11 (2): 147–160.

Boulding, Kenneth Ewart. 1989. *Three Faces of Power*. Newbury Park, CA: Sage Publications.

Bourdieu, Pierre. 1991. *Language and Symbolic Power*. Cambridge, MA: Harvard University Press.

Boutellis, Arthur. 2015. Can the UN Stabilize Mali? Towards a UN Stabilization Doctrine? *Stability: International Journal of Security & Development* 4 (1): 1–16.

Boutellis, Arthur, and Naureen Chowdhury Fink. 2016a. *Waging Peace: UN Peace Operations Confronting Terrorism and Violent Extremism*. New York: International Peace Institute.

2016b. *Mind the Gap: UN Peace Operations and Terrorism and Violent Extremism between Policy and Practice, Opportunities and Risks*. New York: International Peace Institute.

Boutros-Ghali, Boutros. 1992. *An Agenda for Peace: Preventive Diplomacy, Peacemaking, and Peace-Keeping: Report of the Secretary-General Pursuant to the Statement Adopted by the Summit Meeting of the Security Council on 31 January 1992*. New York: United Nations.

1995. *A/RES/51/242: Supplement to an Agenda for Peace*. New York: United Nations.

Bove, Vincenzo, and Leandro Elia. 2011. Supplying Peace: Participation in and Troop Contribution to Peacekeeping Missions. *Journal of Peace Research* 48 (6): 699–714.

2017. Economic Development in Peacekeeping Host Countries. *CESifo Economic Studies*: 1–17.

Bove, Vincenzo, and Andrea Ruggeri. 2016. Kinds of Blue: Diversity in UN Peacekeeping Missions and Civilian Protection. *British Journal of Political Science* 46 (3): 681–700.

Boyle, Michael J. 2014. *Violence after War: Explaining Instability in Post-Conflict States*. Baltimore, MD: Johns Hopkins University Press.

Bozzini, David M. 2011. Low-Tech Surveillance and the Despotic State in Eritrea. *Surveillance & Society* 9 (1/2): 93–113.

Braithwaite, Alex. 2010. Resisting Infection: How State Capacity Conditions Conflict Contagion. *Journal of Peace Research* 47 (3): 311–319.

Brodie, Bernard. 1959. *Strategy in the Missile Age*. Princeton, NJ: Princeton University Press.

Broesder, Wendy A., Tessa P. Op den Buijs, Ad L. W. Vogelaar, and Martin C. Euwema. 2015. Can Soldiers Combine Swords and Ploughshares? The Construction of the Warrior–Peacekeeper Role Identity Survey (WPRIS). *Armed Forces & Society* 41 (3): 519–540.

Brooks, Doug. 2011. Squandering the Potential for Success. *Journal of International Peace Operations*. 6 (4): 4–30.

Brooks, Rosa. 2016. *How Everything Became War and the Military Became Everything: Tales from the Pentagon*. New York: Simon & Schuster.

Brown, Michael J., and Marie-Joelle Zahar. 2015. Social Cohesion ad Peacebuilding in the Central African Republic and Beyond. *Journal of Peacebuilding and Development* 10 (1): 10–15.

Brown, Susan. 1995. Diplomacy by Other Means. In *Namibia's Liberation Struggle: The Two-Edged Sword*, edited by Colin Leys and John S. Saul. London: James Currey.

Browne, Simone. 2015. *Dark Matters: On the Surveillance of Blackness*. Durham, NC: Duke University Press

Bryan, Dominic. 2000. *Orange Parades: The Politics of Ritual, Tradition and Control*. London: Pluto Press.

Brynen, Rex. 1989. PLO Policy in Lebanon: Legacies and Lessons. *Journal of Palestine Studies* 18 (2): 50–51.

Buhaug, Halvard, Jack S. Levy, and Henrik Urdal. 2014. 50 Years of Peace Research: An Introduction to the Journal of Peace Research Anniversary Special Issue. *Journal of Peace Research* 51 (2): 139–144.

Buhaug, Halvard, and Kristian Skrede Gleditsch. 2008. Contagion or Confusion? Why Conflicts Cluster in Space. *International Studies Quarterly* 52 (2): 215–233.

Bukovansky, Mlada. 2002. *Legitimacy and Power Politics: The American and French Revolutions in International Political Culture*. Princeton, NJ: Princeton University Press.

Bunche, Ralph. 1950. Nobel Peace Prize Lecture, December 11. Oslo University, Norway. Available at: www.nobelprize.org/prizes/peace/1950/bunche/acceptance-speech/.

Burgoon, Brian, Andrea Ruggeri, William Schudel, and Ram Manikkalingam. 2015. From Media Attention to Negotiated Peace: Human Rights Reporting and Civil War Duration. *International Interactions* 41 (2): 226–255.

Busby, Joshua W. 2007. Bono Made Jesse Helms Cry: Jubilee 2000, Debt Relief, and Moral Action in International Politics. *International Studies Quarterly* 51 (2): 247–275.

  2010. *Moral Movements and Foreign Policy*. Cambridge University Press.

Byman, Daniel L. 2006. Friends Like These: Counterinsurgency and the War on Terrorism. *International Security* 31 (2): 79–115.

2007. US Counter–Terrorism Options: A Taxonomy. *Survival* 49 (3): 121–150.

2018. Another War in Lebanon? *Lawfare*, 6 September.

Byman, Daniel, and Matthew C. Waxman. 2002. *The Dynamics of Coercion: American Foreign Policy and the Limits of Military Might*. Cambridge: Cambridge University Press.

Cabus, Sofie J., and Kristof de Witte. 2012. Naming and Shaming in a "Fair" Way. On Disentangling the Influence of Policy in Observed Outcomes. *Journal of Policy Modeling* 34 (5): 767–787.

Cakaj, Ledio. 2015. In Unclaimed Land: The Lord's Resistance Army in CAR. In *Making Sense of the Central African Republic*, edited by Tatiana Carayannis and Louisa Lombard. Chicago: University of Chicago Press.

Cammett, Melani C. 2014. *Compassionate Communalism: Welfare and Sectarianism in Lebanon*. Ithaca: Cornell University Press.

Campbell, Susanna P. 2018. *Global Governance and Local Peace*. Cambridge: Cambridge University Press.

Caplan, Richard. 2005. *International Governance of War-Torn Territories: Rule and Reconstruction*. Oxford: Oxford University Press.

2019. *Measuring Peace: Principles, Practices, and Politics*. Oxford: Oxford University Press.

Cara, Anna, and Menelaos Hadjicostis. 2015. As UN Peacekeeping Veers toward Counterterror, the United States Steps In. *Associated Press*, 26 September.

Carayannis, Tatiana, and Louisa Lombard. 2015. A Concluding Note on the Failure and Future of Peacebuilding in CAR. In *Making Sense of the Central African Republic*, edited by Tatiana Carayannis and Louisa Lombard. Chicago: The University of Chicago Press.

Carnahan, Michael, William Durch, and Scott Gilmore. 2006. *Economic Impact of Peacekeeping*. Ottawa: Peace Dividend Trust.

2007. New Data on the Economic Impact of UN Peacekeeping. *International Peacekeeping* 14 (3): 384–402.

Carnegie, Allison, and Christoph Mikulaschek. 2018. The Promise of Peacekeeping: Protecting Civilians in Civil Wars. SSRN.

Caroll, Faye. 1967. *South West Africa and the United Nations*. Lexington: University of Kentucky.

Carr, Edward H. 1946. *The Twenty Years' Crisis, 1919–1939: An Introduction to the Study of International Relations*. London: Macmillan.

Cederman, Lars-Erik, Kristian Skrede Gleditsch, and Halvard Buhaug. 2013. *Inequality, Grievances, and Civil War*. New York: Cambridge University Press.

Celestino, Mauricio Rivera, and Kristian Skrede Gleditsch. 2013. "Fresh Carnations or All Thorn, No Rose? Nonviolent Campaigns and

Transitions in Autocracies." *Journal of Peace Research* 50 (3): 385–400.

Central Intelligence Agency. 2014. *The World Factbook: Central African Republic*. Washington, DC.

2017. *The World Factbook: Namibia*. Washington, DC.

2018. *The World Factbook: Lebanon*. Washington, DC.

Chauvin, Emmanuel. 2018. *La guerre en Centrafrique: a l'ombre du Tchad. Une escalade conflictuelle régionale?* L'Agence Française de Développement. Available at: www.afd.fr/fr/la-guerre-en-centrafrique-lombre-du-tchad-une-escalade-conflictuelle-regionale.

Checkel, Jeffrey T. 1998. The Constructivist Turn in International Relations Theory. *World Politics* 50 (2): 324–348.

1999. Norms, Institutions, and National Identity in Contemporary Europe. *International Studies Quarterly* 43 (1): 83–114.

2008. Process Tracing. In *Proces Tracing: From Metaphor to Analytic Tool*, edited by Andrew Bennett and Jeffrey T. Checkel. Cambridge: Cambridge University Press.

2017. Socialization and Violence: Introduction and Framework. *Journal of Peace Research* 54 (5): 592–605.

Cheng, Christine and Dominik Zaum, eds. 2011. *Post-Conflict Peacebuilding and Corruption: Selling the Peace?* London: Routledge.

Chenoweth, Erica, and Kurt Schock. 2015. Do Contemporaneous Armed Challenges Affect the Outcomes of Mass Nonviolent Campaigns? *Mobilization: An International Quarterly* 20 (4): 427–451.

Chenoweth, Erica, and Maria Stephan. 2011. *Why Civil Resistance Works: The Strategic Logic of Nonviolent Conflict*. New York: Columbia University Press.

Chesterman, Simon, Ian Johnstone, and David M. Malone. 2016. *Law and Practice of the United Nations*. Oxford: Oxford University Press.

Chivers, C. J. 2018. *The Fighters: Americans in Combat*. New York: Simon & Schuster.

Churches Information and Monitoring Service. 1990. We Saw It All. *Observer Reports Namibia*.

Cierco, Teresa. 2013. Evaluating UNMIT's Contribution to Establishing the Rule of Law in Timor-Leste. *Asia-Pacific Review* 20 (1): 79–99.

Cinq-Mars, Evan. 2015. *Too Little, Too Late: Failing to Prevent Atrocities in the Central African Republic*. New York: Global Centre for the Responsibility to Protect. Available at: www.globalr2p.org/media/files/occasionalpaper_car_final.pdf.

Claude, Inis L. Jr. 1966. Collective Legitimization as a Political Function of the United Nations. *International Organization* 20 (3): 367–379.

1996. Peace and Security: Prospective Roles for the Two United Nations. *Global Governance* 2 (3): 289–298.

Clausewitz, Carl von. 1968. *On War*. London: Penguin Classics.

Cliffe, Lionel, ed. 1994. *The Transition to Independence in Namibia*. Boulder, CO: Lynne Rienner.

Clinton, William J. 1999. *A National Security Strategy for A New Century*. Washington, DC: The White House.

Clunan, Anne L. 2009. *The Social Construction of Russia's Resurgence: Aspirations, Identity, and Security Interests*. Baltimore: Johns Hopkins University Press.

Code Blue. 2016. Shocking New Reports of Peacekeeper Sexual Abuse in the Central African Republic. 30 March. Available at: www .codebluecampaign.com/press-releases/2016/3/30.

Cohen, Abner. 1974. *Two-Dimensional Man: An Essay on the Anthropology and Symbolism in Complex Society*. London: Routledge.

Coicaud, Jean-Marc. 2007. *Beyond the National Interest: The Future of UN Peacekeeping and Multilateralism in an Era of U.S. Supremacy*. Washington DC: United State Institute of Peace Press.

Cole, Wade M. 2012. Government Respect for Gendered Rights: The Effect of the Convention on the Elimination of Discrimination against Women on Women's Rights Outcomes, 1981–2004. *International Studies Quarterly* 57 (1): 233–249.

Coleman, Katharina P. 2007. *International Organizations and Peace Enforcement*. Cambridge: Cambridge University Press.

Collier, David, and Henry E. Brady. 2004. *Rethinking Social Inquiry: Diverse Tools, Shared Standards*. Lanham, MD: Rowman and Littlefield.

Collier, David, Henry E. Brady, and Jason Seawright. 2010. Outdated Views of Qualitative Methods: Time to Move On. *Political Analysis* 18 (4): 506–513.

Collier, Paul, Lisa Chauvet, and Haavard Hegre. 2008. The Challenge of Conflicts. In *Global Crises, Global Solutions*, edited by Bjorn Lomborg. Cambridge University Press.

  2009. *Post-Conflict Peacekeeping, In Copenhagen Consensus 2*, edited by Bjorn Lomborg. Cambridge University Press.

de Coning, Cedric. 2011. Civilian Peacekeeping Capacity: Mobilizing Partners to Match Supply and Demand. *International Peacekeeping* 18 (5): 577–592.

  2016a. From Peacebuilding to Sustaining Peace: Implications of Complexity for Resilience and Sustainability. *Resilience* 4 (3): 1–16.

  2016b. Adapting the African Standby Force to a Just-in-Time Readiness Model: Improved Alignment with the Emerging African Model of Peace Operations. In *The Future of African Peace Operations: From the Janjaweed to Boko Haram*, edited by de Coning, Cedric, Linnea Gelot, and John Karlsrud. London: Zed Books.

de Coning, Cedric, Chiyuki Aoi, and John Karlsrud. 2017. *UN Peacekeeping Doctrine in a New Era: Adapting to Stabilisation, Protection and New Threats*. New York: Routledge.

Convergne, Elodie, and Michael R. Snyder. 2015. Making Maps to Make Peace: Geospacial Technology as a Tool for UN Peacekeeping. *International Peacekeeping* 22 (5): 565–586

Cordesman, Anthony H. 2009. *Shape, Clear, Hold and Build: The Uncertain Lessons of the Afghan and Iraq Wars*. Washington, DC: Center for Strategic and International Studies.

Cordier, Andrew, and Wilder Foote, eds. 1974. *Public Papers of the Secretaries-General of the United Nations. Volume 4: Dag Hammarskjöld, 1958–1960*. New York and London: Columbia University Press.

Coyne, Christopher J., and Abigail R. Hall. 2018. *Tyranny Comes Home*. Stanford, CA: Stanford University Press.

Crawford, Neta. 2002. *Argument and Change in World Politics: Ethics, Decolonization, and Humanitarian Intervention*. New York: Cambridge University Press.

Crenshaw, Martha. 2000. The Psychology of Terrorism: An Agenda for the 21st Century. *Political Psychology* 21(2): 405–420.

Crocker, Chester A. 1992. *High Noon in Southern Africa: Making Peace in a Rough Neighborhood*. New York: W.W. Norton and Company.

Crocker, Chester A., Fen Osler Hampson, and Pamela Aall. 1999. Introduction. In *Herding Cats: Multiparty Mediation in a Complex World*, edited by Chester A. Crocker, Fen Osler Hampson, and Pamela Aall. Washington, DC: US Institute of Peace Press.

    2007. Leashing the Dogs of War. In *Leashing the Dogs of War: Conflict Management in a Divided World*, edited by Crocker, Chester A., Fen Osler Hampson, and Pamela R. Aal. Washington, DC: US Institute of Peace Press.

Cruz, Carlos Alberto dos Santos, William R. Phillips, Salvator Cusimano. 2017. Improving Security of United Nations Peacekeepers: We Need to Change the Way We Are Doing Business. December 19. Available at: https://peacekeeping.un.org/sites/default/files/improving_security_of_united_nations_peacekeepers_report.pdf.

Cunliffe, Phillip. 2013. *Legions of Peace: UN Peacekeepers from the Global South*. London: C. Hurst.

Cunningham, David E. 2011. *Barriers to Peace in Civil Wars*. Cambridge: Cambridge University Press.

    2016. Preventing Civil War: How the Potential for International Intervention Can Deter Conflict Onset. *World Politics* 68 (2): 307–340.

Cunningham, Kathleen Gallagher. 2013. Understanding Strategic Choice: The Determinants of Civil War and Nonviolent Campaign in Self-Determination Disputes. *Journal of Peace Research* 50 (3): 291–304.

Cunningham, Kathleen Gallagher, Marianne Dahl, and Anne Frugé. 2017. Strategies of Resistance: Diversification and Diffusion. *American Journal of Political Science* 61 (3): 591–605.

Dahl, Robert A. 1957. The Concept of Power. *Behavioral Science* 2 (3): 201–215.

Dallaire, Roméo, with Brent Beardsley. 2005. *Shake Hands with the Devil: The Failure of Humanity in Rwanda*. New York: Carroll & Graf Publishers.

Daly, Sarah Zukerman. 2016. *Organized Violence after Civil War: The Geography of Recruitment in Latin America*. New York: Cambridge University Press.

de Dardel, Jean-Jacques. 2004. Outreach Strategies in the Wake of NATO and EU Enlargement: Refocusing on the Partnership for Peace. *Connections* 3 (2): 99–106.

Darwin, Charles. 1872. *The Expression of the Emotions in Man and Animals*. London: John Murray.

Davenport, Christian. 2017. Some Things Just Won't Do: Scaling Perceptions of Challenger and Government Tactics. Paper presented at Georgetown University, 24 April.

Day, Graham, and Christopher Freeman. 2005. Operationalizing the Responsibility to Protect – The Policekeeping Approach. *Global Governance* 11 (2): 139–146.

DefenceWeb. 2015. Eastern Africa Standby Force, United States Forge New Partnership. 3 November. Available at: www.defenceweb.co.za/index.php?option=com_content&view=article&id=41262:eastern-africa-standby-force-us-forge-new-partnership&catid=56:Diplomacy%20&%20Peace&Itemid=111.

DeRouen, Karl, Jr., and Jacob Bercovitch. 2012. Trends in Civil War Mediation. In *Peace and Conflict 2012*, edited by J. Joseph Hewitt, Jonathan Wilkenfeld, and Ted Robert Gurr, 59–70. New York: Routledge.

Deschamps, Marie, Hassan B. Jallow, and Yasmin Sooka. 2015. *Taking Action on Sexual Exploitation and Abuse by Peacekeepers*. New York: United Nations.

Diehl, Paul F. 1994. *International Peacekeeping*. Baltimore: Johns Hopkins University Press.

ed. 2004. *The Scourge of War: New Extensions of an Old Problem*. Ann Arbor, MI: The University of Michigan Press.

Diehl, Paul F., and Daniel Druckman. 2010. *Evaluating Peace Operations*. Boulder, CO: Lynne Rienner Publishers.

2018. Multiple Peacekeeping Missions: Analysing Interdependence. *International Peacekeeping* 25 (1): 28–51.

Diehl, Paul F., Jennifer Reifschneider, and Paul R. Hensel. 1996. United Nations Intervention and Recurring Conflict. *International Organization* 50 (4): 683–700.

Dinnen, Sinclair, and Gordon Peake. 2013. More Than Just Policing: Police Reform in Post-Conflict Bougainville. *International Peacekeeping* 20 (5): 570–584.

Dobbin, Frank, Beth Simmons, and Geoffrey Garrett. 2007. The Global Diffusion of Public Policies: Social Construction, Coercion, Competition, or Learning. *Annual Review of Sociology* 33: 449–472.

Dobbins, James. 2003. America's Role in Nation-Building: From Germany to Iraq. *Survival* 45 (4): 87–110.

et al. 2005. *The RAND History of Nation-Building*. Santa Monica, CA: RAND Corporation.

Dominik, Zaum. 2007. *The Sovereignty Paradox: The Norms and Politics of International Statebuilding*. Oxford: Oxford University Press.

Donais, Timothy, 2009. Empowerment or Imposition? Dilemmas of Local Ownership in Post-Conflict Peacebuilding Processes. *Peace & Change* 34 (1):3–26.

Dorn, A. Walter. 2010. United Nations Peacekeeping Intelligence. In *The Oxford Handbook of National Security Intelligence*, edited by Loch K. Johnson. Oxford: Oxford University Press.

2011. *Keeping Watch: Monitoring, Technology & Innovation in UN Peace Operations*. Tokyo: United Nations University Press.

ed. 2014. *Air Power in UN Operations: Wings for Peace*. Farnham: Ashgate.

Dorn, A. Walter, and Christoph Semken. 2015. Blue Mission Tracking: Real-Time Location of UN Peacekeepers. *International Peacekeeping* 22 (5): 545–564.

Downes, Alexander. 2008. *Targeting Civilians in War*. Ithaca, NY: Cornell University Press

Doyle, Michael W., and Nicholas Sambanis. 2000. International Peacebuilding: A Theoretical and Quantitative Analysis. *American Political Science Review* 94 (4): 779–801.

2006. *Making War and Building Peace: United Nations Peace Operations*. Princeton, NJ: Princeton University Press.

Dreyer, Ronald. 1994. *Namibia and Southern Africa: Regional Dynamics of Decolonization 1945–1990*. London: Kegan Paul International.

Dudouet, Véronique. 2013. Dynamics and Factors of Transition from Armed Struggle to Nonviolent Resistance. *Journal of Peace Research* 50 (3): 401–413.

Duffey, Tamara. 2000. Cultural Issues in Contemporary Peacekeeping. *International Peacekeeping* 7 (1): 142–168.

Duffield, Mark. 2012. Challenging Environments: Danger, Resilience and the Aid Industry. *Security Dialogue* 43 (5): 475–492.

Dwan, Renata. 2002. *Executive Policing: Enforcing the Law in Peace Operations*. New York: Oxford University Press.

Dziedzic, Michael, ed. 2016. *Criminalized Power Structures: The Overlooked Enemies of Peace*. London: Rowman & Littlefield.

Dziedzic, Michael, and Michael Seidl. 2005. Special Report: Provincial Reconstruction Teams and Military Relations with International and Nongovernmental Organizations in Afghanistan. Washington, DC: US Institute of Peace.

Edstrom, Hakan, and Dennis Gyllensporre. 2014. Observing War – Making Peace?: Unpacking the Military Strategy of UN Non-Force Missions. *Journal of International Peacekeeping* 18: 290–317.

Eikenberry, Karl W. 2013. The Limits of Counterinsurgency Doctrine in Afghanistan: The Other Side of the COIN. *Foreign Affairs*.

Elliott, Kimberly Ann. 1998. The Sanctions Glass: Half Full or Completely Empty? *International Security* 23 (1): 50–65.

Elliott, Lorraine. 2010. Cosmopolitan Militaries and Cosmopolitan Force. In *Fault Lines of International Legitimacy*, edited by Hilary Charlesworth and Jean-Marc Coicaud, 279–302. New York: Cambridge University Press.

Elron, Efrat. 2007. Israel, UNIFIL II, the UN and the International Community. *Palestine-Israel Journal of Politics, Economics, and Culture* 13 (4). Available at: www.pij.org/details.php?id=973.

Erskine, Emmanuel A. 1989. *Mission with UNIFIL: An African Soldier's Reflections*. London: C. Hurst.

Esarey, Justin, and Jacqueline H. R. DeMeritt. 2017. Political Context and the Consequences of Naming and Shaming for Human Rights Abuse. *International Interactions* 43: 1–30.

Evans, Gareth. 2008. *The Responsibility to Protect: Ending Mass Atrocity Crimes Once and for All*. Washington, DC: Brookings Institution Press.

Fariss, Christopher J. 2014. Respect for Human Rights Has Improved over Time: Modeling the Changing Standard of Accountability. *American Political Science Review* 108 (2): 297–318.

Fearon, James. 1994. Domestic Political Audiences and the Escalation of International Disputes. *American Political Science Review* 88 (3): 577–592.

1995. Rationalist Explanations for War. *International Organization* 49 (3): 379–414.

Fearon, James, and Alexander Wendt. 2002. Rationalism v. Constructionism: A Skeptical View. In *Handbook of International Relations*, edited by Walter Carlsnaes, Thomas Risse, and Beth A. Simmons. Thousand Oaks, CA: Sage Publications.

Feaver, Peter D. 2011. The Right to Be Right: Civil-Military Relations and the Iraq Surge Decision. *International Security* 35 (4): 87–125.

Feeley, Malcolm M. 1979. *The Process Is the Punishment: Handling Cases in a Lower Criminal Court*. New York: Russell Sage Foundation.

Feil, Scott R. 1998. *Preventing Genocide: How the Early Use of Force Might Have Succeeded in Rwanda*. New York: Carnegie Corporation.

Ferguson, James. 1990. *The Anti-Politics Machine: "Development," Depoliticization and Bureaucratic Power in Lesotho*. Cambridge: Cambridge University Press.

Findlay, Trevor. 2002. *The Use of Force in UN Peace Operations*. Oxford: Oxford University Press.

Finnemore, Martha. 1996a. Norms, Culture, and World Politics: Insights from Sociology's Institutionalism. *International Organization* 50 (2): 325–347.

1996b. *National Interests in International Society*. Ithaca, NY: Cornell University Press.

2003. *The Purpose of Intervention: Changing Beliefs about the Use of Force*. Ithaca, NY: Cornell University Press.

Finnemore, Martha, and Kathryn Sikkink. 1998. International Norm Dynamics and Political Change. *International Organization* 52 (4): 887–917.

Fjelde, Hanne, Lisa Hultman, and Desiree Nilsson. 2019. Protection through Presence: UN Peacekeeping and the Costs of Targeting Civilians. *International Organization* 73 (1).

Fligstein, Niel. 1990. *The Transformation of Corporate Control*. Harvard, MA: University Press.

Fortna, Virginia Page. 2004a. Does Peacekeeping Keep Peace? International Intervention and the Duration of Peace after Civil War. *International Studies Quarterly* 48 (2): 269–292.

2004b. Interstate Peacekeeping: Causal Mechanisms and Empirical Effects. *World Politics* 56 (4): 481–519.

2008. *Does Peacekeeping Work? Shaping Belligerents' Choices after Civil War*. Princeton, NJ: Princeton University Press.

2015. Do Terrorists Win? Rebels' Use of Terrorism and Civil War Outcomes. *International Organization* 69 (3): 519–556.

Fortna, Virginia Page, and Lise Morjé Howard. 2008. Pitfalls and Prospects in the Peacekeeping Literature. *Annual Review of Political Science* 11: 283–301.

Fortna, Virginia Page, and Reyko Huang. 2012. Democratization after Civil War: A Brush-Clearing Exercise. *International Studies Quarterly* 56 (4): 801–806.

Foucault, Michel. 1977. *Discipline and Punish: The Birth of the Prison*. New York: Vintage Books.

1998. *The History of Sexuality: The Will to Knowledge*, London: Penguin.

François, Pierre-Olivier. 2015. *The UN: Last Station before Hell*. Documentary Film. Paris: Arté/Alegria.

Franklin, James. 2008. Shame on You: The Impact of Human Rights Criticism on Political Repression in Latin America. *International Studies Quarterly* 52 (1): 187–211.

Friedman, Brett. 2014. No COIN for You? The Most Stagnant Debate in Strategic Studies. *War on the Rocks*, 30 January. Available at: https://warontherocks.com/2014/01/no-coin-for-you-the-most-stagnant-debate-in-strategic-studies/.

Friis, Karsten M. 2010. Peacekeeping and Counter-Insurgency: Two of a Kind? *International Peacekeeping* 17 (1): 49–66.

Fujii, Lee Ann. 2014. Five Stories of Accidental Ethnography: Turning Unplanned Moments in the Field into Data. *Qualitative Research* 15 (4): 525–539.

Galtung, Johan. 1976. *Peace, War and Defense: Essays in Peace Research, Vol. II*. Oslo: International Peace Research Institute.

Galula, David. 1963. *Pacification in Algeria, 1956–1958*. Santa Monica, CA: RAND Corporation.

1964. *Counterinsurgency Warfare: Theory and Practice*. Westport, CT: Praeger.

Gentile, Gian. 2013. *Wrong Turn: America's Deadly Embrace of Counterinsurgency*. New York: The New Press.

George, Alexander. 1991. *Forceful Persuasion: Coercive Diplomacy as an Alternative to War*. Washington, DC: United States Institute of Peace.

George, Alexander, and Andrew O. Bennett. 2005. *Case Studies and Theory Development in the Social Sciences*. Cambridge, MA: The MIT Press.

Gerring, John. 2007. *Case Study Research: Principles and Practice*. New York: Cambridge University Press.

Getmansky, Anna. 2013. You Can't Win if You Don't Fight: The Role of Regime Type in Counterinsurgency Outbreaks and Outcomes. *The Journal of Conflict Resolution* 57 (4): 709–734.

Ghali, Mona. 1993. UNIFIL, 1978-Present. In *Evolution of UN Peacekeeping: Case Studies and Comparative Analysis*, edited by William J. Durch. New York: St. Martin's Press.

Ghobarah, Hazem Adam, Paul Huth, and Bruce Russett. 2003. Civil Wars Kill and Maim People: Long after the Shooting Stops. *American Political Science Review* 97 (2): 189–202.

Giddens, Anthony. 1987. *Volume Two of A Contemporary Critique of Historical Materialism*. Cambridge: Polity.

Giffen, Alison. 2010. *Addressing the Doctrinal Deficit: Developing Guidance to Prevent and Respond to Widespread or Systematic Attacks Against Civilians*. Washington, DC: Stimson Center.

Gilligan, Michael, and Ernest J. Sergenti. 2008. Do UN Interventions Cause Peace? Using Matching to Improve Causal Inference. *Quarterly Journal of Political Science* 3 (1): 89–122.

Gilligan, Michael, and Stephen J. Stedman. 2003. Where Do the Peacekeepers Go?. *International Studies Review* 5 (4): 37–54.

Gilliom, John. 2001. *Overseers of the Poor: Surveillance, Resistance, and the Limits of Privacy*. Chicago: University of Chicago Press.

Gilpin, Robert. 1975. *US Power and the Multinational Corporation: The Political Economy of Foreign Direct Investment*. New York: Basic Books.

Girod, Desha. 2015. *Explaining Post-Conflict Reconstruction*. New York: Oxford University Press.

Gisselquist, Rachel, ed. 2017a. *Fragility, Aid, and Statebuilding: Understanding Diverse Trajectories*. New York: Routledge.

2017b. *Development Assistance for Peacebuilding*. New York: Routledge.

Glawion, Tim, Lotje de Vries, and Andreas Mehler. 2018. Handle with Care! A Qualitative Comparison of the Fragile States Index's Bottom Three Countries: Central African Republic, Somalia and South Sudan. *Development & Change* 0: 1–24.

Global Center for the Responsibility to Protect. 2018. Member State Endorsements: The Kigali Principles on the Protection of Civilians. Available at: www.globalr2p.org/resources/1007.

Goddard, Stacie. 2008. When Right Makes Might: How Prussia Overturned the European Balance of Power. *International Security* 33 (3): 110–142.

Goddard, Stacie E., Daniel H. Nexon. 2016. The Dynamics of Global Power Politics: A Framework for Analysis. *Journal of Global Security Studies* 1 (1): 4–18.

Goertz, Gary, Paul F. Diehl, and Alexandru Balas. 2016. *The Puzzle of Peace: The Evolution of Peace in the International System*. New York: Oxford University Press.

Goksel, Timur. 2007. Mr. UNIFIL Reflects on a Quarter Century of Peacekeeping in Southern Lebanon. *Journal of Palestinian Studies*. 36 (3): 50–77.

Goldberg, Mark Leon. 2015. Why President Obama Is Hosting a Summit on UN Peacekeeping. *UN Dispatch*, 28 September. Available at: www.undispatch.com/why-president-obama-is-hosting-a-summit-on-un-peacekeeping/.

Goldstein, Joshua S. 2011. *Winning the War on War*. Hialeah: Dutton.

Goodman, Ryan, and Derek Jinks. 2013. *Socializing States: Promoting Human Rights through International Law*. New York: Oxford University Press.

Gordon, Peake. 2011. Partnerships and International Policing: The Reach and Limits of Policy Processes. *International Peacekeeping* 18 (5): 612–626.

Goulding, Marrack. 2002. Public Participation and International Peacekeeping. *Owning the Process: Public Participation in Peacemaking* 13: 86–89.

———. 2003. *Peacemonger*. Baltimore: Johns Hopkins University Press.

Gowan, Richard. 2015a. CAR Scandal Reflects UN Peacekeeping's Loss of Strategic Direction. *World Politics Review*, 8 June. Available at: www.worldpoliticsreview.com/articles/15941/car-scandal-reflects-u-n-peacekeeping-s-loss-of-strategic-direction.

———. 2015b. Ten Trends in UN Peacekeeping. *Global Peace Operations Review: Annual Compilation*, 17 June. Available at: https://peaceoperationsreview.org/thematic-essays/10-trends-in-peace-operations/.

———. 2015c. Can U.N. Peacekeepers Fight Terrorists? *Global Peace Operations Review*, 30 June. Available at: http://peaceoperationsreview.org/commentary/can-u-n-peacekeepers-fight-terrorists/.

———. 2015d. How the UN Can Help Create Peace in a Divided World. *Huffington Post*, 7 October. Available at: www.huffingtonpost.ca/centre-for-international-policy-studies/un-world-powers_b_8248628.html.

Gowan, Richard, and Alexandra Novosseloff. 2010. Le renforcement de la Force intérimaire des Nations Unies au Liban: Etude des processus décisionnels au sommet. *Annuaire français de relations internationals*. XI: 245–267.

Grant, J. Andrew. 2012. The Kimberly Process at Ten: Reflections on a Decade of Efforts to End the Trade in Conflict Diamonds. In *High-Value Natural Resources and Peacebuilding*, edited by Päivi Lujala and Siri Aas Rustad. London: Earthscan.

Greener, Bethan K. 2011. The Rise of Policing in Peace Operations. *International Peacekeeping* 18 (2): 183–195.

Greenhill, Kelly M. 2010. The Company You Keep: International Socialization and the Diffusion of Human Rights Norms. *International Studies Quarterly* 54 (1): 127–145.

Greenhill, Kelly M., and Peter Krause, eds. 2018. *Coercion: The Power to Hurt in International Politics*. New York: Oxford University Press.

Greig, J. Michael, and Paul F. Diehl. 2005. The Peacekeeping–Peacemaking Dilemma. *International Studies Quarterly* 49 (4): 621–646.

Groth, Siegfried. 1995. *Namibia: The Wall of Silence*. Wuppertal: Peter Hammer Verlag.

Guéhenno, Jean-Marie. 2002. On the Challenges and Achievements of Reforming UN Peace Operations. *International Peacekeeping*, 9 (2): 69–80.

   2015a. World Peace Is Increasingly Elusive. *Time*, 23 September. Available at: http://time.com/4038857/is-world-peace-possible/.

   2015b. *The Fog of Peace*. Washington, DC: Brookings Institution Press.

Gupta, Dipankar. 2000. *Culture, Space and the Nation-State*. New Delhi: Sage.

Guterres, António Manuel de Oliveira. 2018. Action for Peacekeeping (A4P). Secretary-General's Remarks to Security Council High-Level Debate on Collective Action to Improve UN Peacekeeping Operations. Available at: www.un.org/sg/en/content/sg/statement/2018-03-28/secretary-generals-remarks-security-council-high-level-debate.

   2018. Remarks to Security Council High-Level Debate on Collective Action to Improve UN Peacekeeping Operations. 28 March. www.un.org/sg/en/content/sg/speeches/2018-03-28/collective-action-improve-un-peacekeeping-operations-remarks.

Gwin, Peter, 2015. Chaos in the Heart of Africa. *National Geographic*. https://video.nationalgeographic.com/video/gwin-bleasdale-war-africanglive.

Haas, Ernst B. 1990. *When Knowledge Is Power: Three Models of Change in International Organizations*. Berkeley, CA: University of California Press.

Haass, Richard N. and Meghan L. O'Sullivan, eds. 2000. *Honey and Vinegar: Incentives, Sanctions, and Foreign Policy*. Washington, DC: Brookings Institution Press.

Habermas, Jurgen. 1981. *Theory of Communicative Action*. Cambridge: Polity Press.

Hafner-Burton, Emilie. 2008. Sticks and Stones: Naming and Shaming the Human Rights Enforcement Problem. *International Organization* 62 (4): 689–716.

Hall, Peter A. 1986. *Governing the Economy: The Politics of State Intervention in Britain and France*. Oxford: Oxford University Press.

Hall, Peter A., and Rosemary C. R. Taylor. 1996, Political Science and the Three New Institutionalisms. *Political Studies* 44 (5): 936–957.

Hampton, Daniel. 2014. *Creating Sustainable Peacekeeping Capability in Africa*. Africa Security Brief No. 27. National Defense University Africa Center for Strategic Studies.

Hansen, Annika. 2002. Civil-Military Cooperation: The Military, Paramilitary, and Civilian Police in Executive Policing. In *Executive Policing: Enforcing the Law in Peace Operations*, edited by Renata Dwan, 67–84. Oxford: Oxford University Press.

Harland, David. 2004. Legitimacy and Effectiveness in International Administration. *Global Governance* 10 (1): 15–19.

Harlech-Jones, Brian. 1997. *A New Thing? The Namibian Independence Process, 1989–1990*. Windhoek: EIN Publications.

Hauchard, Amaury. 2018. China, Russia Rise in CAR as Western Influence Shrinks. *Mail and Guardian*, 24 May.

Hazelton, Jacqueline L. 2017. The "Hearts and Minds" Fallacy: Violence, Coercion, and Success in Counterinsurgency Warfare. *International Security* 42 (1): 80–113.

Hearn, Roger. 1999. *UN Peacekeeping in Action: The Namibian Experience*. Commack, NY: Nova Science Publishers.

Heiberg, Marianne. 1991. Peacekeepers and Local Populations: Some Comments on UNIFIL. In *The UN and Peacekeeping: Results, Limitations, and Prospects*, edited by Indar Jit Rikhye and Kjell Skjelsbaek. New York: Palgrave MacMillan.

Heiduk, Felix. 2015. Rethinking "Policebuilding." *Cooperation & Conflict* 50 (1): 69–86.

Hellman, Joel, Geraint Jones, and Daniel Kaufmann. 2000. Seize the State, Seize the Day: State Capture, Corruption, and Influence in Transition. *Policy Research Working Paper 2444*. Washington, DC: World Bank Group.

Hémez, Rémy. 2016. Operation Sangaris: A Case Study in Limited Military Intervention. *Military Review* 96 (6): 72–80.

Hémez, Rémy, and Aline Leboeuf. 2016. Retours sur Sangaris: Entre stabilization et protection des civils. *Etudes de l'Ifri. Focus Stratégique*, no. 67.

Hendrix, Cullen S., and Wendy H. Wong. 2013. When Is the Pen Truly Mighty? Regime Type and the Efficacy of Naming and Shaming in Curbing Human Rights Abuses. *British Journal of Political Science*, 43 (3): 651–672.

Higgins, Rosalyn. 1969. *United Nations Peacekeeping, 1946–1967: Documents and Commentary, Volume I, The Middle East*. Oxford: Oxford University Press.

High-Level Conference on the Protection of Civilians. 2015. The Kigali Principles on the Protection of Civilians. Available at: http://

civilianprotection.rw/wp-content/uploads/(2015/09/REPORT_PoC_ conference_Long-version.pdf.

Hill, Daniel W., Jr., Will H. Moore, and Bumba Mukherjee. 2013. Information Politics versus Organizational Incentives: When Are Amnesty International's "Naming and Shaming" Reports Biased? *International Studies Quarterly*, 57 (2): 219–232.

Hillen, John. 1998. *Blue Helmets: The Strategy of UN Military Operations*. Washington, DC: Brassey's.

Hills, Alice. 2012. Lost in Translation: Why Nigeria's Police Don't Implement Democratic Reforms. *International Affairs* 88 (4): 739–755.

Hirschmann, Gisela. 2017. UN Peacekeeping and the Protection of Due Process Rights: Learning How to Protect the Rights of Detainees. In *Protecting the Individual from International Authority*, edited by Monika Heupel and Michael Zürn, 186–202. New York: Cambridge University Press.

Hobbes, Thomas. 2017. *Leviathan*. London: Penguin Classics.

Hoffmann, Stanley. 1975. Notes on the Elusiveness of Modern Power. *International Journal* 30 (2): 183–206.

Holt, Victoria, Glyn Taylor, and Max Kelly. 2009. *Protecting Civilians in the Context of UN Peacekeeping Operations: Successes, Setbacks and Remaining Challenges*. New York: United Nations. Office for the Coordination of Humanitarian Affairs.

Holt, Victoria, and Tobias Berkman. 2006. *The Impossible Mandate? Military Preparedness, the Responsibility to Protect, and Modern Peace Operations*. Washington, DC: The Henry L. Stimson Center.

Hopf, Ted. 2010. The Logic of Habit in International Relations *European Journal of International Relations*. 16 (4): 539–561.

Hovland, Carl I., Arthur A. Lumsdaine, and Fred D. Sheffield. 1949. *Experiments on Mass Communication. (Studies in Social Psychology in World War II), Vol. 3*. Princeton, NJ: Princeton University Press.

Hovsepian, Nubar, ed. 2008. *The War on Lebanon: A Reader*. Northampton, MA: Olive Branch Press.

Howard, Lise Morjé. 2002. "UN Peace Implementation in Namibia: The Causes of Success" in *International Peacekeeping* 9 (1): 99–132.

2008. *UN Peacekeeping in Civil Wars*. Cambridge: Cambridge University Press.

2010. Sources of Change in United States-United Nations Relations. *Global Governance* 16 (4): 485–503.

2012. The Ethnocracy Trap. *Journal of Democracy* 23 (4): 155–169.

2014. Kosovo and Timor Leste: Neotrusteeship, Neighbors, and the United Nations. *Annals of the American Academy of Political and Social Science* 656 (1): 116–135.

2015a. Peacekeeping, Peace Enforcement, and UN Reform. *Georgetown Journal of International Affairs* 16 (2): 6–13.

2015b. US Foreign Policy Habits in Ethnic Conflict. *International Studies Quarterly* 59 (4): 721–734.

Howard, Lise Morjé, and Alexandra Stark. 2017–18. How Civil Wars End: The International System, Norms, and the Role of External Actors. *International Security* 42 (3): 127–171.

Howard, Lise Morjé, and Anjali Kaushlesh Dayal. 2018. The Use of Force in UN Peacekeeping. *International Organization* 72 (1): 71–103.

Hughes, Tim. 2006. Conflict Diamonds and the Kimberley Process: Mission Accomplished – or Mission Impossible? *South African Journal of International Affairs* 13 (2): 115–130.

Hultman, Lisa. 2010. Keeping Peace or Spurring Violence? Unintended Effects of Peace Operations on Violence against Civilians. *Civil Wars* 12 (1–2): 29–46.

Hultman, Lisa, and Dursun Peksen. 2017. Successful or Counterproductive Coercion? The Effect of International Sanctions on Conflict Intensity. *Journal of Conflict Resolution* 61 (6): 1315–1339.

Hultman, Lisa, Jacob Kathman, and Megan Shannon. 2013. United Nations Peacekeeping and Civilian Protection in Civil War. *American Journal of Political Science* 57 (4): 875–891.

2014. Beyond Keeping Peace: United Nations Effectiveness in the Midst of Fighting. *American Political Science Review* 108 (4): 737–753.

Humphreys, Macartan, and Jeremy M. Weinstein. 2006. Handling and Manhandling Civilians in Civil War. *American Political Science Review* 100 (3):429–447.

2007. Demobilization and Reintegration. *Journal of Conflict Resolution* 51 (4): 531–567.

Huntington, Samuel P. 1957. *The Soldier and the State*. Cambridge, MA: Harvard University Press.

Hurd, Ian. 2002. Legitimacy, Power, and the Symbolic Life of the UN Security Council. *Global Governance* 8: 35.

2007. *After Anarchy: Legitimacy and Power in the United Nations Security Council*. Princeton, NJ: Princeton University Press.

Huth, Paul K. 1999. Deterrence and International Conflict: Empirical Findings and Theoretical Debate. *Annual Review of Political Science* 2: 25–48.

ICRC. Rule 71. Weapons That Are by Nature Indiscriminate. IHL Database. Available at: https://ihl-databases.icrc.org/customary-ihl/eng/docs/v1_rul_rule71#Fn_F4806E7_00032.

Institute for Economics and Peace. 2015. *Global Terrorism Index Report*. New York.

International Crisis Group. 2006. Israel/Palestine/Lebanon: Climbing Out of the Abyss. Middle East Report N°57, 25 July.

2007. Central African Republic Anatomy of a Phantom State. Available at https://d2071andvip0wj.cloudfront.net/central-african-republic-anatomy-of-a-phantom-state.pdf.

2014. The Central African Republic's Hidden Conflict. Crisis Group Africa Briefing 105, 12 December. Available at: www.crisisgroup.org/africa/central-africa/central-african-republic/central-african-republics-hidden-conflict.

Isaac, Jeffrey. 1987. *Power and Marxist Theory*. Ithaca, NY: Cornell University Press.

Issa, Antoun. 2016. Lebanon Has a New President (Not That It Matters). *Foreign Policy*, 1 November.

Jackson, Patrick. 2006. *Civilizing the Enemy: German Reconstruction and the Invention of the West*. Ann Arbor, MI: University of Michigan Press.

Jackson, Patrick and Daniel Nexon. 2009. Paradigmatic Faults in International Relations Theory. *International Studies Quarterly*. 53 (4): 907–930.

Jakobsen, Peter V. 2000. Focus on the CNN Effect Misses the Point: The Real Media Impact on Conflict Management Is Invisible and Indirect. *Journal of Peace Research* 37 (2): 131–143.

James, Alan. 1983. Painful Peacekeeping: The United Nations in Lebanon 1978–1982. *International Journal*. 38 (4): 613–634.

1990. *Peacekeeping in International Politics*. London: Macmillan/International Institute for Strategic Studies.

Jardine, Eric, and Simon Palamar. 2013. From Medusa Past Kantolo: Testing the Effectiveness of Canada's Enemy-Centric and Population-Centric Counterinsurgency Operational Strategies. *Studies in Conflict & Terrorism* 36 (7): 588–608.

Jaster, Robert. 1985. *South Africa in Namibia: The Botha Strategy*. Lanham, MD: University Press of America.

1990. The 1988 Peace Accords and the Future of South Western Africa. Adelphi Papers 53. London: International Institute for Strategic Studies.

Jennings, Kathleen M. 2015. Life in a 'Peace-kept' City: Encounters with the Peacekeeping Economy. *Journal of Intervention and Statebuilding* 9 (3): 296–315.

Jennings, Kathleen M., and Morten Bøås. 2015. Transactions and Interactions: Everyday Life in the Peacekeeping Economy. *Journal of Intervention and Statebuilding* 9 (3): 281–295.

Jentleson, Bruce W., and Christopher A. Whytock. 2005. Who 'Won' Libya? *International Security* 30 (3): 47–86.

Jervis, Robert. 1982. Deterrence and Perception. *International Security* 7 (3): 3–30.

Jervis, Robert, Richard N. Lebow, and Janice G. Stein. 1985. *The Psychology of Deterrence*. Baltimore: Johns Hopkins University Press.

Johansson, Patrik. 2009. The Humdrum Use of Ultimate Authority: Defining and Analyzing Chapter VII Resolutions. *Nordic Journal of International Law* 78 (3): 309–342.

Johnstone, Ian. 2011. *The Power of Deliberation: International Law, Politics and Organizations*. Oxford: Oxford University Press.

2016. Between Bureaucracy and Adhocracy: Crafting a Spectrum of Peace Operations. Global Peace Operations Review, 31 March.

Joint Chiefs of Staff. 2016. Joint Publication 3–07 Stability Operations. Available at: www.dtic.mil/doctrine/new_pubs/jp3_07.pdf.

Jones, Bruce D. 2001. *Peacemaking in Rwanda: The Dynamics of Failure*. Boulder, CO: Lynne Reinner.

2015. *Why the United States needs UN Peacekeeping*. Brookings Institute, 10 December 2015. Available at: www.brookings.edu/blogs/order-from-chaos/posts/2015/12/10-un-peacekeeping-serves-us-strategic-interests-jones.

Joshi, Madhav. 2013. United Nations Peacekeeping, Democratic Process, and the Durability of Peace after Civil Wars. *International Studies Perspective* 14 (3): 362–382.

Kalyvas, Stathis N. 2006. *The Logic of Violence in Civil War*. New York: Cambridge University Press.

Kalyvas, Stathis N., and Laia Ballcells. 2010. International System and Technologies of Rebellion: How the End of the Cold War Shaped Internal Conflict. *American Political Science Review* 104 (3): 415–429.

Kalyvas, Stathis N., and Matthew Adam Kocher. 2009. The Dynamics of Violence in Vietnam: An Analysis of the Hamlet Evaluation System (HES). *Journal of Peace Research* 46 (3): 335–355.

Kapiszewski, Diana, Lauren M. MacLean, and Benjamin L. Reed. 2015. *Field Research in Political Science: Practices and Principles*. Cambridge: Cambridge University Press.

Kaplan, Eben. 2010. Profile: Hassan Nasrallah, Secretary-General of Hezbollah. Council on Foreign Relations.

Karakaya, Süveyda. 2018. Globalization and Contentious Politics: A Comparative Analysis of Nonviolent and Violent Campaigns. *Conflict Management and Peace Science* 35 (4): 315–335.

Karim, Sabrina, and Kyle Beardsley. 2016. Explaining Sexual Exploitation and Abuse in Peacekeeping Missions: The Role of Female Peacekeepers and Gender Equality in Contributing Countries. *Journal of Peace Research* 53 (1): 100–115.

Karlsrud, John. 2013. Special Representatives of the Secretaries-General as Norm Arbitrators? Understanding Bottom-Up Authority in UN Peace-keeping. *Global Governance* 19 (4): 525–544.

2014. Peacekeeping 4.0: Harnessing the Potential of Big Data, Social Media and Cyber Technology. In *Cyber Space and International Relations*, edited by J. F. Kremer and B. Müller. Berlin: Springer.

2015. The UN at War: Examining the Consequences of Peace Enforce-ment Mandates for the UN Peacekeeping Operations in the CAR, the DRC and Mali. *Third World Quarterly* 36 (1): 40–54.

2018. *The UN at War: Peace Operations in a New Era*. Palgrave Macmillan.

Karlsrud, John, and Frederik Rosen. 2013. In the Eye of the Beholder? The UN and the Use of Drones to Protect Civilians. *International Journal of Security and Development* 2 (2): 1–10.

Karns, Margaret. Ad Hoc Multilateral Diplomacy: The United States, the Contact Group, and Namibia. *International Organization* 41 (1): 93–123.

Kassem, Susann. 2017. Peacekeeping, Development and Counterinsurgency: The United Nations Interim Force in Lebanon and "Quick Impact Projects." In Karim Makdisi and Vijay Prashad, eds. 2016. *Land of the Blue Helmets: The UN in the Arab World*. Berkeley, CA: University of California Press.

Kathman, Jacob D. 2011. Civil War Diffusion and Regional Motivations for Intervention. *Journal of Conflict Resolution* 55 (6): 847–876.

Kathman, Jacob D. and Reed M. Wood. 2016. Stopping the Killing during the "Peace": Peacekeeping and the Severity of Postconflict Civilian Victimization. *Foreign Policy Analysis* 12(2): 149–169.

Katjavivi, Peter. 1988. *A History of Resistance in Namibia*. London: James Currey.

Katzenstein, Peter J., ed. 1996. *The Culture of National Security: Norms and Identity in World Politics*. New York: Columbia University Press.

Kaufman, Asher. 2013. *Contested Frontiers in the Syria-Lebanon-Israel Region: Cartography, Sovereignty, and Conflict*. Washington, DC: Woodrow Wilson Press.

Keck, Margaret E., and Kathryn Sikkink, eds. 1998. *Activists beyond Borders: Advocacy Networks in International Politics*. Ithaca, NY: Cornell University Press.

Kelley, Judith. 2012. *Monitoring Democracy When International Election Observation Works, and Why It Often Fails*. Princeton, NJ: Princeton University Press.

Kelly, Fergus. 2018. UN Renews Mandate for Central African Republic Peacekeeping Mission. *The Defense Post*, 14 December.

Kelly, Max, and Alison Giffen. 2011. *Military Planning to Protect Civilians: Proposed Guidance for UN PKOs*. Washington, DC: Stimson Center.

Kende, Mathias. 2018. *The Trade Policy Review Mechanism: A Critical Analysis*. Oxford: Oxford University Press.

Keohane, Robert O., and Lisa Martin. 1995. The Promise of Institutionalist Theory. *International Security*, 20(1): 39–51.

Keohane, Robert O., and Joseph S. Nye. 1977. *Power and Interdependence: World Politics in Transition*. Boston: Little Brown.

Kertzer, David I. 1988. *Ritual, Politics, and Power*. New Haven, CT: Yale University Press.

Kertzer Joshua D. 2016. *Resolve in International Politics*. Princeton, NJ: Princeton University Press.

Kier, Elizabeth. 1997. *Imagining War*. Princeton, NJ: Princeton University Press.

Kilembe, Faouzi. 2015. Local Dynamics in the PK5 District of Bangui. In *Making Sense of the Central African Republic*, edited by Tatiana Carayannis and Louisa Lombard. London: Zed Books.

King, Gary, Robert O. Keohane, and Sidney Verba, 1994. *Designing Social Inquiry: Scientific Inference in Qualitative Research*. Princeton, NJ: Princeton University Press.

Kleinfeld. Philip. 2018. Part I, Special Report: The Central Africa Republic: Little Peace to Keep, but 4.7 Million Lives to Live. Integrated Regional Information Networks (IRIN), May.

Klotz, Audie. 1995. Norms Reconstituting Interests: Global Racial Equality and US Sanctions against South Africa. *International Organization* 49 (3): 451–478.

Kokopakpa, Leger Serge. 2018. Civilians Killed in Central African Republic Were "Manipulated," *U.N. Reuters*, 12 April.

Koops, Joachim, and Giulia Tercovich. 2016. Europe's Return to United Nations Peacekeeping: Challenges, Opportunities and Ways Ahead. *International Peacekeeping* 5: 597–609

Koursany, Fleury. 2017. Diamonds Bring New Life to War-Torn Central African Republic. Bloomberg, 23 July.

Krain, Matthew. 2012. J'accuse! Does Naming and Shaming Perpetrators Reduce the Severity of Genocides or Politicides? *International Studies Quarterly* 56 (3): 574–589.

Krasno, Jean, Don Daniel, and Bradd Hayes, eds. 2003. *Leveraging for Success in UN Peace Operations*. Westport, CT: Greenwood Publishing Group.

Krause, Peter. 2013. The Structure of Success: How the Internal Distribution of Power Drives Armed Group Behavior and National Movement Effectiveness," *International Security* 38 (3): 72–116.

Krebs, Ronald R. 2005. One Nation under Arms? Military Participation Policy and the Politics of Identity. *Security Studies* 14 (3): 529–564.

Krebs, Ronald R., and Patrick Thaddeus Jackson. 2007. Twisting Tongues and Twisting Arms: The Power of Political Rhetoric. *European Journal of International Relations* 13 (1): 35–66.

Kreike, Emmanuel. 2004. *Re-Creating Eden: Land Use, Environment, and Society in Southern Angola and Namibia.* Portsmouth: Heinemann.

Kupchan, Charles A. 2010. Enemies into Friends: How the United States Can Court Its Adversaries. *Foreign Affairs* 89 (2): 120–134.

Kydd, Andrew. 2003. Which Side Are You On? Bias, Credibility, and Mediation. *American Journal of Political Science* 47 (4): 597–561.

Lake, David. A. 2011. Why "Isms" Are Evil: Theory, Epistemology, and Academic Sects as Impediments to Understanding and Progress. *International Studies Quarterly* 55 (2): 465–480.

  2016. *The Statebuilder's Dilemma: On the Limits of Foreign Intervention.* Ithaca, NY: Cornell University Press.

Lakoff, George, and Mark Johnson. 1980. *Metaphors We Live By.* Chicago: University of Chicago Press.

Landgren, Karin. 2015. Reflections on a Career in Peace Operations. *Global Peace Operations Review.* 16 July.

  2018. Nailing Down the Primacy of Politics in UN Peacekeeping: An Insider Perspective. *IPI Global Observatory* (blog). Available at: https://theglobalobservatory.org/2018/08/nailing-down-primacy-of-politics-un-peacekeeping-an-insider-perspective/.

Larson, Charles. 1983. *Persuasion: Reception and Responsibility.* Belmont: Wadsworth Publishing Group.

Le Borgne, Eric, and Thomas J. Jacobs. 2016. Lebanon Promoting Poverty Reduction and Shared Prosperity. Washington, DC: World Bank Group.

Lebovic, James, and Erik Voeten. 2006. The Politics of Shame: The Condemnation of Country Human Rights Practices in the UNCHR. *International Studies Quarterly* 50(4): 861–888.

  2009. The Cost of Shame: International Organizations and Foreign Aid in the Punishing of Human Rights Violators. *Journal of Peace Research* 46 (1): 79–97.

Lebow Richard N., and Janice Gross Stein. 1989. Rational Deterrence Theory. *World Politics* (41): 208–224.

  1990. Deterrence, the Elusive Dependent Variable. *World Politics* 42 (1): 336–369.

Lehmann, Ingrid A. 1999. *Peacekeeping and Public Information: Caught in the Crossfire.* London: Frank Cass.

Lepin, Marie. 2015. UN Quick Impact Projects: A Stepping Stone for United Nations Missions Effectiveness through the Creation of a Confidence Building System. MA Thesis, CUNY Academic Works.

Levitsky, Steven, and Lucan A. Way. 2010. *Competitive Authoritarianism: Hybrid Regimes after the Cold War*. New York: Cambridge University Press.

Leys, Colin. 1989. Whose Security Is This? *The Namibian*, 10 October.

Leys, Colin, and John S. Saul, ed. 1995. *Namibia's Liberation Struggle: The Two-Edged Sword*. London: James Currey.

Libel, Tamir. 2016. *European Military Culture and Security Governance: Soldiers, Scholars and Defence Universities*. New York: Routledge.

Lieber, Robert. 2012. *Power and Willpower in the American Future: Why The United States Is Not Destined to Decline*. Cambridge: Cambridge University Press.

Lindberg, Nancy and David Rothkopf. 2015. Four Lessons for Fighting Violent Extremists – Without Guns. *Foreign Policy*. Available from http://foreignpolicy.com/2015/09/29/four-lessons-for-fighting-extremists-without-guns-obama-united-nations-summit/.

Lipson, Michael. 2007. Peacekeeping: Organized Hypocrisy. *European Journal of International Relations* 13 (1):5–34.

Lombard, Louisa. 2016. *State of Rebellion: Violence and Intervention in the Central African Republic*. London: Zed Books.

Lombard, Louisa, and Sylvain Batianga-Kinzi. 2015. Violence, Popular Punishment, and War in the Central African Republic. *African Affairs* 114 (454): 52–71.

Lombard, Louisa, and Tatiana Carayannis. 2015. Making Sense of CAR: An Introduction. In *Making Sense of the Central African Republic*, edited by Tatiana Carayannis and Louisa Lombard. London: Zed Books.

Losh, Jack. 2018. Child Soldiers in Africa: Recruitment in CAR Civil War Is Surging, with the U.N. Struggling to Assist Children. *Newsweek*, 6 June.

Lukes, Steven. 1974. *Power: A Radical View*. New York; London: Macmillan Education.

Luttwak, Edward. 1999. Give War a Chance. *Foreign Affairs*, July/August: 36–44.

Lyall, Jason. 2010. Do Democracies Make Inferior Counterinsurgents? Reassessing Democracy's Impact on War Outcomes and Duration. *International Organization* 64 (1): 167–192.

Lyall, Jason, and Isaiah Wilson. 2009. Rage against the Machines: Explaining Outcomes in Counterinsurgency Wars. *International Organization* 63 (1): 67.

Lynn-Jones, S. M. 1995. Offense-Defense Theory and Its Critics. *Security Studies* 4 (4): 660–691.

Lyon, David. 2001. *Surveillance Society: Monitoring Everyday Life*. Buckingham: Open University Press.

2007. *Surveillance Studies: An Overview*. Cambridge: Polity.

Lyon, David, Kirstie Ball, and Kevin Haggerty (eds.). 2012. *Routledge Handbook of Surveillance Studies*. New York: Routledge.

Mac Ginty, Roger, and Olivier Richmond. 2013. The Local Turn in Peace Building: a Critical Agenda for Peace. *Third World Quarterly* 34 (5): 763–783.

Mack, Andrew. 1975. Why Big Nations Lose Small Wars: The Politics of Asymmetric Conflict. *World Politics* 27 (2): 175–200.

Madley, Benjamin. 2005. From Africa to Auschwitz: How German South West Africa Incubated Ideas and Methods Adopted and Developed by the Nazis in Eastern Europe. *European History Quarterly* 35 (3): 429–464.

Mahoney, James and Kathleen Thelen. 2009. *Explaining Institutional Change: Ambiguity, Agency and Power*. New York: Cambridge University Press.

Makdisi, Karim. 2014. Reconsidering the Struggle Over UNIFIL in Southern Lebanon. *Journal of Palestine Studies* 43 (2): 24–41.

2017. Constructing Security Council Resolution 1701 for Lebanon in the Shadow of the "War on Terror." *International Peacekeeping*. 18 (1): 4–20.

Makdisi, Karim, Rami Khouri and Martin Waehlisch, eds. 2015. *Interventions in Conflict: International Peacemaking in the Middle East*. New York: Palgrave Macmillan.

Makdisi, Karim, Timor Goksel, Hans Bastian Hauck, and Stuart Reigeluth. 2009. UNIFIL II: Emerging and Evolving European Engagement in Lebanon and the Middle East. *Euro-Mesco Paper*. 76 (1): 25.

Makdisi, Karim, and Vijay Prashad, eds. 2016. *Land of the Blue Helmets: The UN in the Arab World*. Berkeley, CA: University of California Press.

Mandela, Nelson. 2004. *In His Own Words*. New York: Little Brown.

March, James G. and Johan P. Olsen. 1998. Juxtaposing Rationalism and Constructivism: The Institutional Dynamics of International Political Orders. *International Organization* 52 (4): 943–969.

Marchal, Roland. 2014. As Violence Persists, International Intervention in CAR Falls Short. International Peace Institute, Global Observatory. Available at: https://theglobalobservatory.org/2014/02/as-violence-persists-international-intervention-in-car-falls-short/.

2015. CAR and the Regional (Dis)order. In *Making Sense of the Central African Republic*, edited by Tatiana Carayannis and Louisa Lombard. London: Zed Books.

Marten, Kimberly Zisk. 2006. *Enforcing the Peace: Learning from the Imperial Past.* New York: Columbia University Press.

Martin, Lisa L. 1992. *Coercive Cooperation: Explaining Multilateral Economic Sanctions.* Princeton, NJ: Princeton University Press.

McCormick, Ty. 2015. Feature: One Day, We Will Start a Big War. Foreign Policy. https://foreignpolicy.com/2015/10/28/one-day-we-will-start-a-big-war-central-african-republic-un-violence/.

McDermott, Anthony, and Kjell Skjelsbaek, eds. 1991. *The Multinational Force in Beirut 1982–1994.* Miami, FL: Florida International University Press.

McGreal, Chris. 2015. What's the Point of Peacekeepers When They Don't Keep the Peace? *The Guardian,* 17 September 2015.

McGregor, Andrew. 2018. How Russia Is Displacing the French in the Struggle for Influence in the Central African Republic. *Eurasia Daily Monitor* 15 (74). Available at https://jamestown.org/program/how-russia-is-displacing-the-french-in-the-struggle-for-influence-in-the-central-african-republic/.

McGuire, W. J. 1968. Personality and Attitude Change: An Information Processessing Theory. In *Psychological Foundations of Attitudes,* edited by A. G. Greenwald, T. C. Brock, and T. M Ostrom, 171–196. New York: Academic Press.

McHenry, Donald F. 1990. Foreword. *Nation Building: The UN and Namibia.* Washington, DC: The National Democratic Institute for International Affairs.

McNamara, Kathleen R. 1998. *The Currency of Ideas: Monetary Politics in the European Union.* Ithaca, NY: Cornell University Press.

Mearsheimer John J. 1983. *Conventional Deterrence.* Ithaca, NY: Cornell University Press.

2001. *The Tragedy of Great Power Politics.* New York: Norton.

Meernik, James, Rosa Aloisi, Marsha Sowell, and Angela Nichols. 2012. The Impact of Human Rights Organizations on Naming and Shaming Campaigns. *Journal of Conflict Resolution* 56 (2): 233–256.

Mehler, Andreas. 2009. Peace and Power Sharing in Africa: A Not So Obvious Relationship. *African Affairs* 108 (432): 453–473.

Melander, Erik. 2009. Selected to Go Where Murderers Lurk? The Preventive Effect of Peacekeeping on Mass Killings of Civilians. *Conflict Management and Peace Science* 26 (4): 389–406.

Melber, Henning, ed. 2003. *Re-Examining Liberation in Namibia: Political Culture Since Independence.* Stockholm: Nordiska Afrikainstitutet.

Melin, Molly M., and Isak Svensson. 2009. Incentives for Talking: Accepting Mediation in International and Civil Wars. *International Interactions* 35 (3): 249–271.

Mercer, Jonathan. 2010. Emotional Beliefs. *International Organization* 64 (1): 1–31.

Milner, Helen V. 1997. *Interests, Institutions, and Information: Domestic Politics and International Relations*. Princeton, NJ: Princeton University Press.

Monteiro, Nuno. 2014. *Theory of Unipolar Politics*. Cambridge: Cambridge University Press.

Moore, Adam. 2013. *Peacebuilding in Practice: Local Experience in Two Bosnian Towns*. Ithaca, NY: Cornell University Press.

Moskos, Charles C. 1976. *Peace Soldiers: The Sociology of a United Nations Military Force*. Chicago: University of Chicago Press.

Mosley, Layna ed. 2013. *Interview Research in Political Science*. Ithaca, NY: Cornell University Press.

Moyo, Dambisa. 2009. *Dead Aid: Why Aid Is Not Working and How There Is a Better Way for Africa*. New York: Farrar, Straus, and Giroux.

Muggah, Robert. 2018. The U.N. Can't Bring Peace to the Central African Republic: But It Can Help Solve Local Conflicts. Here's How. Foreign Policy, 16 August.

Muggah, Robert, and Chris O'Donnell. 2015. Next Generation Disarmament, Demobilization and Reintegration. *Stability: International Journal of Security and Development* 4(1): 1–30.

Murdie, Amanda, and David R. Davis. 2010. Problematic Potential: The Human Rights Consequences of Peacekeeping Interventions in Civil Wars. *Human Rights Quarterly* 32 (1): 49–72.

Murdie, Amanda, and Johannes Urpelainen. 2015. Why Pick on Us? Environmental INGOs and State Shaming as a Strategic Substitute. *Political Studies*, 63(2): 353–372.

Myint-U, Thant and Amy Scott. 2007. *The UN Secretariat: A Brief History*. New York: International Peace Academy.

Nachmias, Nitza. 1996. The Impossible Peacekeeping Mission: UNIFIL. *Peacekeeping and International Relations*. 25 (5): 14–15.

Nagl, John A. 2005. *Learning to Eat Soup with a Knife: Counterinsurgency Lessons from Malaya and Vietnam*. Chicago: University of Chicago Press.

Narang, Neil. 2014. Humanitarian Assistance and the Duration of Peace after Civil War. *The Journal of Politics* 76 (2): 446–460.

Nepstad, Sharon Erickson. (2011). *Nonviolent Revolutions: Civil Resistance in the Late 20th Century*. New York: Oxford University Press.

Newby, Vanessa. 2018. *Peacekeeping in South Lebanon: Credibility and Local Cooperation*. Syracuse, NY: Syracuse University Press.

Newman, Abraham L., and Elliot Posner. 2018. *Voluntary Disruptions: International Soft Law, Finance, and Power*. Oxford: Oxford University Press.

Nexon, Daniel, and Patrick Thaddeus Jackson. 2009. Paradigmatic Faults in International Relations Theory. *International Studies Quarterly* 53 (4): 907–940.

Nikitin, Alexander. 2013. The Russian Federation. In *Providing Peacekeepers: The Politics, Challenges, and Future of United Nations Peacekeeping Contributions*, edited by Alex Bellamy and Paul Williams. Oxford: Oxford University Press.

Norheim-Martinsen, Per Martin, and Jacob Aasland Ravndal. 2011. Towards Intelligence-Driven Peace Operations? The Evolution of UN and EU Intelligence Structures. *International Peacekeeping*, 18:4, 454–467

North, Douglass C. 1990. *Institutions, Institutional Change and Economic Performance*. New York: Cambridge University Press.

Novosseloff. Alexandra. 2015a. United Nations Interim Force in Lebanon. In Joachim A. Koops, Norrie Macqueen, Thierry Tardy, and Paul D. Williams eds. *The Oxford Handbook of United Nations Peacekeeping Operations*. Oxford: Oxford University Press.

2015b. Expanded United Nations Interim Force in Lebanon. In Joachim A. Koops, Norrie Macqueen, Thierry Tardy, and Paul D. Williams eds. *The Oxford Handbook of United Nations Peacekeeping Operations*. Oxford: Oxford University Press.

2018. *The Many Lives of a Peacekeeping Mission: The UN Operation in Côte d'Ivoire*. New York: International Peace Institute.

Novosseloff, Alexandra, and Thierry Tardy. 2016. France and the Evolution of the UN Peacekeeping Doctrine. In *UN Peacekeeping Doctrine towards the Post-Brahimi Era? Adapting to Stabilization, Protection and New Threats*, edited by Chiyuki Aoi, Cedric de Coning, and John Karlsrud. Abingdon: Routledge.

Ntchatcho, Herman. 1993. Political Amnesty and Repatriation of Refugees in Namibia. In *African Yearbook of International Law*, edited by Abdulqawi Yusuf. London: Martinus Nijhoff Publishers.

Nujoma, Sam. 2001. *Where Others Wavered*. Bedford: Panaf Books.

Nyamutata, Conrad. 2013. Engaging or Shaming? An Analysis of UN's Naming and Shaming of Child Abusers in Armed Conflict. *Journal of International Humanitarian Legal Studies*, 2013, 4 (1): 151–173.

Nzwili, Fredrick. 2015. African Catholics Embrace Jubilee Year as Time for Muslim Understanding. *Washington Post*, 21 December.

Nye, Joseph S., Jr. 2009. *Soft Power: The Means to Success in World Politics*. New York: Public Affairs.

Ochoa, Christiana, and Patrick Keenan. 2011. Regulating Information Flows, Regulating Conflict: An Analysis of United States Conflict Minerals Legislation. *Goettingen Journal of International Law* 129.

Official Gazette Extraordinary of South West Africa. 1980. Proclamation by the Administrator General for the Territory of South West Africa. No. AG8. Windhoek, 24 April.

Oksamytna, Kseniya. 2018. Policy Entrepreneurship by International Bureaucracies: The Evolution of Public Information in UN Peacekeeping. *International Peacekeeping* 25 (1): 79–104.

Olin, Nathaniel. 2015. Pathologies of Peacekeeping and Peacebuilding in CAR. In *Making Sense of the Central African Republic*, edited by Tatiana Carayannis and Louisa Lombard. London: Zed Books.

Olson, Mancur. 2000. *Power and Prosperity*. New York: Basic Books.

Olsson, Louise. 2001. Gender Mainstreaming in Practice: The United Nations Transitional Assistance Group in Namibia. *Journal of International Peacekeeping* 8 (2): 1–16.

Oswald, Bruce. 2011. Detention by United Nations Peacekeepers: Searching for Definition and Categorisation. *Journal of International Peacekeeping* 15 (1–2): 118–151.

Ourdan, Rémy. 2018. En Centrafrique, Bangui sous la menace d'une attaque de rebelles. *Le Monde*, 25 April.

Oxfam. 2012. For Me, But Without Me, Is Against Me: Why Efforts to Stabilize the Eastern Congo Are Not Working. Oxfam Lobby Briefing.

Oye, Kenneth A. 1993. *Economic Discrimination and Political Exchange: World Political Economy in the 1930s and 1980s*. Princeton, NJ: Princeton University Press.

Paddon Rhoads, Emily. 2011. Partnering for Peace: Implications and Dilemmas. *International Peacekeeping* 18 (5): 516–533.

   2016. *Taking Sides in Peacekeeping: Impartiality and the Future of the United Nations*. Oxford: Oxford University Press.

Pampinella, Stephen. 2015. The Effectiveness of Coercive and Persuasive Counterinsurgency Practices since 1945. *Civil Wars* 17 (4): 503–526.

Pape, Robert A. 1997. Why Economic Sanctions Do Not Work. *International Security* 22 (2): 90–136.

   2003. The Strategic Logic of Suicide Terrorism. *American Political Science Review* 97 (3): 343–361.

   2005. *Dying to Win: The Strategic Logic of Suicide Terror*. New York: Random House.

Paris, Roland. 2004. *At War's End: Building Peace after Civil Conflict*. Cambridge and New York: Cambridge University Press.

   2010. Saving Liberal Peacebuilding. *Review of International Studies*, 36 (2): 337–365.

Patrick, Wendy L. 2013. *Using the Psychology of Attraction in Christian Outreach: Lessons from the Dark side*. New York: Peter Lang.

Paul, Christopher, Colin P. Clarke, and Beth Grill. 2010. *Victory Has a Thousand Fathers: Sources of Success in Counterinsurgency.* National Defense Research Institute. Santa Monica, CA: RAND Corporation. Available at: www.rand.org/pubs/monographs/MG964.html.

Paul, Christopher, Colin P. Clarke, Beth Grill, and Molly Dunigan. 2016. Moving beyond Population-Centric vs. Enemy-Centric Counterinsurgency. *Small Wars & Insurgencies* 27 (6): 1019–1042.

Paulson, Joshua. 2005. *Waging Nonviolent Struggle: 20th Century Practice and 21st Century Potential,* edited by Gene Sharp. Manchester, NH: Extending Horizons Books.

Perazzone, Stephanie. 2017. Reintegrating Former Fighters in the Congo: Ambitious Objectives, Limited Results. *International Peacekeeping* 24 (2): 254–279.

Pérez de Cuéllar, Javier. 1997. *Pilgrimage for Peace: A Secretary-General's Memoir.* New York: St. Martin's.

Perloff, Richard M. 1993. *The Dynamics of Persuasion.* Mahwah, NY: Lawrence Erlbaum Associates.

2014. *The Dynamics of Persuasion.* 5th edn. New York: Routledge.

Perry, Tom and Oliver Holmes. 2014. Former PM Hariri back in Lebanon for First Time in Three Years. *Reuters.* 8 August.

Peter, Mateja. 2015. Between Doctrine and Practice: The UN Peacekeeping Dilemma. *Global Governance: A Review of Multilateralism and International Organizations* 21 (3): 351–370.

Pettersson, Thérése and Kristine Eck. 2018. Organized Violence, 1989–2017. *Journal of Peace Research* 55 (4).

Petraeus, David. 2010. Counterinsurgency Concepts: What We Learned in Iraq. *Global Policy.* 1 (1): 116–117.

Pfaeltzer, Juliette J. W. 2014. Naming and Shaming in Financial Market Regulations: A Violation of the Presumption of Innocence? *Utrecht Law Review* 10 (1): 134–148.

Piarroux, Renaud, et al. Understanding the Cholera Epidemic, Haiti. *Emerging Infectious Diseases* 17 (7): 1161–1168.

Pierson, Paul. 2004. *Politics in Time: History, Institutions, and Social Analysis.* Princeton, NJ: Princeton University Press.

Porch, Douglas. 1986. Bugeaud, Gallieni, Lyautey: The Development of French Colonial Warfare. In *Makers of Modern Strategy: From Machiavelli to the Nuclear Age,* edited by Peter Paret. Princeton, NJ: Princeton University Press.

2013. *Counterinsurgency: Exposing the Myths of the New Way of War.* New York: Cambridge University Press.

Posen, Barry R. 1993. The Security Dilemma and Ethnic Conflict. *Survival* 35 (1): 27–47.

Pouligny, Béatrice. 2006. *Peace Operations Seen from Below: UN Missions and Local People*. Bloomfield, CT: Kumarian Press.

Pouliot, Vincent. 2008. The Logic of Practicality: A Theory of Practice of Security Communities. *International Organization* 62 (2): 257–288.

Powell, Robert. 1999. *In the Shadow of Power*. Princeton, NJ: Princeton University Press.

2004. Bargaining and Learning While Fighting. *American Journal of Political Science* 48 (2):344–61.

2012. Persistent Fighting and Shifting Power. *American Journal of Political Science* 56 (3):620–37.

Powell, Walter, and Paul J. Dimaggio, eds. 1991. *The New Institutionalism in Organizational Analysis*. Chicago: University of Chicago Press.

Power, Samantha. 2013. Remarks by Ambassador Samantha Power, U.S. Permanent Representative to the United Nations, At the EU/ OCHA Ministerial Breakfast on the Central African Republic. 25 September.

2014. Remarks by Ambassador Samantha Power: Reforming Peacekeeping in a Time of Conflict. American Enterprise Institute. Available at: www.aei.org/publication/remarks-ambassador-samantha-power-reforming-peacekeeping-time-conflict/.

2015. Remarks on Peacekeeping in Brussels. *United States Mission to the United Nations*, 9 March 2015. Available at: http://usun.state.gov/remarks/6399.

Press, Daryl. 2004. The Credibility of Power: Assessing Threats during the "Appeasement" Crises of the 1930s. *International Security*. 29 (1): 136–169.

2005. *Calculating Credibility: How Leaders Assess Military Threats*. Ithaca, NY: Cornell University Press.

Price, Monroe E., and Nicole Stremlau. 2016. Strategic Communications and the Avoidance of Violent Conflict. In *Communication and Peace: Mapping an Emerging Field*, edited by Julia Hoffmann and Virgil Hawkins. Abington: Routledge.

Price, Richard, and Christian Reus-Smit. 1998. Dangerous Liaisons?: Critical International Theory and Constructivism. *European Journal of International Relations* 4 (3): 259–294.

Price, Robert. 1991. *Apartheid State in Crisis: Political Transformation in South Africa, 1975–1990*. Oxford: Oxford University Press.

Prioul, Christian. 1981. *Entre Oubangui et Chari vers 1890*. Paris: Société d'éthnographie.

Pugh, Michael. 2004. Peacekeeping and Critical Theory. *International Peacekeeping* 11 (1): 39–58.

2005. The Political Economy of Peacebuilding: A Critical Theory Perspective. *International Journal of Peace Studies* 10 (2): 23–42.

Pugh, Michael N. Cooper, and M. Turner, eds. 2008. *Whose Peace? Critical Perspective on the Political Economy of Peacebuilding.* Basingstoke: Palgrave.

Qian, Nancy. 2015. Making Progress on Foreign Aid. *Annual Review of Economics* 7 (1): 277–308.

Quester, George. 2003. *Offense and Defense in the International System.* New Brunswick, NJ: Transaction Publishers.

Raj, Shannon. 2011. Blood Electronics: Congo's Conflict Minerals and the Legislation that Could Cleanse the Trade. *Southern California Law Review* 84 (4): 981–1035.

Ratner, Steven R. 1995. *The New UN Peacekeeping: Building Peace in Lands of Conflict after the Cold War.* New York: St. Martin's Press.

Regan, Patrick M. 2002. Third-Party Interventions and the Duration of Intrastate Conflicts. *Journal of Conflict Resolution* 46 (1): 55–73.

Regan, Patrick, and Frank Aydin. 2006. Diplomacy and Other Forms of Intervention in Civil War. *Journal of Conflict Resolution* 50 (5): 736–756.

Renshon, Jonathan. 2017. *Fighting for Status: Hierarchy and Conflict in World Politics.* Princeton, NJ: Princeton University Press.

Reynaert, Julie. 2011. MONUC/MONUSCO and Civilian Protection in the Kivus. *International Peace Information Service.* Available at: www.ipisresearch.be/.

Ricks, Thomas E. 2009. *The Gamble: General David Petraeus and the American Military Adventure in Iraq, 2006–2008.* Easter Rutherford, NJ: Penguin.

Rieker, Pernille. 2017. *French Foreign Policy Practices in the Age of Globalization and Regional Integration: Challenging Grandeur.* New York: Palgrave Macmillan.

Risse, Thomas. 2000. "Let's Argue!": Communicative Action in World Politics. *International Organization* 54 (1): 1–39.

Rogerson, Christian M. 1980. A Future University of Namibia? The Role of the United Nations Institute for Namibia. *Journal of Modern African Studies.* 18 (4): 675–683.

Rohland, Klaus, and Sarah Cliffe. 2002. The East Timor Reconstruction Program: Successes, Problems and Tradeoffs. Working Papers Conflict Prevention and Reconstruction Unit. Washington, DC: World Bank Group.

Rolandsen, Øystein H. 2015. Small and Far Between: Peacekeeping Economies in South Sudan. *Journal of Intervention and Statebuilding* 9 (3): 353–371.

Risse, Thomas, Stephen C. Roppe, and Kathryn Sikkink, eds. 1999. *The Power of Human Rights: International Norms and Domestic Change.* New York: Cambridge University Press.

Rosén, Frederik, and John Karlsrud. 2014. The MONUSCO UAVs: The Implications for Actions and Omissions. *Conflict Trends* 4: 42–48.

Ross, Marc Howard. 2009. *Culture and Belonging in Divided Societies: Contestation and Symbolic Landscapes.* Philadelphia: University of Pennsylvania Press.

Ross, Michael L. 2004. What Do We Know about Natural Resources and Civil War? *Journal of Peace Research* 41 (3): 337–356.

Rubin, Herbert J., and Irene S. Rubin. 2005. *Alternative Interviewing: The Art of Hearing Data.* Thousand Oaks, CA: Sage Publications.

Rubinstein, Robert A. 2005. Intervention and Culture: An Anthropological Approach to Peace Operations *Security Dialogue* 36 (4): 527–544.

Ruffa, Chiara. 2014. What Peacekeepers Think and Do: An Exploratory Study of French, Ghanaian, Italian, and South Korean Armies in the United Nations Interim Force in Lebanon. *Armed Forces & Society.* 40 (2): 199–225.

2017a. *Imagining War and Keeping Peace: Military Cultures in Peace Operations.* Philadelphia: University of Pennsylvania Press.

2017b. Military Cultures and Force Employment in Peace Operations. *Security Studies.* 26 (3): 391–422.

Ruggeri, Andrea, Han Dorussen, and Theodora-Ismene Gizelis. 2017. Winning the Peace Locally: UN Peacekeeping and Local Conflict. *International Organization,* 71 (1): 163–185.

Ruggeri, Andrea. Theodora-Ismene Gizelis, and Han Dorussen. 2012. Managing Mistrust: An Analysis of Cooperation with UN Peacekeeping in Africa. *Journal of Conflict Resolution* 57 (3): 387–409.

2013. Managing Mistrust: An Analysis of Cooperation with UN Peacekeeping in Africa. *Journal of Conflict Resolution* 57 (3): 387–409.

Ruggie, John G. 1992. Multilateralism: The Anatomy of an Institution. *International Organization.* 46 (3): 561–598.

1993. Wandering in the Void: Charting the UN's New Strategic Role. *Foreign Affairs* 72: 26–31.

1998. *Constructing the World Polity: Essays on International Institutionalization.* New York: Routledge.

Russell, Bertrand. 1938. *Power: A New Social Analysis.* New York: W. W. Norton & Company.

Rwanda, Government of. 2015. The Kigali Principles on the Protection of Civilians.

Sagan, Scott D. 1993. *The Limits of Safety: Organizations, Accidents, and Nuclear Weapons.* Princeton, NJ: Princeton University Press.

Saideman, Stephen, and Marie-Joëlle Zahar, eds. 2008. *Intra-State Conflicts, Governments and Security: Dilemmas of Deterrence and Assurance.* London: Routledge.

Salehyan, Idean. 2009. *Rebels without Borders*. Ithaca, NY: Cornell University Press.

Salehyan, Idean, and Kristian Skrede Gleditsch. 2006. Refugees and the Spread of Civil War. *International Organization* 60 (2): 335–366.

Salem, Paul. 2006. The Future of Lebanon. *Foreign Affairs*. 85 (6): 13–22.

Sambanis, Nicholas. 1999. The United Nations Operation in Cyprus: A New Look at the Peacekeeping-Peacemaking Relationship. *International Peacekeeping* 6 (1): 79–108.

Saul, John, and Colin Leys. 2003. Truth, Reconciliation, Amnesia: The "Ex-Detainees" Fight for Justice. In *Re-Examining Liberation in Namibia: Political Culture Since Independence*, edited by Henning Melber. Stockholm: Nordiska Afrikainstitutet.

Saulnier, Pierre. 1998. *Le Centrafrique: Entre mythe et réalité*. Paris: L'Harmattan.

Schelling, Thomas C. 1960. *The Strategy of Conflict*. Cambridge, MA: Harvard University Press.

1963. *The Strategy of Conflict*. Cambridge, MA: Harvard University Press.

1966. *Arms and Influence*. New Haven, CT: Yale University Press.

1967. Some Questions on Civilian Defense. In *Civilian Resistance as a National Defense: Nonviolent Action against Aggression*. Harrisburg, PA: Stackpole, 1967.

Schock, Kurt. 2013. The Practice and Study of Civil Resistance. *Journal of Peace Research* 50 (3): 277–290.

Schutte, Sebastian, and Nils B. Weidmann. 2011. Diffusion Patterns of Violence in Civil Wars. *Political Geography* 30 (3): 143–152.

Schwartz, J. 2015. The Conflict Minerals Experiment. *Harvard Business Law Review*. Available at: https://papers.ssrn.com/sol3/papers.cfm?abstract_id=2548267.

Seawright, Jason, and John Gerring. 2008. Case Selection Techniques in Case Study Research: A Menu of Qualitative and Quantitative Options. *Political Research Quarterly* 61 (2): 294–308.

Seay, Laura. 2012. What's Wrong with Dodd-Frank 1502? *Center for Global Development* Working Paper 284. Available at: www.cgdev.org/sites/default/files/1425843_file_Seay_Dodd_Frank_FINAL.pdf.

Seethaler, Franziska 2016. *Assessing the Impact of DDR Programmes: Possibilities and Challenges*. New York: United Nations University.

Sending, Ole Jacob. 2010. Learning to Build a Sustainable Peace: Ownership and Everyday Peacebuilding. Norwegian Institute of International Affairs. CMI Report 4.

Sengupta, Somini. 2014. Unarmed Drones Aid UN Peacekeeping Missions in Africa. *New York Times*, 2 July.

2015a. Police Officer with U.N. Force in Central African Republic Is Accused of Rape. *New York Times*, 11 August.

2015b. U.N. Official Resigns Amid Accusations of Sex Abuse by Peacekeepers. *New York Times*, 12 August.

2015c. 3 Peacekeepers Accused of Rape in Central African Republic. *New York Times*, 19 August.

Sharp, Gene 1973. *The Politics of Nonviolent Action: The Methods of Nonviolent Action*. P. Sargent Publisher.

1999. Nonviolent Action. In *Encyclopedia of Violence, Peace, and Conflict*, edited by Lester Kurtz and Jennifer Turpin. New York: Academic Press.

Shaykhutdinov, Renat. 2010. Give Peace a Chance: Nonviolent Protest and the Creation of Territorial Autonomy Arrangements. *Journal of Peace Research* 47 (2): 179–191.

Shesterinina, Anastasia, and Brian L. Job. 2016. Particularized Protection: UNSC Mandates and the Protection of Civilians in Armed Conflict. *International Peacekeeping* 23 (2): 240–273.

Sil, Rudra, and Peter Katzenstein. 2010. Analytic Eclecticism in the Study of World Politics: Reconfiguring Problems and Mechanisms across Research Traditions. *Perspectives on Politics* 8 (2): 411–431.

Simmons, Beth A. 2009. *Mobilizing for Human Rights: International Law in Domestic Politics*. New York: Cambridge University Press.

Sisk, Timothy D. 1996. *Power Sharing and International Mediation in Ethnic Conflicts*. New York: Carnegie Corporation.

Skocpol, Theda. 1979. *States and Social Revolutions: A Comparative Analysis of France, Russia, and China*. New York and Cambridge: Cambridge University Press.

Skogmo, Bjorn. 1989. *International Peacekeeping in Lebanon (1978–88)*. Boulder, CO: Lynne Rienner.

Sloan, James. 2014. The Evolution of the Use of Force in UN Peacekeeping. *Journal of Strategic Studies* 37 (5): 674–702.

Small, Melvin, and J. David Singer. 1982. *Resort to Arms: International and Civil War, 1816–1980*. Beverly Hills, CA: Sage Publications.

Smith, Stephen W. 2015. CAR's History: The Past of a Tense Present. In *Making Sense of the Central African Republic*, edited by Tatiana Carayannis and Louisa Lombard. London: Zed Books.

Soeters, Joseph, Donna Winslow, and Alise Weibull. 2003. Military Culture. In *Handbook of the Sociology of the Military*, edited by Giuseppe Caforio. Handbooks of Sociology and Social Research, 237–254. New York: Kluwer.

Solli, Audun, Benjamin de Carvalho, Cedric de Coning, and Mikkel F. Pedersen. 2011. Training in Vain? Bottlenecks in Deploying Civilians for UN Peacekeeping. *International Peacekeeping* 18 (4): 425.

Sotomayor, Arturo C. 2014. *The Myth of the Democratic Peacekeeper: Civil-Military Relations and the United Nations*. Baltimore: Johns Hopkins University Press.

Sprenger, Sebastian. 2008. Office Looking at Warfighter Needs: Gao Urges Better "Outreach" Effort for Dod's Responsive Space Plans. *Inside Missile Defense* 14 (15): 1, 8–9.

Stanley, Elizabeth A. Widen the Window: Training Your Brain and Body to Thrive during Stress and Recover from Trauma. New York: Avery/Penguin Random House, 2019.

Starr, Amory, Luis Fernandez, Randall Amster, Lesley Wood, and Manuel Caro. 2008. The Impacts of State Surveillance on Political Assembly and Association: A Socio-Legal Analysis. *Qualitative Sociology* 31 (3): 251–270.

Stearns, Jason. 2015. Can Force Be Useful in the Absence of a Political Strategy? Lessons from the UN Missions to the DR Congo. *Global Peace Operations Review*. Available at: http://peaceoperationsreview .org/thematic-essays/can-force-be-useful-in-the-absence-of-a-political-strategy-lessons-from-the-un-missions-to-the-dr-congo/

Steenkamp, Willem. 1989. *South Africa's Border War 1966–1989*. Gibraltar: Ashanti.

Steffek, Jens. 2005. Incomplete Agreements and the Limits of Persuasion in International Politics. *Journal of International Relations and Development* 8: 229–256.

Steinmo, Sven. 1993. *Taxation and Democracy: Swedish, British and American Approaches to Financing the Modern State*. New Haven, CT: Yale University Press.

Strandow, Daniel. 2006. *Sanctions and Civil War: Targeted Measures for Conflict Resolution*. Uppsala: Department of Peace and Conflict Research.

Straus, Scott. 2008. *The Order of Genocide: Race, Power, and War in Rwanda*. Ithaca, NY: Cornell University Press.

  2015. *Making and Unmaking Nations War, Leadership, and Genocide in Modern Africa*. Ithaca, NY: Cornell University Press.

Sullivan, Rachel, and Susan Stigant. 2014. Central African Republic: Religious Leaders Call for Dialogue Backed by Grassroots. United States Institute of Peace, 20 November. Available at: www.usip.org/publica tions/2014/11/central-african-republic-religious-leaders-call-dialogue-backed-grassroots.

Sun, Tzu. 1971. *The Art of War*. Translated with an Introduction by Samuel B. Griffith and Foreword by B. H. Liddell Hart. Oxford: Oxford University Press.

Taebi, Behnam, and Azar Safari. 2017. On Effectiveness and Legitimacy of 'Shaming' as a Strategy for Combatting Climate Change. *Science and Engineering Ethics* 23 (5): 1289–1306.

Tannenwald, Nina. 1997. The Nuclear Taboo: The United States and the Normative Basis of Nuclear Non-Use. *International Organization* 53 (3): 433–68.

Tanner, Samuel, and Benoit Dupont. 2015. Police Work in International Peace Operation Environments: A Perspective from Canadian Police Officers in the MINUSTAH. *Policing & Society* 25 (6):663–680.

Tardy, Thierry. 2014. The Reluctant Peacekeeper: France and the Use of Force in Peace Operations. *Journal of Strategic Studies* 37 (5): 770–792.

2016. France: The Unlikely Return to UN Peacekeeping. *International Peacekeeping* 23 (5): 610–629.

Tardy, Thierry, and Dominik Zaum. 2016. France and the United Kingdom in the Security Council. In *The UN Security Council in the 21st Century*, edited by Sebastian von Einsiedel, David M. Malone, and Bruno S. Ugarte, 121–138. Boulder, CO: Lynne Rienner.

Tejpar, J. 2009. *How Do Peace Support Operations Impact on Conflict Regions' Economies?* Stockholm: Fo¨rsvarets forskningsantalt (FOI).

Terman, Rochelle, and Erik Voeten. 2018. The Relational Politics of Shame: Evidence from the Universal Periodic Review. *The Review of International Organizations* 13 (1): 1–23.

Thakur, Ramesh. 1987. The United Nations Interim Force in Lebanon. In *International Peacekeeping in Lebanon: UN Authority and Multinational Force*. Boulder, CO: Westview Press.

The International Institute for Strategic Studies. 2017. *The Military Balance*. London.

The United States Institute of Peace. 2018. Creating a Stable Peace in the Central African Republic. Conference, Library of Congress, Washington DC, 27 June.

The White House. 1994. United States Policy on Reforming Multilateral Peace Operations. Washington, DC. Available at: http://nsarchive.gwu .edu/NSAEBB/NSAEBB53/rw050394.pdf.

2014. Fact Sheet: Summit on Peacekeeping. 26 September. Available at: www.whitehouse.gov/the-press-office/2014/09/26/fact-sheet-summit-un-peacekeeping.

2015. United States Support to United Nations Peace Operations. Washington, DC. Available at: www.defense.gov/Portals/1/Docu ments/pubs/2015peaceoperations.pdf.

The World Bank. 2018. Lebanon. Available at: https://data.worldbank.org/ country/lebanon.

Thelen, Kathleen, Sven Steinmo, and Frank Longstreth, eds. 1992. *Structuring Politics: Historical Institutionalism in Comparative Analysis*. New York: Cambridge University Press.

Theobald, Andrew. 2015. The United Nations Truce Supervision Organization. In *The Oxford Handbook of United Nations Peace-keeping Operations*, edited by Joachim A. Koops, Norrie Macqueen, Thierry Tardy, and Paul D. Williams. Oxford: Oxford University Press.

Thomas, Jakana. 2014. Rewarding Bad Behavior: How Governments Respond to Terrorism in Civil War. *American Journal of Political Science* 58 (4): 804–818.

Thompson, Alexander. 2009. *Channels of Power: The UN Security Council and US Statecraft in Iraq*. Ithaca, NY: Cornell University Press.

Thornberry, Cedric. 2004. *A Nation Is Born: The Inside Story of Namibia's Independence*. Windhoek: Gamsberg Macmillan Publishers.

Traub, James. 2015. Can Attack Helicopters Save U.N. Peacekeeping? *Foreign Policy*, 28 September.

Trenkov-Wermuth, Calin. 2010. *United Nations Justice: Legal and Judicial Reform in Governance Operations*. New York: United Nations University Press.

UN Development Programme. 2017. Human Development Index. Available at: http://hdr.undp.org/en/content/human-development-index-hdi.

UN General Assembly. 2000. *Comprehensive Review of the Whole Question of Peacekeeping Operations in All Their Aspects*. Fifty-fifth session, Item 87 of the Provisional Agenda, A/55/305S/2000/809. Available at: www.un.org/en/ga/search/view_doc.asp?symbol=A/55/305.

UN Information Department. 2013. Press Release. 15 May. Available from www.un.org/press/en/2013/sc11010.doc.htm.

UNHCR. 2004. Quick Impact Projects: A Provisional Guide. UNHCR Geneva.

UNIFL. 2018. FAQS. Available at: https://unifil.unmissions.org/faqs.

United Nations. 1945. *Charter of the United Nations and Statute of the International Court of Justice*. New York: United Nations.

  1948. A/RES/50, 29 May 1948.

  1988. Soldiers for Peace. Audiovisual. Available from www.unmultimedia.org/avlibrary/asset/2005/2005952/.

  1989. *Yearbook of the United Nations: Volume 43*. New York: United Nations.

  1990. *Yearbook of the United Nations: Volume 44*. The Hague: Martinus Nijhoff Publishers.

  1996. *The Blue Helmets: A Review of United Nations Peace-Keeping*. New York: United Nations Department of Public Information.

  1999a. Report of the Independent Inquiry into the Actions of the United Nations during the 1994 Genocide in Rwanda. 16 December 1999. S/1999/1257.

1999b. Report of the Secretary-General Pursuant to General Assembly Resolution 53/35: The Fall of Srebrenica. A/54/549.

2000. *Report of the Panel on United Nations Peace Operations [Brahimi Report]*. New York: United Nations.

2006. Approved Resources for Peacekeeping Operations for the Period from 1 July 2005 to 30 June 2006. A/C.5/60/27.

2008. Department of Peacekeeping Operations and Department of Field Support. *United Nations Peacekeeping Operations: Principles and Guidelines*. New York: United Nations.

2009a. Approved resources for Peacekeeping Operations for the Period from 1 July 2008 to 30 June 2009. A/C.5/63/23.

2009b. *Peacebuilding in the Immediate Aftermath of Conflict*. New York: United Nations.

2013. *Report of the Secretary-General on the Situation in Mali*, 26 March 2013. New York: United Nations. S/2013/189.

2014a. Peacebuilding in the Aftermath of Conflict. New York: United Nations. A/69/399-S/2014/694.

2014b. *Guidelines on Understanding and Integrating Local Perceptions in UN Peacekeeping*. New York: United Nations.

2014c. Multidimensional Integrated Stabilization Mission in Mali. *Standard Operating Procedure: Intelligence Cycle Management*. Bamako: United Nations.

2014d. *UN Police towards 2020: Serve and Protect to Build Peace and Security: A Vision and Multi-Year Strategy*. New York: United Nations.

2015a. MONUSCO, Civil Affairs. Available at: http://monusco .unmissions.org/LinkClick.aspx?fileticket=sbKJDmIIJWQ%3D&tabid= 10715&mid=13709&language=en-US.

2015b. *Performance Peacekeeping*. New York: United Nations.

2015c. *Global Study: Preventing Conflict, Transforming Justice, Securing the Peace*. New York: United Nations. 14 October.

2015d. *Security Council Reiterates Sanctions Decision against Those Undermining Peace, Stability in Central African Republic*. 20 October.

2015e. *Report of the High-Level Independent Panel on Peace Operations on Uniting Our Strengths for Peace: Politics, Partnership and People* ("HIPPO Report"). New York: United Nations. A/70/95-S/2015/446.

2015f. *Conflict-Related Sexual Violence. Report of the Secretary-General*. 23 March.

2016a. Fresh Allegations of Sexual Abuse Made against UN Peacekeepers in Central African Republic. 5 January. Available at: www.un.org/apps/ news/story.asp?NewsID=52941#.VtAZyG1qhM0.

2016b. Security Council Counter-Terrorism Committee. United Nations. Available at: www.un.org/en/sc/ctc/practices.html.

2016c. The 'New Horizon' Process. Available at: www.un.org/en/peace keeping/operations/newhorizon.shtml.

2017a. *Annual Report 2017: UN for Lebanon.* New York: United Nations. Available at: https://reliefweb.int/sites/reliefweb.int/files/ resources/UNreportfinal_Year 2017.pdf.

2017b. Peacekeeping Fact Sheet. September. Available from www.un.org/ en/peacekeeping/documents/bnotelatest.pdf.

2017c. United Nations Peacekeeping Fatalities. Available at: www.un.org/ en/peacekeeping/resources/statistics/fatalities.shtml.

2018. Approved Resources for Peacekeeping Operations for the Period from 1 July 2017 to 30 June 2018. A/C.5/71/24.

2018b. Conduct in UN Field Missions: Sexual Exploitation and Abuse. Status by Mission. Available from https://conduct.unmissions.org/sea-investigations.

2018c. Global Peacekeeping Data as of July 2018. https://peacekeeping .un.org/en/data.

2018d. List of Peacekeeping Operations 1948–2018. Available at: https:// peacekeeping.un.org/sites/default/files/180413_unpeacekeeping-opera tionlist_2.pdf.

2018e. Outreach Division. Available at: www.un.org/en/sections/depart ment-public-information/department-public-information/outreach-div ision/index.html.

2018f. Ranking of Military and Police Contributions to UN Operations. Available at: https://peacekeeping.un.org/en/ranking-of-military-and-police-contributions.

United Nations Chiefs of Police Summit. 2018. Concept Note. United Nations, New York, NY, 20–21 June. https://police.un.org/sites/ default/files/uncops2018-concept-note-en.pdf.

United Nations Council for Namibia. 1974. *Establishment of the Institute for Namibia.* A/AC 131.34, 7.

United Nations Counter-Terrorism Center. 2013/14. Kingdom of Saudi Arabia Donates USD 100 Million for the United Nations Counter-Terrorism Centre. *The Beam.* Available at: www.un.org/es/terrorism/ ctitf/pdfs/The%20Beam%20Vol%208.pdf.

United Nations Department for Peacekeeping Operations. 2017. Available at: www.un.org/en/peacekeeping/about/dpko/.

United Nations Department of Field Support. 2017. Available at: www.un.org/en/peacekeeping/about/dfs/.

United Nations Department of Peacekeeping Operations. 2010. *Second Generation Disarmament, Demobilization and Reintegration (DDR) Practices in Peace Operations.* New York: United Nations. Available at: www.un .org/en/peacekeeping/documents/2GDDR_ENG_WITH_COVER.pdf.

United Nations Department of Political Affairs. 2017. Available at: www.un.org/undpa/en/overview.

United Nations Development Programme. 2016. *Community Security and Armed Violence Reduction.* Available at: www.undp.org/content/ undp/en/home/ourwork/democratic-governance-and-peacebuilding/ rule-of-law–justice-and-security/community-security-and-armed-vio lence-areduction.html.

United Nations General Assembly. 2014. Report of the Office of Internal Oversight Services. *Evaluation of the Implementation and Results of Protection of Civilians Mandates in United Nations Peacekeeping Operations.* New York: A/68/787.

United Nations Peacekeeping. 2018. What Is Peacekeeping. Available at: www.un.org/en/peacekeeping/operations/peacekeeping.shtml.

United Nations Security Council. 2010. *Report of the Secretary-General on the Protection of Civilians in Armed Conflict.* S/2010/579.

United States Army, John A. Nagl, David H. Petraeus, James F. Amos, Sarah Sewall. 2006. *The U.S. Army/Marine Corps Counterinsurgency Field Manual, FM-3-24.* Chicago: Chicago University Press.

United States Department of State. 2012. The Lord's Resistance Army Fact-sheet. 23 March. Available at https://2009–2017.state.gov/r/pa/prs/ps/ 2012/03/186734.htm.

  2013. *African Contingency Operations Training and Assistance (ACOTA) Program.* Available at: www.state.gov/r/pa/prs/ps/2013/02/ 203841.htm.

  2016a. *Global Peace Operations Initiative (GPOI).* Available at: www.state.gov/t/pm/ppa/gpoi/.

  2016b. *The Global Coalition to Counter ISIL.* Available at: www.state.gov/s/seci/.

United States General Accounting Office. 2018. Cost Estimate for Hypothetical U.S. Operation Exceeds Actual Costs for Comparable UN Operation. GAO-18-243, February.

Urquhart, Brian. 1972. *Hammarskjold.* New York: Alfred A. Knopf.

  1987. *A Life in Peace and War.* London: Norton.

  1989. Foreword. *International Peacekeeping in Lebanon (1978–88).* By Bjoern Skogmo. Boulder, CO: Lynne Rienner.

  1998. *Ralph Bunche: An American Odyssey.* New York: W. W. Norton & Company

Uzonyi, Gary. 2015. Refugee Flows and State Contributions to Post-Cold War UN Peacekeeping Missions. *Journal of Peace Research* 52 (6): 743–757.

Varhola, Laura R., Thomas E. Sheperd. 2013. Africa and the United States – A Military Perspective. *American Foreign Policy Interests* 35 (6): 325–332.

Vilmer, Jean-Baptiste, Jean Gène and Olivier Schmitt. 2015. Frogs of War: Explaining the New French Interventionism. *War on the Rocks*, 14 October 2015. Available at: http://warontherocks.com/2015/10/frogs-of-war-explaining-the-new-french-military-interventionism/.

Voeten, Erik. 2001. Outside Options and the Logic of Security Council Action. *American Political Science Review* 95 (4): 845–857.

2005. The Political Origins of the UN Security Council's Ability to Legitimize the Use of Force. *International Organization* 59 (3): 527–557.

Vogel, Christoph. 2014. *Islands of Stability or Swamps of Insecurity? MONUSCO's Intervention Brigade and the Danger of Emerging Security Voids in Eastern Congo*. Brussels: Egmont Institute.

de Vries, Hugo. 2015. *Going around in Circles: The Challenges of Peacekeeping and Stabilization in the Democratic Republic of Congo*. The Hague: Netherlands Institute of International Relations Clingendael.

2016. The Ebb and Flow of Stabilization in the Congo. *PSRP Briefing Paper 8*. Nairobi: Rift Valley Institute.

Walker, Christopher, and Jessica Ludwig. 2017. The Meaning of Sharp Power: How Authoritarian States Project Influence. *Foreign Affairs*. 17 November.

de Waal, Alex. 2014. When Kleptocracy Becomes Insolvent: Brute Causes of the Civil War in South Sudan. *African Affairs* 113 (452): 347–369.

Wallis, Jim. 2014. 100 Most Influential People: Imam Omar Kobine Layama, Archbishop Dieudonné Nzapalainga and The Rev. Nicolas Guérékoyame-Gbangou. *Time*, 23 April.

Wallis, Kim. 2006. Seán MacBride and Namibia. *History Ireland*. 4 (14).

Walsh, James I. 2005. Persuasion in International Politics: A Rationalist Account. *Politics and Policy*, 33 (4).

Walt, Stephen M. 1987. *The Origin of Alliances*. Ithaca, NY: Cornell University Press.

Walter, Barbara. 1997. The Critical Barrier to Civil War Settlement. *International Organization* 51 (3):335–364.

2002. *Committing to Peace: The Successful Settlement of Civil Wars*. Princeton, NJ: Princeton University Press.

Walter, Barbara, Lise Howard, and V. Page Fortna. 2019. The Extraordinary Relationship between Peacekeeping and Peace. Working Paper.

Waltz, Kenneth. 1979. *Theory of International Politics*. Long Grove, IL: Waveland Press.

Weber, Max. 1978. *Economy and Society*. Berkeley, CA: University of California Press.

Wedeen, Lisa. 2010. Reflections on Ethnographic Work in Political Science. *Annual Review of Political Science*, 13: 255–272.

Weiland, Heribert, and Matthew Braham, eds. 1994. *The Namibian Peace Process: Implications and Lessons for the Future.* A Review of an International Conference Jointly Organized by the Arnold Bergstraesser Institute and the International Peace Academy, 1–4 July 1992, Freiburg, Germany. Arnold Bergstraesser Institut.

Weinberger, Naomi J. 1983. Peacekeeping Options in Lebanon. *Middle East Journal.* 37 (3): 344.

1995. How Peacekeeping Becomes Intervention: Lessons from the Lebanese Experience. In Milton Esman and Shibley Telhami, eds. *International Organizations and Ethnic Conflict.* Ithaca, NY: Cornell University Press.

Weingast, Barry R. 2002. Rational-Choice Institutionalism. In *Political Science: State of the Discipline*, edited by Ira Katznelson and Helen V. Milner, 660–692. New York: W. W. Norton.

Welz, Martin. 2016. Multi-Actor Peace Operations and Inter-Organizational Relations: Insights from the Central African Republic. *International Peacekeeping* 23 (4): 568–591.

Wendt, Alexander. 1999. *Social Theory of International Politics.* Cambridge and New York: Cambridge University Press.

Werner, Suzanne, and Amy Yuen. 2005. Making and Keeping Peace. *International Organization* 59 (2):261–292.

Whalan, Jeni. 2013. *How Peace Operations Work.* New York: Oxford University Press.

What's in Blue. 2018. Central African Republic: Briefing and Informal Interactive Dialogue. 20 June. Available at: www.whatsinblue.org/2018/06/central-african-republic-briefing-and-informal-interactive-dialogue.php.

Wiharta, Sharon, Neil Melvin, and Xenia Avezov. 2012. *The New Geopolitics of Peace Operations: Mapping the Emerging Landscape.* Stockholm: Stockholm International Peace Research Institute.

de Wijk, Rob. 2005. *The Art of Military Coercion: Why the West's Military Superiority Scarcely Matters.* Amsterdam: Mets and Schilt.

Williams, Paul D. 2015. Keeping a Piece of Peacekeeping. *Foreign Affairs,* 6 October.

2018. Strategic Communications for Peace Operations: The African Union's Information War Against al-Shabaab. *Stability: International Journal of Security and Development* 7(1): 3.

William Wunderle and Andre Briere. 2008. US Foreign Policy and Israel's Qualitative Military Edge: The Need for a Common Vision. *Washington Institute for Near East Policy*, Policy Focus #80, January.

Wills, Siobhan. 2009. *Protecting Civilians: Obligations of Peacekeepers.* Oxford: Oxford University Press.

Wilson, Scott, and Craig Whitlock. 2011. Small U.S. Force to Deploy to Uganda, Aid Fight against Lord's Resistance Army. *Washington Post*, 14 October.

Wohlers. Laurence D. 2015. A Central African Elite Perspective on the Struggles of the Central African Republic. In *Making Sense of the Central African Republic*, edited by Tatiana Carayannis and Louisa Lombard. Chicago: University of Chicago Press.

Wohlforth, William C. 1993. *The Elusive Balance: Power and Perceptions during the Cold War*. Ithaca: Cornell University Press.

Wolfe, Lauren. 2013. The U.N. Is Not Serious About Its Peacekeeper Rape Problem. *Foreign Policy*, 13 August.

Wood, Elizabeth. 2003. *Insurgent Collective Action and Civil War in El Salvador*. Cambridge: Cambridge University Press.

World Bank. 2018. *Breaking the Cycle of Conflict and Instability*. Available at: http://documents.worldbank.org/curated/en/444491528747992733/pdf/127056-WP-PUBLIC-BreakingTheCycleOfConflitAndInstabilityIn CAR.pdf.

Wren, Christopher. 1989. Rebel Hunters in Namibia Train for Less Violent Times as Ordinary Police. *New York Times*, 9 January, A3.

1990. Outjo Journal: UN Namibia Team Makes Some Unlikely Friends. *New York Times*, 19 January, A4.

Wuthnow, Robert. 2009. *Boundless Faith: The Global Outreach of American Churches*. Berkeley, CA: University of California Press.

Yee, Albert S. 1996. The Causal Effects of Ideas on Policies. *International Organization* 50 (1): 69–108.

Young, Steven. 2015. Responsible Sourcing of Metals: Certification Approaches for Conflict Minerals and Conflict-Free Metals. *The International Journal of Life Cycle Assessment* 23 (7): 1429–1447.

Zahar, Marie-Joëlle. 2012. Norm Transmission in Peace- and State-Building: Lessons from Democracy Promotion in Sudan and Lebanon. *Global Governance* 18 (1): 73–88.

Zanotti, Laura. 2006. Taming Chaos: A Foucauldian View of UN Peacekeeping, Democracy and Normalization. *International Peacekeeping* 13 (2): 150–167.

Zaum, Dominik. 2007. *The Sovereignty Paradox: The Norms and Politics of International Statebuilding*. Oxford: Oxford University Press.

Zimbardo, Philip, and Michael Leippe. 1991. *The Psychology of Attitude Change and Social Influence*. Philadelphia: Temple University Press.

United Nations Documents

A/RES/3111, 12 December 1973
S/12636, 10 April 1978
S/12827, 29 August 198
S/15287, 12 July 1982
S/20346, 22 December 1988
S/20346, 22 December 1988
S/20412, 23 January 1989
S/20566, 4 April 1989
S/20658, 26 May 1989
S/20872, 28 September 1989
S/20883, 6 October 1989
S/29412, 16 March 1989
S/RES/425, 19 March 1978
S/RES/435, 29 September 1978
S/RES/439, 13 November 1978
S/RES/629, 16 January 1989
S/RES/632, 16 February 1989
S/RES/640, 29 August 1989
S/RES/643, 31 October 1989
S/RES/1701, 11 August 2006
Unpublished UN Report #1
Unpublished UN Report #2
A/55/305, 21 August 2000
S/RES/2127, 5 December 2013
S/RES/2149, 10 April 2014
A/70/95, 17 June 2015

Reports of the Secretary-General on the Central African Republic

S/2013/677, 15 November 2013
S/2013/787, 31 December 2013
S/2014/142, 3 March 2014
S/2014/562, 1 August 2014
S/2014/857, 28 November 2014
S/2014/928, 22 December 2014
S/2015/576, 29 July 2015
S/2015/003, 5 January 2015
S/2015/227, 1 April 2015
S/2015/344, 4 June 2015

S/2016/133, 12 February 2016
S/2016/305, 1 April 2016
S/2016/565, 22 June 2016
S/2016/824, 29 September 2016
S/2017/94, 1 February 2017
S/2017/865, 18 October 2017
S/2018/125, 15 February 2018

Index

For EU product safety concerns, contact us at Calle de José Abascal, 56–1°,
28003 Madrid, Spain or eugpsr@cambridge.org.

www.ingramcontent.com/pod-product-compliance
Ingram Content Group UK Ltd.
Pitfield, Milton Keynes, MK11 3LW, UK
UKHW020334140625
459647UK00018B/2138